LEADERSHIP

IN EARLY CARE AND EDUCATION

Sharon L. Kagan and Barbara T. Bowman, Editors

A 1996–97 NAEYC Comprehensive Membership Benefit

National Association for the Education of Young Children
Washington, D.C.

National Association for the Education of Young Children
1509 16th Street, NW
Washington, DC 20036-1426
202-232-8777 or 800-424-2460
Website: http://www.naeyc.org/naeyc

The National Association for the Education of Young Children (NAEYC) attempts through its publications program to provide a forum for discussion of major issues and ideas in our field. We hope to provoke thought and promote professional growth. NAEYC wishes to thank the editors, contributors, and all who donated their time to the development of this book as a contribution to our profession.

Library of Congress Catalog Number: 96-72625
ISBN Catalog Number: 0-935989-81-1
NAEYC Order Number: 209

Printed in the United States of America.

For Marilyn "Micky" Segal

A courageous and gentle leader—
one who is ahead of her time
and an inspiration to us all.

Editors

Sharon Lynn Kagan, senior associate at Yale University's Bush Center in Child Development and Social Policy, is recognized nationally and internationally for her work in the field of early care and education. She is a frequent consultant to the White House, Congress, the National Governors' Association, the U.S. Departments of Education and Health and Human Services, and numerous national foundations, corporations, and professional associations. She sits on more than 40 national boards and panels, serving as chair or co-chair of many of them. She is former chair of the Family Resource Coalition board of directors and a past member of the NAEYC Governing Board, President Clinton's education transition team, and national commissions on Head Start and Chapter 1.

A prolific writer of 10 volumes and 100 articles, she has examined policy development for children and families, family support, early childhood pedagogy, strategies for collaboration and service integration, and evaluation of social programs. She recently completed the *Quality 2000* national study.

Barbara T. Bowman, an authority on early education and a nationally recognized advocate for improved and expanded training for practitioners who work with children and families, is president and co-founder of the Erikson Institute for Advanced Study in Child Development. She teaches courses in early education and administration at Erikson, which is affiliated with Loyola University Chicago. Her current research focuses on how to introduce developmentally appropriate practice and authentic assessment in the early grades.

A past president of NAEYC, she has served on numerous national boards and a variety of professional committees. She is a frequent consultant on parent support programs and has directed training projects for Head Start teachers, caregivers of infants at risk for morbidity or mortality, and preschool primary teachers and administrators.

Contributors

Helen K. Blank, director of child care at the Children's Defense Fund, works to expand support for positive early care and education experiences for children, especially those from low-income families. She is credited with leading the large-scale effort to pass the first comprehensive federal child care legislation since World War II, and she has worked to promote the expansion of Head Start and its continued focus on community-based, high-quality services. The author of numerous studies, she developed *CDF Reports* and the Child Watch project to monitor the effects of federal cutbacks on children and families.

Paula Jorde Bloom is a professor of early childhood education at National-Louis University in Wheeling, Illinois. She has taught preschool and kindergarten, designed and directed a child care center, and served as administrator of a campus laboratory school. Her current research interests are organizational climate and occupational stress as they relate to job satisfaction in early childhood settings. She is the author of numerous journal articles and several books.

Sue Bredekamp is director of professional development and accreditation for the National Association for the Education of Young Children. She also directs NAEYC's National Institute for Early Childhood Professional Development. She is editor of the association's position statements on accreditation, developmentally appropriate practice, and curriculum and assessment, as well as of the guidelines for preparation of early childhood professionals.

Richard M. Clifford is a senior investigator at the Frank Porter Graham Child Development Center and research associate professor in education at the University of North Carolina at Chapel Hill. He also is director of the Early Childhood Leadership Development Program and associate director of the National Center for Early Learning and Development. He is co-author of a widely used instrument for evaluating learning environments for young children, and he was a leader in the design and implementation of the North Carolina Smart Start early childhood initiative. He currently serves as president of NAEYC.

Dwayne A. Crompton has dedicated himself to the advancement of social issues, particularly for the very young and especially within his community. He has been a preschool teacher, an elementary teacher, a public school administrator, and a child care agency director. For 19 years he has been executive director of KCMC Child Development Corporation in Kansas City, which reaches out through its many programs to help thousands of children and families in northwestern Missouri. In 1995 he received the Children Defense Fund's Innovative Leadership Award.

Josué Cruz Jr. is a professor of early childhood education at the University of South Florida in Tampa. Former secretary of the NAEYC Governing Board, he currently is a board member of the Council for Early Childhood Professional Recognition. He specializes in professional development and preparation and is now conducting a national study on the licensure of teachers for young children and an analysis of state-mandated curriculum guidelines and standards for early childhood instruction.

Mary L. Culkin is an assistant research professor at the University of Colorado Health Sciences Center, School of Nursing, and an adjunct professor in the early childhood program at the Naropa Institute. Her involvement in the development of several programs for young children and their families led to a research focus on the role of administrators as managers and leaders of community-based programs. She also works on early care and education cost and quality issues and a professional development program for administrators and teachers in child care settings.

Alice Walker Duff is the co-founder and executive director of Crystal Stairs, Inc., one of California's largest private/nonprivate child development agencies, which provides service, research, and advocacy. She is a principal author of the Cultural Masterplan for the City of Los Angeles. She has served on a number of boards and committees that protect and expand child care services. In 1995 she received the Hunger Fighter of the Year Award from the California Hunger Coalition.

Linda M. Epinosa is an associate professor of education at the University of Missouri–Columbia. She has had experience as a preschool teacher, child care center director, elementary school principal, central office administrator, state program director, and corporate vice president of education. Her research interests focus on the design and evaluation of optimal learning environments for young children at risk for school failure. She is the past treasurer of the NAEYC Governing Board and currently serves on the National Academy of Sciences Research Roundtable on Head Start.

Ellen Galinsky is president and co-founder of the Families and Work Institute, a nonprofit center for policy research on the changing workforce and changing family lives. A prolific researcher and author, she currently directs the National Study of the Changing Workforce and the Early Education Quality Improvement Study, as well as three studies examining the impact of state, community, and business efforts to improve the quality of early care and education. She also coordinates a public awareness campaign to promote young children's healthy development and school readiness. She is past president of NAEYC.

Marilyn Henry is director of program development and communications at the Council for Early Childhood Professional Recognition. She began her career in early care and education in the early 1970s as field coordinator for the North Carolina Federation of Child Development Centers. She worked as staff writer for the National Black Child Development Institute and was one of the first editors of *The Black Child Advocate.*

Lilian G. Katz is a professor of early childhood education at the University of Illinois (Urbana-Champaign), where she also serves as director of the ERIC Clearinghouse on Elementary and Early Childhood Education. A past president of NAEYC, she now chairs the board of directors of the National Society for the Study of Education. Founding editor-in-chief of the *Early Childhood Research Quarterly,* she is the author of more than 100 publications, including articles, chapters, and books about early childhood education, teacher education, and parenting. She lectures widely throughout the world.

Judy Langford, a nationally known expert in the field of family support, advises foundations, state and federal agencies, and private organizations on child and family issues. She is a senior consultant for and the former executive director of the Family Resource Coalition, a national organization of more than 2,500 family resource programs and practitioners, and former executive director of The Ounce of Prevention Fund, a public/private partnership providing technical assistance, training, and evaluation for more than 40 projects in Illinois. She serves on a number of national advisory boards and review panels.

Anne Mitchell is president of Early Childhood Policy Research, an independent consulting firm launched in 1991 to specialize in policy research and planning in early care and education for government agencies, foundations, and national nonprofit organizations. Previously she was associate dean of the research division at Bank Street College of Education. Using her experiences as director of child care centers, she founded Bank Street's graduate program in early childhood leadership in 1981.

Evelyn K. Moore was a founder of the National Black Child Development Institute and now serves as its executive director. Since 1970 she has raised more than $20 million to support the work of the Institute, which has become a leading voice for African American children and their families. A recipient of many awards, she maintains a busy writing and speaking schedule on topics related to the welfare of children. She also serves on several national boards and advisory committees.

Gwen Morgan has provided vision for policy development in the field of early care and education for more than 26 years. Recognized as a leading national authority on child care regulation, she writes extensively on a wide range of policy, regulation, and training topics, and she has guided the development of thousands of students in the field. She is founding director of the Center for Career Development in Early Care and Education and co-founder of Work/Family Directions and Wheelock College's Advanced Seminars in Child Care Administration.

Susan Muenchow, executive director of the Florida Children's Forum, administers an extensive nonprofit child care resource-and-referral network, which serves more than 100,000 families a year. Her work in early childhood services has included co-authoring a book on Head Start, directing a governor's Constituency for Children, directing and expanding Florida's subsidized child care program, working for the Bush Center in Child Development and Social Policy and the Carnegie Council on Children at Yale University, and covering children and youth issues as a correspondent for the *Christian Science Monitor.*

Roger Neugebauer, along with his wife Bonnie, publishes *Child Care Information Exchange,* a management magazine for directors of early childhood programs that goes to more than 25,000 early childhood professionals in the United States and 10 foreign countries. He is a former member of the governing board of the National Association of Child Care Resource and Referral Agencies and has been appointed to numerous national advisory panels.

Michelle J. Neuman is a research assistant at Yale University's Bush Center in Child Development and Social Policy. Her research focuses on early care and education policy, family support, children's transitions to school, school readiness, and family policy in France. She graduated in 1995 from Princeton University with a degree from the Woodrow Wilson School of Public and International Affairs and a certificate in French language and culture.

Marce Verzaro-O'Brien is an early childhood and policy consultant and the former administrator of the Erie County/Buffalo Head Start Program in New York. As curriculum director for the Early Childhood Professional Development Network, she is responsible for implementing the National Head Start Association's quality initiative. She is engaged in a case study of the Ohio Head Start Collaboration Project and is the public policy Early Head Start specialist at Western Kentucky's Technical Assistance Support Center. She is a member of the NAEYC Governing Board.

Carol Brunson Phillips is executive director of the Council for Early Childhood Professional Recognition, which serves as the home of the Child Development Associate National Credentialing Program and the Head Start Fellows Program. She is the liaison for the exchange between the schools in Reggio Emilia, Italy, and the early childhood community in the United States. As a member of the human development faculty at Pacific Oaks College for 13 years, she specialized in early childhood education and cultural influences on development.

Patricia Siegel is executive director of the California Child Care Resource and Referral Network. Cofounder and senior policy advisor of the National Association of Child Care Resource and Referral Agencies, she actively helps shape state and federal policy for children and families. Her current work includes the Child Care Initiative Project, California's public-private partnership to expand the supply of licensed quality child care by recruiting new family child care providers.

Maurice R. Sykes, deputy superintendent of the Center for Systemic Educational Change in the District of Columbia Public Schools and former executive director of D.C.'s early childhood program, is a nationally recognized expert in the fields of early childhood education, urban education, and educational policy. He examined urban education initiatives at the U.S. Department of Education and was senior associate at the Institute for Educational Leadership. He has led numerous demonstration projects, training institutes, curriculum design teams, and collaborative efforts.

Valora Washington, program director for the W.K. Kellogg Foundation, provides administrative leadership in a wide range of key program areas, including youth, families and neighborhoods, and higher education. She is former vice president and professor at Antioch College and previously held faculty and administrative posts at American University, Howard University, and the University of North Carolina at Chapel Hill. She is the author of six books and more than 40 journal articles, and she serves on several commissions.

Bernice Weissbourd is well-known as an early childhood educator and as initiator and leader of the family support movement. In 1976 she founded Family Focus, a not-for-profit agency providing comprehensive programs for families of children from birth, and in 1981 created the Family Resource Coalition, a national organization serving as a resource on family support programs and policies. She is the author or editor of numerous publications and a lecturer at the University of Chicago's school of social services administration. She has served on many national boards and advisory committees.

Marcy Whitebook is founding director and senior research policy advisor of the National Center for the Early Childhood Work Force (formerly the Child Care Employee Project). She began her career as a preschool teacher, and in recent years she was a principal investigator for the National Child Care Staffing Study and co-author of the *Early Childhood Mentoring Curriculum.*

Contents

Preface

The quality of any field or organization is dependent on the quality of its leaders. In early care and education, leadership has never been as critical to the field's advancement as it is now. This is so for several reasons. First, long-held concerns about the status of early care and education services recently have been empirically confirmed, with studies finding that many programs threaten the healthy development of young children *and* that leadership plays a key role in quality enhancement. Second, anticipated growth of early childhood services, as well as the changing nature and numbers of individuals entering the profession, spurs interest in the training of a leadership cadre. Third, because important efforts to nurture leadership have emerged in recent years, there is a need to consolidate lessons from the field with understandings of leadership strategies and theories from other fields. If the field is to ensure the adequacy of its present and future child care and early educational system, new leadership development efforts that are multidimensional—focusing on pedagogical, administrative, and advocacy/policy leadership—must be conceptualized and implemented.

Coinciding with emerging interest in and demand for leadership development, this volume was created with the goal of providing a forum to examine current understandings about leadership and to explore future possibilities for its development. Its focus is leadership development within the field of early care and education, a field that embraces many kinds of programs (e.g., family child care, for-profit and non-profit center-based care, Head Start, and school-based early childhood education) and many kinds of allied services (e.g., resource-and-referral agencies, child care administration, regulation, teacher/provider preparation, and research).

Leadership development has been a topic of concern in early care and education, with many excellent contributions by noted scholars and thinkers (e.g., Spodek, Saracho, & Peters 1988; VanderVen 1988; Bloom & Sheerer 1992; Rodd 1994). Despite this attention to leadership, the field does not have a commonly accepted definition of leadership, nor has it engaged in a systematic and collaborative discussion of the properties of leadership. Moreover, early care and education has not attempted to fuse relevant practical and theoretical ideas about leadership or forecast leadership needs and strategies to address those needs. *Leadership in Early Care and Education* is designed to do just that—provoke discussion and evoke fresh thinking and fresh action.

To be sure, this volume does not stand alone. A bevy of leadership efforts are under way; the volume is designed to augment these efforts. We invited contributions by people currently engaged in leadership initiatives. We sought to include voices from across the field—those of practitioners, policymakers, academics, and researchers.

In constructing the volume, we sought the input of many diverse individuals not only in serving as chapter authors and commentators but also in shaping and structuring the volume's contents and recommendations. Though we alone are responsible for the volume, we are deeply appreciative of the many contributions of an outstanding advisory team—Sue Bredekamp, Dwayne Crompton, Linda Espinosa, Evelyn Moore, Gwen Morgan, and Carol Brunson Phillips. In addition, Michelle Neuman lent her talents, editorial artistry, and patience to the work. All their ideas and insights have substantively guided our thinking.

Any serious discussion of leadership can be approached from many vantage points. We wish that the words of many other early childhood leaders could have dotted these pages. That so many fine leaders are not contributors to this volume reflects the page limitations associated with any single publication rather than any limitation in our respect and admiration for our colleagues and their work. We trust that, through the diverse voices herein, the ideas and contributions of many are represented. We also hope that our effort will give rise to other efforts and other opportunities for diverse opinions to be expressed.

Leadership in early care and education has many facets, including but not limited to management and administration. The volume assumes that real leadership is not necessarily synonymous with job title or job function—that is, that many people, irrespective of their titles, exert profound leadership on the field. It also assumes that formal degrees alone do not create a leader. Thus, leadership is broadly defined in this volume. It is a fragile commodity, earned over time. It can accrue to individuals and to organizations. At its core is a deep knowledge of the field, a willingness to take risks, and a breadth of vision and thinking that transcends individual programs, services, or orientations. Leadership in early care and education is innovative but sensitive to history, diversity, and context, and it is collaborative yet bold—precisely, but not incidentally, the qualities we hope to have embraced in this volume.

The contents of the volume

Section 1 of the volume defines leadership from two perspectives. Sharon L. Kagan and Barbara T. Bowman, in chapter 1, provide an opening discussion of the new nature of leadership in early care and education, focusing on current challenges. Ideas about how to address the challenges are presented, as is the salience of the issue for the new century. In chapter 2 Gwen Morgan reviews the history of leadership development in and outside the field, presenting implications of historical efforts for contemporary practice.

Section 2 presents a broadened framework for considering leadership. It expands conventional notions of leadership as management or administration, suggesting that leadership in early care and education actually has many functions or parts. In chapter 3 Lilian G. Katz explores the pedagogical function of leadership, discussing how pedagogy is formed and how those who form it constitute a special cadre of leaders. Maurice R. Sykes provides commentary on the chapter. Mary L. Culkin discusses administrative leadership in chapter 4. Culkin presents notions about managers as leaders and infuses her work with new understanding about the changing roles of managers and administrators. Commentary is provided by Paula Jorde Bloom. In chapter 5 Helen K. Blank discusses the advocacy function of leadership, focusing on the role of advocates and policy advisors as early childhood leaders. Susan Muenchow offers commentary. Dwayne A. Crompton, in chapter 6, presents a vision of early childhood educators as community leaders, enunciating the multiple roles and responsibilities that these individuals assume at the community level. Marce Verzaro-O'Brien comments on the chapter. The section on the functions of leadership concludes with a chapter by Sharon L. Kagan and Michelle J. Neuman, who suggest that proactive leadership demands a willingness to challenge convention, to think broadly, and to think ahead of the curve. Commentary on chapter 7 is provided by Valora Washington.

Section 3 examines the leadership context from diverse perspectives, addressing constraints and possibilities and the actual challenges of creating a durable leadership capacity, given the realities of the field. Chapter 8, by Evelyn K. Moore, presents an overview of the institutional and racial biases that inhibit training for diverse leadership and offers new ideas on how to alter these biases. Josué Cruz Jr. provides commentary. Marcy Whitebook, in chapter 9, discusses adequate recognition and compensation for teachers and workers in the field; her work focuses on the overall devaluing of the early childhood profession. Alice Walker Duff offers commentary. In chapter 10 Anne Mitchell discusses the fragmentation of training and delivery systems, stressing how these structural characteristics of the field affect leadership development. Roger Neugebauer comments on the chapter. Linda M. Espinosa, in chapter 11, discusses personal considerations associated with leadership development. Richard M. Clifford provides commentary.

Section 4 turns to new paths in leadership development. It presents specific issues facing many diverse institutions and organizations as they consider alternative approaches to leadership development. In chapter 12 Barbara T. Bowman discusses the ways in which two- and four-year colleges might restructure themselves and their offerings to address the leadership challenge. New roles for professional organizations are addressed by Sue Bredekamp in chapter 13. She explains how multiple organizations can work individually and collaboratively to revitalize commitments to future leaders. Chapter 14 focuses on new roles for non-college/university-based training efforts. Marilyn Henry and Carol Brunson Phillips offer an analysis of how leadership is and can be fostered through the Child Development Associate credential, mentoring programs, and other national efforts. In chapter 15 Patricia Siegel addresses the roles of resource-and-referral agencies as critical community-based organizations that foster leadership development among providers and parents. In chapter 16 Ellen Galinsky examines the roles of mediating organizations—including research, advocacy, membership and professional organizations, and foundations—in fostering a leadership agenda. Judy Langford and Bernice Weissbourd, in chapter 17, discuss the role of parent leadership in a family-support model of early care and education.

Section 5 is a critical chapter, "Moving the Leadership Agenda," that builds on the ideas discussed throughout the volume. It presents the Leadership Working Group's set of action recommendations to help advance a leadership agenda for early care and education.

* * * * *

No volume of this magnitude could have been completed without the support of many individuals. First, we wish to acknowledge the support of the A.L. Mailman Family Foundation for the financial resources that enabled the production of this effort. Marilyn Segal, Luba Lynch, and Vickie Frelow of the Mailman Foundation provided the ongoing technical and spiritual support necessary for this volume to be as much a process as a document. Second, we again wish to acknowledge the support and input of the Leadership Working Group, without whom this volume would have had a different shape, different content, and different focus. We are profoundly indebted to our fine colleagues. Third, we wish to thank all the authors and commentators; without their spirit of dedication and inventiveness, this volume would lack the spark and ingenuity that we intended. Finally, we wish to thank our publisher, the National Association for the Education of Young Children, and our editor, Carol Copple, for all their support. At Yale University, we thank Jane Murray for her constant help throughout all phases of this effort, and at Erikson Institute our appreciation is extended to Sharon Dudley.

Oliver Wendell Holmes said it well: "I find the great thing in this world is not so much where we stand, as in what direction we are moving. To reach the port of heaven we must sail sometimes with the wind and sometimes against it, but we must sail and not drift, nor lie at anchor" (from *The Autocrat of the Breakfast-Table,* 1858). It is to that sail—a collective voyage toward a durable leadership capacity—that this volume is dedicated.

—Sharon L. Kagan and Barbara T. Bowman
February 1997

References

Bloom, P. J., & M. Sheerer. 1992. The effects of leadership training on child care program quality. *Early Childhood Research Quarterly* 7 (4): 579–94.

Rodd, J. 1994. *Leadership in early childhood: The pathway to professionalism.* New York: Teachers College Press.

Spodek, B., O. Saracho, & D. Peters, eds. 1988. *Professionalism and the early childhood practitioner.* New York: Teachers College Press.

VanderVen, K. 1988. Pathways to professional effectiveness for early childhood educators. In *Professionalism and the early childhood practitioner,* eds. B. Spodek, O. Saracho, & D. Peters. New York: Teachers College Press.

Overview

Chapter 1

Leadership in Early Care and Education: Issues and Challenges

Sharon L. Kagan and Barbara T. Bowman

American early care and education is at a crossroad. On the one hand, rhetorical interest in and support for early care and education have expanded considerably in the public and private sectors, with more media and press attention being accorded young children than ever before. In the private sector, prestigious national groups, including the Business Roundtable and the Committee for Economic Development (1993), have turned their attention to young children and the early years of life. Such interest from the corporate sector is mirrored in localities throughout the nation, with business, civic, and religious leaders becoming increasingly involved in planning, funding, and supporting early care and education.

On the other hand, a contradictory policy stance exists. States' commitments to young children have grown, with the number of states operating early childhood initiatives nearly tripling between 1979 and 1992 and now investing a national total of about $665 million to provide more than 290,000 young children with such services (Adams & Sandfort 1994; Adams & Poersch 1996). Conversely, at the federal level, where there is a strong focus on consolidating government programs, such commitments are sparse. As a result of new welfare reform, expanded need for child care will cause unprecedented demand for limited places in child care programs. Although this increased demand has been met with additional—although still insufficient—funding (Adams & Poersch 1996), little attention is paid to the quality of services provided. Child care is being approached primarily as a custo-

dial service to enable parents to get off public assistance. Quality child care, once rising to the American social agenda, now seems to be on the back burner.

Such polar strategies—federal limitations and state expansions—generate new challenges for the early childhood field. Aside from coping with the uncertainty and the havoc that such uncertainty creates, early care and education specialists are forced to create the quality early care and education system demanded by the public at the same time quality safeguards are being torn asunder by the movement to deregulate and to require fewer standards.

Long intuited, the current problematic status of early childhood service quality, quantity, and accessibility is now being empirically documented (Cost, Quality, & Child Outcomes Study Team 1995). Indeed, research results are so dire that we must ask: How can a field continue to exist without radical reform when 86% of its services are empirically judged to be poor or mediocre? How can a field continue to exist with high staff turnover rates, poor and declining compensation, and a diminishing supply of qualified practitioners? Or when services are so inequitably distributed that at-risk children—those who need and benefit from them most—have the least access (U.S. General Accounting Office 1993)?

However untenable the present quality and equity situation is, it is likely to become worse, thereby exacerbating the need for sturdy and strong leadership in the field. Changes in the American family over the past decades—the increases in marital instability, the delay and decline of marriage, births outside of marriage, and maternal employment—have profoundly affected the field of early care and education. As numbers of single-parent families, reconstituted families, and working mothers soar, the traditional American family—married parents with the mother caring for children full time—is no longer the norm. Increasing workforce participation by mothers with young children means that the number of children in nonparental care has risen and will likely continue to rise. Infants and toddlers constitute the fastest growing subgroup of children in early care and education programs. Further, at the threshold of the most massive welfare reform in decades, many thousands of children will enter care as their mothers meet welfare employment mandates.

Even if such an increase were not accelerated by welfare reform, basic demographics predict an expanded population of young children, and of poor young children in particular, who will need early childhood services (U.S. General Accounting Office 1993). Additionally, the likelihood that far greater numbers of families will want early care and education is being fueled by new attention to the importance of the early years and new learnings about the early development of brain capacity (Carnegie Task Force 1994). The first National Education Goal—that by the year 2000 all children will start school ready to learn—further highlights the significance of children's early learning experiences. Parents are realizing the importance of the early years to their children's long-term development and are seeking quality out-of-home settings that optimize that development. In short, to meet the developmental and educational needs of all children, as well as the employment demands of their parents, early care and education will expand dramatically.

These sociodemographic and policy trends have contributed to the development of an increasingly complex set of early care and education services. Characterized by uncoordinated growth, programs emerge episodically and inconsistently, emanating from different legislative mandates, funding streams, regulatory systems, and administrative agencies. Some programs fall under the jurisdiction of state departments of education, others are overseen by departments of health, and still others by departments of welfare or social services (Kagan et al. 1995). A recent study documented 90 different federal programs administered by 11 federal agencies and 20 offices (U.S. General Accounting Office 1995). Equally inconsistent, state-supported programs vary from state to state and even within states. Not surprisingly, regulatory policy in early care and education is marked by inconsistent standards and enforcement across and within states, with many programs—family child care, school based, church based, part day—legally exempt from licensing requirements. In other words, there is variation regarding what is regulated, which programs are regulated, and whether or not these standards are enforced.

The field must also cope with the changing of funding levels and programs stimulated, in part, by welfare reform. With the recent trend toward program proliferation and devolution, governing and navigating the sea of state and local early care and education services is likely to become even more difficult. More than any time in history, the social and political context is challenging the fate of early care and education.

The polemics and the problems

There is little question that the field of early care and education is at a critical juncture. We must put an end to the delivery of inferior services; the alternative is to continue providing services that harm children and families and ultimately threaten the intellectual and social capital of the nation. In truth, we have no choice. We must dramatically improve the quality of services, concentrating efforts and resources where they can best be felt.

Those who understand the pressing need for quality early care and education are calling for systemic changes, including coordinated delivery systems, community-based planning, streamlined data collection, and clearer regulatory and enforcement strategies (Sugarman 1993; Kamerman & Kahn 1995). Even more profound are the needs that relate to the human capacity of the field, including the capacity to compensate workers equitably, engender access to quality training, and enhance the leadership capacity of the field. Efforts to address compensation have been admirably addressed in the literature and in action, including nationwide "worthy wage" campaigns (Whitebook, Hnatiuk, & Bellm 1994). Similarly, inventive efforts are under way to bolster and streamline training opportunities, with a great deal of emphasis on issues of transdisciplinary training and training for directors (Azer, Capraro, & Elliott 1996). Less attention, however, has been systematically accorded the development of a durable and perpetuating leadership capacity for the field. In some ways, this is peculiar, given all the emphasis placed by other fields on leadership. With global competition and the downsizing of corporate America has come the need for new kinds of leadership, and a plethora of leadership institutes have sprung up in nearly every field and industry (Kelley 1992).

Not limited to practice, leadership has theoretical roots dating back to the 1930s (Gulick 1937; Barnard 1938), with work on organizational and structural leadership emerging later (Bennis 1966; Gardner 1976; Simon 1976). More recent literature offers new perspectives on leadership that stress collaborative leadership (Gray 1989), the power of learning organizations (Senge 1990), and the need for inclusive leadership (Cortes 1996; Olson 1996).

Well established across many fields is the pivotal role of leaders in achieving and maintaining an institution's quality. How the individuals at the helm craft their mission, understand the organizational culture, manage for quality, and create capacity in others—all these aspects of leadership determine organizational effectiveness and well-being. Leadership is a preferred domain for investment in most institutions—one that yields long-term, cost-efficient rewards. Early care and education should not be an exception to this reality. Faced with mounting pressures from contextual changes, the early care and education field must focus on the way it views and approaches leadership. In the past, leadership was equated with management, with leaders in early care and education typically being center directors or administrators. The leadership cadre was not representative of the racial and ethnic diversity of the field; the content of practitioner training was often narrowly focused and seldom emphasized leadership development; and access to leadership development was not widespread. While some of these trends persist today, they cannot be allowed to continue into the future. These issues matter, and they matter a lot. Early care and education has become a complex field serving a large and diverse population of children and families. If the nation is to ensure the quality of children's early care and education experiences, new leadership development efforts must be considered. We can no longer ignore the necessity for the field to expand and develop its leadership capacity.

Yet historic and operational considerations make leadership in early care and education interesting conceptually and challenging pragmatically. First, early care and education has had a historic commitment to open admission to the field, giving workers without preservice training or credentials the opportunity to work in programs as they often—but not always—pursue some form of credential. This notion of open access is unique among service fields (Mitchell 1996). To some, this suggests a willingness to trade formal study for life experience. This commitment to open admission to the field has necessitated heavy reliance on inservice training for workers and leaders. This reliance on inservice training has been helpful to individuals who have been able to participate, but not all workers or leaders have had such opportunity. With discretionary dollars nearly nonexistent and a loose organizational apparatus unable to foot the bill, early educators were de facto denied access to entrepreneurial—and often expensive—inservice workshops and institutes. It is interesting to note that when opportunities for inservice leadership development were made available, it was usually via Head Start training or other special efforts, and they were not open to early educators in general. As a result, there is limited access to leadership development throughout the entire field.

A number of current realities exacerbate these concerns. Given increasing options for female employment in other fields, even fewer qualified individuals are attracted to the early care and education field. Further, many potential workers are deterred by the minimal compensation and perceived lack of opportunities for career advancement and leadership. Many of those who do work in early care and education do not value it as a profession; turnover remains high. Viewing work in early care and education as a short-term commitment, many in the field do not see the value of making long-term investments in either professional or leadership development.

When it comes to the recruitment and training of minorities, the situation is even more problematic. Important research by the National Black Child Development Institute (1993) documents the paucity of African American leadership in a field that serves large numbers of African American children and indicates that the situation—always problematic—is becoming acute. Moreover, without the force of mandate or state requirements for leadership positions or without potential rewards, there are few incentives for individuals to pursue such training or for it to be provided. Typical of the loose entry requirements that characterize the entire field, the lack of leadership mandate and incentives reflects a historic inattention to the nurturance and support of workers at any level. Thus, a number of contextual factors—open admission, lack of inservice training opportunities, low status of the field, insufficient minority representation in leadership positions, lack of mandates and incentives—create formidable attitudinal and practical obstacles to the development of leadership in the field.

A second set of issues underscores the leadership challenge in early care and education. Indeed, the field has been slow to understand and interpret theory from other fields. Gwen Morgan, founding director of the Center for Career Development in Early Care and Education at Wheelock College, notes that "our field rejects other fields as not relevant" (personal communication, 29 November 1994). This is true for many facets of the field and is especially true in the leadership domain, which could benefit from informative work in business administration, sociology, and psychology. It seems that our field has created ideas about leadership in a somewhat ad hoc manner, without building on major theoretical constructs—including, for example, stakeholder theory, situational leadership, and/or contingency theory. There may be clear reasons for this. Past models and traditional leadership theory may not have been appropriate to the early childhood field in that they reflected a hierarchical, top-down, male-oriented orientation. Newer leadership approaches, however, support collaborative leadership and respect the role of gender in leadership development; these are more in concert with early childhood principles and practices and bode well for the potential of knowledge transfer across the disciplines.

A third set of issues that must be addressed if the field is to tackle leadership with seriousness is the lack of definition of an early care and education leader. Conventionally, leadership has been equated with management, so that leaders were typically center directors or other child care administrators. As noted earlier, this narrow definition was sufficient when the field and the context in which it existed were less complex than they are today. A broadened definition of leadership has now emerged, with leaders occupying positions as researchers, advocates, conceptualizers, and teacher trainers, to name a few. But are teachers—master teachers, who elect to work directly with children—"leaders"? A false hierarchy of leadership may exist, one wherein leaders are only those who set their sights outside classrooms or family child care homes.

Not unrelated is the tendency to equate leadership with a specific job role or function. In this view, leadership functions and characteristics are determined by the institution or position rather than the qualities and capacities of individuals. This raises an even more fundamental problem: the field has not defined whether there is a particular set of skills associated with leadership and, if so, what skills are important. For example, is self-knowledge a component of leadership? In short, it is not yet clear what constitutes a leader, whether leaders are defined by role or individual characteristics, and what skills, competencies, and training leaders should have. It is precisely because there is no consensual definition or understanding of what is meant by leadership that this volume came into existence. Our intent is to air different perspectives on leadership in hopes of advancing discussion and action.

Finally, and perhaps most fundamentally, leadership in early care and education cannot be defined until the field defines what constitutes early care and education. Does it include all the services that young children receive, including health services, social services, and family support? Or is early care and education only the core or primary services such as child care, Head Start, prekindergarten, or family child care programs? Does early care and education include those individuals who work in capacities that create the infrastructure—resource and referral, research, planning and coordination, or teacher preparation?

The promise

Herculean as these challenges appear, many promising efforts are under way to address them. Dialogue about what constitutes early care and education is moving forward (April 19th Group 1996). This volume suggests that early care and education is composed of the core and the infrastructural services that support the core. It includes family support but does not—for the purposes of this discussion—include health, mental health, or social services.

A diverse group of players—researchers, advocates, and community organizers (including some authors in this volume)—are working to define leadership, both conceptually and practically. With this work, new attitudes toward leadership are emerging in the field. For example, until recently, *Young Children*, the journal of the profession, published little on leadership per se; most articles addressing leadership focused primarily on supervision and administration. Influenced by the new leadership work in general and new needs in the field, those attitudes have changed. Rodd (1994), though writing from an Australian perspective, discusses aspects of leadership (including decisionmaking, team-building, and conflict resolution) that will be extremely helpful to early childhood leaders and practitioners. Bowman (1994) writes about cultural differences and the need to allow children and adults to express competence in diverse ways. Phillips (1994) directly addresses the training of leaders, noting the differing historical traditions involved in preparing individuals to work in schools and in child care and other early childhood settings. Kagan (1994) discusses the inapplicability of conventional leadership norms to early care and education, and Morgan (this volume) works consistently to promote the utilization of applicable leadership theories from other disciplines.

The breadth of definition that is being considered is reflected in the range of leadership efforts under way. Some are designed to foster leadership capacity in the policy/advocacy domain (e.g., the Children's Defense Fund's Expanding Advocacy for Child Care

Project). Other initiatives focus on enhancing the capacity of organizations and their affiliates (e.g., the National Association for the Education of Young Children's Affiliate Development Process). Still others work to promote local leadership and community planning through the provision of national technical assistance (e.g., Families and Work Institute EQUIP; Child Care Action Campaign and Council of Chief State School Officers' Child Care and Education: Forging the Link). In addition, the National Conference of State Legislatures is providing leadership support on early care and education to legislators and legislative staff, while the National Center for Children in Poverty is working with urban child care administrators in the Urban Child Care Project. And a group of major national foundations has funded an important new leadership capacity-building effort at Wheelock College's Center for Career Development in Early Care and Education.

Other significant efforts train leaders in antibias education (e.g., Pacific Oaks College's Culturally Relevant Anti-Bias Leadership Education Project [CRABLE]). And still others promote professional development through an array of efforts (e.g., through NAEYC's Professional Development Institute). The Center for Career Development in Early Care and Education is working through its Partners in Change project, as well as through other avenues, to create career development systems that enhance leadership training opportunities. The National Center for the Early Childhood Work Force's mentoring programs support the acquisition of knowledge and skills by novice caregivers and enhance the professional development of more skilled and experienced teachers; mentor teachers are rewarded symbolically and financially to encourage their commitment to the early care and education field (Whitebook & Sakai 1995). Moreover, NAEYC has taken subsequent steps to advance leadership in the field through its Spring Leadership Conference and it Professional Development Institute, as well as through other activities that advance individual and Affiliate development.

Finally, professional organizations conduct ongoing leadership efforts, often in conjunction with their national conferences. Examples of these important leadership efforts include a preconference day devoted to leadership at the National Black Child Development Institute annual meeting and institutes held in conjunction with the NAEYC and National Head Start Association conferences. In addition, the National Head Start Association offers leadership institutes specifically for Head Start personnel. In short, new and broader conceptions of leadership are emerging, and opportunities for leadership and professional development are expanding. The field is moving forward.

Charting the course

As thrilling as these efforts are, far more remains to be done. Facing the polemics and problems and building on the promise, we suggest taking four major steps to foster further leadership development in early care and education. First, we need to come to some consensus around the definition, however broad, of leadership in early care and education, drawing on historical conceptions and attitudes toward leadership in this field and other fields. A generally accepted definition will enable the field to take the second step: understand what leadership does. Leadership has many functions: pedagogical, management, advocacy, community, and conceptual. We must explore the nature of each to learn what purposes leadership serves. Third, because we know that leadership development does not occur in a vacuum, we must be sensitive to the context in which individuals and organizations become leaders and to the context in which they will lead. In particular, we need to pay attention to the barriers and opportunities and the strengthens and weaknesses in the current system so that we recognize the elements on which to build, as well as those that need improvement. The fourth and final step entails exploring new paths to leadership. It calls for examining the different roles various organizations—from educational institutions to professional organizations—can take to support leadership development.

Leadership in Early Care and Education adds its voice to the chorus of concern regarding the historic lack of support for the field, for personnel in the field, and for leaders who are the nation's unsung heroes. This volume aims to take the four major steps outlined above to further the dialogue around a broadened understanding of leadership. Throughout these chapters, authors and commentators allude to the issues discussed above. The problems are not all solved, but many are clearly identified. Finally, the recommendations (in chapter 18) that conclude this volume suggest far more specific strategies. These strategies are ours, *all of ours,* to chart.

References

Adams, G., & N.O. Poersch. 1996. *Who cares? State commitment to child care and education.* Washington, DC: Children's Defense Fund.

Adams, G., & J. Sandfort. 1994. *First steps, promising futures: State prekindergarten initiatives in the early 1990s.* Washington, DC: Children's Defense Fund.

April 19th Group. 1996. *Guiding principles for a child care/early education system.*

Azer, S.L., K.L. Capraro, & K.A. Elliott. 1996. *Working toward making a career of it: A profile of career development initiatives in 1996.* Boston: Center for Career Development in Early Care and Education, Wheelock College.

Barnard, C. 1938. *The functions of the executive.* Cambridge, MA: Harvard University Press.

Bennis, W. 1966. *Changing organizations.* New York: McGraw-Hill.

Bowman, B. 1994. The challenge of diversity. *Phi Delta Kappan* 76 (3): 218–24.

Carnegie Task Force on Meeting the Needs of Young Children. 1994. *Starting points: Meeting the needs of our youngest children.* New York: Carnegie Corporation of New York.

Committee for Economic Development. 1993. *Why child care matters: Preparing young children for a more productive America.* New York: Author.

Cortes, E. 1996. Organizing communities and constituents for change. In *Reinventing early care and education: A vision for a quality system,* eds. S.L. Kagan & N.E. Cohen. San Francisco: Jossey-Bass.

Cost, Quality, and Child Outcomes Study Team. 1995. *Cost, quality, and child outcomes in child care centers. Public report.* 2d ed. Denver: Economics Department, University of Colorado.

Gardner, S. 1976. Roles for general purpose governments in human services. *Human Services Monograph Series 2* (August).

Gray, B. 1989. *Collaborating: Finding common ground for multiparty problems.* San Francisco: Jossey-Bass.

Gulick, L. 1937. Notes on the theory of organization. In *Papers on the science of administration,* eds. L. Gulick & L. Urwick. New York: Augustus Kelley.

Kagan, S.L. 1994. Leadership: Rethinking it—Making it happen. *Young Children* 49 (5): 50–54.

Kagan, S.L., S. Goffin, S. Golub, & E. Pritchard. 1995. *Toward systemic reform: Service integration for young children and their families.* Falls Church, VA: National Center for Service Integration.

Kamerman, S.B., & A.J. Kahn. 1995. *Starting right: How America neglects its youngest children and what we can do about it.* New York: Oxford University Press.

Kelley, R. 1992. *The power of followership: How to create leaders people want to follow and followers who lead themselves.* New York: Doubleday.

Mitchell, A. 1996. Licensing: Lessons from other occupations. In *Reinventing early care and education: A vision for a quality system,* eds. S.L. Kagan & N.E. Cohen. San Francisco: Jossey-Bass.

National Black Child Development Institute. 1993. *Paths to African American leadership positions in early childhood education: Constraints and opportunities.* Washington, DC: Author.

Olson, L. 1996. Leadership standards target teaching, learning. *Education Week* (4 September): 5.

Phillips, C. 1994. The challenge of training and credentialing early childhood educators. *Phi Delta Kappan* 76 (3): 214–17.

Rodd, J. 1994. *Leadership in early childhood: The pathway to professionalism.* New York: Teachers College Press.

Senge, P. 1990. *The fifth discipline: The art and practice of the learning organization.* New York: Doubleday.

Simon, H.A. 1976. *Administrative behavior: A study of decision-making processes in administrative organizations.* 3d rev. ed. New York: Free Press.

Sugarman, J. 1993. *Building local strategies for young children and their families.* Washington, DC: Center in Effective Services for Children.

U.S. General Accounting Office. 1993. *Poor preschool-aged children: Numbers increase but most not in preschool.* 93-411. Washington, DC: Author.

U.S. General Accounting Office. 1995. *Early childhood programs: Multiple programs and overlapping target groups.* 95-4FS. Washington, DC: Author.

Whitebook, M., P. Hnatiuk, & D. Bellm. 1994. *Mentoring in early care and education: Refining an emerging career path.* Washington, DC: National Center for the Early Childhood Work Force.

Whitebook, M., & L. Sakai. 1995. *The potential of mentoring: An assessment of the California early childhood mentor teacher program.* Washington, DC: National Center for the Early Childhood Work Force.

Chapter 2

Historical Views of Leadership

Gwen Morgan

As the early care and education field seeks to expand leadership opportunities and strengthen leadership development, it is important to explore existing knowledge of leadership. This chapter begins by examining studies from fields other than our own. Much of the general understanding of leaders and leadership comes from business research, and although some of this material has filtered to early childhood practitioners through journals, workshops, consultations, and college courses, many early childhood professionals are not familiar with it. Yet much can be learned from the experience of others as we try to understand leadership in our own field. The next section discusses the application of this research on leadership to the early childhood field. In particular, I will enumerate some of the factors that may inhibit leadership development and the ingredients necessary to prepare early childhood leaders.

Background

Studies on leadership began early in this century (see Schein 1980 for a comprehensive history) and initially focused on improving work output through time and motion analyses. In the course of these studies, psychologists found that how workers felt about the workplace, how they organized and identified with their groups, and how they were treated by management greatly influenced the amount and quality of the work they did.

One of the early themes in the study of organizations was personality traits associated with leadership (see McClelland 1994 for a review). However, interest in these was short-lived, and by 1970 identification of traits was out of fashion, primarily because it was found that a set of traits did not predict performance or leadership success (McClelland 1994). In view of the limited usefulness of lists of personality traits, psychologists turned their attention to the need

to match their leadership styles with the differing needs of workers (Graves 1966; Maslow [1954] 1987) and the many different roles played by the heads of organizations (Mintzberg 1973).

Competencies—both generic ones and those specific to different roles and levels in a field—also have been studied. The competency movement, which dates from late 1960s, has influenced public education and many other fields, including early care and education (Spencer, McClelland, & Spencer 1994). A competency is an underlying characteristic of an individual that is causally related to effective or superior job performance (Boyatzis 1982). Competencies can be motives, traits, self-concepts, attitudes/values, and content knowledge of skills. Any individual characteristic that can be measured and shown to differentiate significantly superior from average performance is included in the bundle of characteristics referred to as competencies. It is from this work that the early childhood field drew the idea of identifying competencies for early childhood teachers and caregivers, which resulted in the Child Development Associate (CDA) credentialing system.

In the generic research on competencies, experts identify six clusters: achievement, helping/service, influence, managerial, cognitive problem solving, and personal effectiveness. Different competencies are found between jobs and at varying levels of the same job. The one competency that distinguishes superior performance in the greatest number of fields and roles is information-seeking behavior. Success in today's world often is more dependent on knowing how to get information than on the acquisition of a specific body of knowledge.

A concept to emanate from early studies of leadership was a distinction between transformational and transactional leadership (Selznick 1957; Burns 1978; Peters & Waterman 1982; Kanter 1983; Bass 1985; Bennis & Nanus 1985). Tichy and Devanna (1986) describe *transformational* leaders as change agents and visionaries, able to deal with complexity, ambiguity, and uncertainty. *Transactional* leaders are able to facilitate the development of a mutually supportive community (Francis & Young 1979; Jentz & Wofford 1979; Woodcock & Francis 1981). Transactional leaders are described as value driven, persuasive, strong, predictable, essential to team building, and skilled in anecdotal communication (Francis & Young 1979). According to Bennis and Nanus (1985), transformational leaders influence and inspire others, while transactional leaders or managers lead by employing the technical skills necessary to get the job done. Transformational leadership is an art rather than a science, focusing on policy rather than execution and being concerned with values rather than facts. Most experts believe that a leader of an organization needs both transactional and transformational skills.

The role of leader is also defined by the form of an organization's structure and culture. A different style of leadership is essential when organizations are highly participatory or responding to rapid change. The shift toward knowledge-based organizations creates a different set of leadership tasks (Senge 1990; Schein 1993). Hennig and Jardin (1976) suggest that organizations and fields in which women predominate—such as early care and education—also may need different qualities in their leaders.

General systems theory (Bertalanffy 1968), introduced in the 1950s and applied to businesses and large service systems, is based on the application of organic concepts of biology to large complex systems. This approach was popularized by Graham Allison (1971), who showed that while policy emerges on the large stage, other events are happening concurrently at the personal and organizational level that either support or subvert the policy. The deliberate use of several vantage points to view systems was a blow to linear, Newtonian thinking and led to a more textured view of how organizations work.

Today's literature has replaced linear thinking with more complex models of organizations and leadership. Rather than making decisions driven by short-term results, leaders today are mission driven, highly sensitive to consumer values, and inclined to include a broader list of stakeholders in their priorities (De Pree 1987; Autry 1991; Heifetz 1994; Micklethwait & Wooldridge 1996). For example, the Johnson & Johnson credo (Collins & Porras 1994) orders the priorities among the company's missions and lists responsibility to customers, employees, management, the communities of which the company is a member, and the stockholders, in that order. Systems approaches, which include defining multiple audiences and encouraging teamwork and concepts of total quality management, are spreading throughout business and governmental

organizations (Deal & Peterson 1994). Bolman and Deal (1991) suggest that frames for understanding systems include the organizational structure, human resources, political realities, and symbolic processes.

Another extension of general systems theory is found in the literature on complexity and chaos (Waldrop 1992). This approach accepts complexity and change as constants. According to Tichy and Devanna, "One way to sum up the problem of bureaucracy (or any system for that matter) is to point out that today's solutions have embedded in them the next round of problems and that what makes for good fit and alignment at a particular time will probably be out of sync under another set of conditions" (1986, 219). However, resistance to change is difficult to dismantle and reassemble in a more effective way.

All new organizational models require leaders who are able to make far-reaching transformational changes in the way people work and who can convince members of the organization to accept and participate in change (Bennis 1966; Jones 1986). While change initially is experienced as a loss, gradually the pain is overcome and people begin to function in new ways. The organization becomes creative and innovative, and its members continue to learn, until the organization freezes into a new static pattern.

Another new conception of leadership arises from the notion of self-renewing organizations. These organizations embrace errors and emphasize risk taking, innovation, goal setting, and goal revision. Their decisionmaking process values intuition and creativity, can live with paradox, and puts less emphasis on purely analytic approaches.

Drucker (1966, 1974, 1990, 1993) articulated general concepts of missions and marketing that are widely applicable today, and he continues to initiate innovative ideas (see also Hesselbein, Goldsmith, & Beckhard 1997). Leaders are encouraged to ask questions and probe below any superficial level of answers: What business are you in? What groups are your customers? What do your customers value? How does what you offer your customers relate to what they value? These basic marketing concepts, essential to quality in a service just as they are for a product, are greatly needed in the field of early child care and education, where adversarial relationships between parents and teachers are sometimes complacently sustained.

The combination of policies and principles known as total quality management (TQM) is a set of interrelated factors that lead to constant change and improvement (Deming 1986). In this decade TQM has become widespread across many sectors, combining a customer orientation, team building, empowerment of workers, improved systems of work flow, benchmarking, and a total commitment to quality by everybody in an organization. Competition, long considered important to leadership, has been highly valued in the business world because it prevents overstability, a characteristic thought to undermine excellence. However, business has always avoided inappropriate competition, such as that caused by narrow functional divisions in the same organization.

Strategic analysis and thinking has undergone several transformations during the past several decades (Mintzberg 1994, 1995). One line of thought, stakeholder analysis, maintains that the leader's job is not just relating to the internal employees and the shareholders but negotiating with a large number of other organizations and individuals who have a stake in the enterprise. The old business or military concept of "span of control," with the manager being responsible only for what can be controlled, has been replaced by the challenging concept of negotiation with a large number of stakeholders, over whom the manager has little or no control (Freeman 1984).

A number of factors influence the environment in which leadership is practiced and therefore affect how leadership can be exerted. For instance, the social context (values and beliefs, social/economic status, preferred relating styles) mediates the effect of leadership qualities and behavior. Among the more salient contextual issues for the field of early care and education are authority, followership, and gender, all of which interact in organizations to define leadership.

Authority is not a trait but a broad concept that operates across a variety of social domains and contexts—for example, religion, politics, government, education, health, and family relationships (Schein 1980). A few important points about authority are relevant to leadership. First, authority is not innate; it does not reside in the person who has authority. Instead, it is granted to the leader by the followers. For that reason, as we try to understand the dance of leaders and followers, we need to understand the reasons people grant authority to other people (Siu 1979; Schein 1980; Sennett 1980; Mintzberg 1983; Kotter 1985). Second, there is a distinction between authoritarian and authoritative relationships. *Authoritarian* relationships are based on a status gap between leader and follower in which both are committed to the perpetuation of that gap, thus enslaving both the leader and the follower. An *authoritative* relationship is one in which there is a status gap, but the parties are committed to reducing or removing the gap—the teacher is committed to the growth of the student, the parent is committed to the growth of the child, and the mentor is committed to the growth of the protégé. The relationship contributes to the further growth of each party, empowering all.

Leaders and followers are inextricably related; there cannot be one without the other. Leadership is a relationship and not a stand-alone set of competencies. The successful leader needs to have followers (Barnard 1938; Kelley 1991). Relationships between leaders and followers are colored by the leader's assumptions about why people work. According to McGregor (1958), leaders hold two views of workers: in the first, the "jackass fallacy," they assume people have to be forced to work or must be motivated by extrinsic rewards; in the other, they believe workers are motivated to work and do so if recognized, valued, and involved. Chester Barnard (1938) wrote as early as the 1930s about the need to develop *followership*, but this strand of organizational psychology needs more exploration.

With transactional and transformational skills replacing older ideas of authoritarian leadership, collaborative leadership is the current trend. Heroic, single male executives are no longer the stereotype of business leaders. Shared leadership is more commonly described. Women bring distinct characteristics to leadership roles (Hennig & Jardin 1976; Kanter 1983; Kinney 1992; Morrison 1992). For instance, women managers often possess the collaborative and communication skills that are in high demand in today's world. Women are likely to espouse a more collaborative leadership style (Lawler, Mohrman, & Ledford 1992). Because the overwhelming majority of early care and education workers are female, this literature is highly relevant to our field.

Application of leadership concepts to the early childhood field

The director or administrator's role is essential for achieving quality in the early childhood organization (Decker & Decker 1984; Greenman & Fuqua 1984; Bloom & Sheerer 1992), yet this role continues to be undervalued.

Defining leaders' roles and responsibilities

Leaders of direct-service organizations are usually accountable for recruitment, supervision, staff development, progressive discipline, motivation, and creation of a healthy and mutually supportive community. In addition, leaders are responsible for community relations and for finding and managing financial resources. The field has been slow to recognize the knowledge and skills needed for this role. Perhaps out of fear of creating rewards and incentives that would attract teachers away from direct work with children, the field has been reluctant to devise formal preparation programs for the role of director.

Directors, or administrators, of early childhood programs wear many hats. A manager's role has to do with projecting the future, making wise decisions about expenditures and expectations of future income, and agonizing over the trilemma of salaries, fees, and ratios (Morgan 1995). Strategies and techniques developed in other fields for improving the work culture are enormously useful to leaders in our field. They go beyond the examination of the conditions in which people work to an examination of how to help people-oriented organizations work more effectively together through team building, conflict resolution, and group goal setting and decisionmaking (Schein 1987, 1993; Bloom & Sheerer 1992; Rodd 1994). Program quality is more likely to be achieved if the person accountable for it has knowledge and experience in the specific field rather than in another field. Bloom and colleagues (1991) found that after participating in leadership training, others perceived Head Start directors' and some lead teachers' improved level of competence.

Newer literature on directors' roles stresses the need for family-centered service and interprofessional collaboration with other community helpers (Kagan et al. 1992; Morgan 1995). Schorr (1992) points out that, by "groping along," program managers often lack the skills needed to manage. She identifies challenges for directors: finding new ways to recruit, selecting and supervising workers, putting together diverse sources of support in ingenious ways, and creating a nonbureaucratic, outcome-oriented organizational culture.

Just as directors are essential for program quality in centers, principals make a difference in whether programs in their schools are developmentally appropriate. This model of supportive leadership is rare; most principals have little knowledge of early childhood programming. Many of the current efforts in school reform are geared to restoring leadership and decisionmaking to the local school, removing the crippling red tape of large bureaucracy. The success of such reforms lies not only in the success of the school-based management strategy or charter schools but in the ability of the principal to provide leadership and support.

One popular reform effort proposed a new goal for schools: success for all children (Seeley 1981). For all children to be successful, leaders must create new relationships between students and teachers, develop a stronger partnership with parents and the community, and liberate the school from outside control. Further, the principal and teacher leaders must be able to embrace new concepts and new ways of thinking, rejecting old mental pathways.

Leaders as advocates

Advocacy is another dimension of leadership that needs attention. The *Guidelines for Preparation of Early Childhood Professionals* says, "At each of these [educational] levels, the professional is expected to advocate for policies designed to improve conditions for children, families, and the profession" (NAEYC 1996, 3). To do this, leaders must be able to take multiple perspectives rather than narrow academic or service viewpoints. To improve conditions for children and families, professionals need to understand the history and issues that surround important policies, regulations, funding, and role of the government and the private sector in influencing what happens in the field. While advocacy on behalf of children and families is well established in the field, advocacy on behalf of the profession is a newer idea. It is common for other professions to use their power and influence to benefit members, but our field has been more inclined to use its influence in more altruistic ways. Altruism is a basic—and commendable—characteristic of the field, but it may be that we need to plan strategically to represent our own interests in the policy arena.

The reward system

Prestige and earnings are two factors that play an important role in early childhood leadership. The U.S. Labor Department considers prestige and earnings a function of the substantive complexity of work performed within an occupation. There has been a tendency in early care and education to lump the entire field into one role, without differentiating the level of expertise or the complexity of the work. This means that different roles have not led to differentiated compensation, despite differences in the complexity of tasks. The field would profit from the Department of Labor's studies on complexity as a useful way to establish criteria for compensation (Spenner 1990; Rowan 1994).

Characteristics of the field that inhibit leadership development

The field of early care and education has several characteristics which, singly and in combination, impede leadership development. Among the most significant are the following.

Too narrow a definition of leadership. For the field of early care and education to move ahead, an important and essential change is a more diverse leadership. The field has made some headway in defining roles for work with children and to a lesser extent with parents, but it is weak in producing leaders who can work together across traditional divisions of race, social class, and culture. Even though the early childhood field is dominated by women—as a group, stronger in interpersonal, collaborative skills (Lawler, Mohrman, & Ledford 1992)—we have not developed the skills necessary to collaborate across diverse cultures. Here, some large corporations, motivated by the world stage on which they now compete, may be ahead of the helping professions and have lessons we can use.

Ambivalence about authority. Another area of concern is the attitude about authority that permeates the field. Many early childhood professionals are reluctant to become involved in authority relationships. As a field, we need to get comfortable with roles of leadership, responsibility, influence, and authority. Leadership is not compatible with powerlessness. Authority rests both with the leader and with the follower, and both need to develop new beliefs and expectations regarding leader and follower roles.

Lack of systems thinking. "You can't just fix one thing" sums up systems thinking. In the early childhood field this means we need to work toward improvement of the whole system; working only on one problem may make things worse. Lawrence K. Frank (1962), an early systems thinker in the early childhood field, emphasized the importance of a holistic view of children and the social contexts in which they live. He lamented the discipline orientations (psychology, sociology, anthropology) that separate children's development into "anonymous units" (physical, social, emotional, cognitive), ignoring the need to synthesize both the studies and the children. He advises us to take a broader view of children within society rather than a narrow, programmatic approach.

Scarce resources and inappropriate competition. Some competition is healthy, such as the competition among centers to serve children and families well. But we also are involved in some inappropriate competition. Early care and education programs are in competition for scarce resources, and fierce turf battles are common, preventing us from joining forces to increase our resources. Children's programs are also in competition with programs for school-age and adolescent youth as well as for the homeless and aged populations. In some instances, centers compete with family child care. Despite the pressure to get as much as we can for our own service, early childhood professionals must learn to cooperate and collaborate with other human services (Kagan et al. 1992; Morgan 1995). Presidents of major companies in the American

Business Collaboration (ABC) have committed massive funding to support improvements in child care— "to do together what none of us could do alone" (ABC internal communication 1993).

Narrow preparation for our roles. We have not always encouraged our leaders to seek wider domains or to take on roles outside the classroom. Many who enter the field are initially attracted to work with children and are often distrustful of power, hierarchies, and the equating of money with service. However, our values may inhibit our leadership. Direct-service idealism is a quality that should not be lost, but a more realistic stance is also desirable since it offers leaders the opportunity to influence broader venues, such as public policies, systems, and collaboration (VanderVen 1992).

Summary

Much can be learned from the generic study of leadership in other fields, particularly from business. A few basic ideas that could be of great value to leaders in our field include the following.

• Understand that leadership is a set of reciprocal relationships, not a static quality.

• Reinforce holistic thinking and planning through knowledge about how systems work.

• Develop a more extensive knowledge base and a theoretical framework concerning roles, competencies, and teams specific to early childhood professions.

• Accept authority and its place in relationships with children, parents, followers, and other leaders.

• Acknowledge the distinction between and the value of different forms of leadership.

• Match the complexity of work with compensation to reward higher levels of preparation and personal growth.

• Work to advance concepts that focus on families as well as on children.

It is time at this moment in history that we focus on leadership. Learning from others is essential if the field of early care and education is to move quickly enough to meet the challenges it faces.

References

Allison, G. 1971. *Essence of decision: Explaining the Cuban missile crisis.* Boston: Little Brown.
Autry, J.A. 1991. *Love and profit: The art of caring leadership.* New York: William Morrow.
Barnard, C. 1938. *The functions of the executive.* Cambridge, MA: Harvard University Press.

Bass, B.M. 1985. *Leadership and performance beyond expectations.* New York: Free Press.

Bennis, W. 1966. *Changing organizations.* New York: McGraw-Hill.

Bennis, W.G., & B. Nanus. 1985. *Leaders: Strategies for taking charge.* New York: Harper & Row.

Bertalanffy, L.V. 1968. *General systems theory.* New York: George Braziller.

Bloom, P.J., & M. Sheerer. 1992. The effects of leadership training on child care program quality. *Early Childhood Research Quarterly* 7: 579–604.

Bloom, P.J., M. Sheerer, N. Richard, & J. Britz. 1991. The *Head Start Leadership Training Program: Final report to the Department of Health and Human Services, Head Start Division.* Evanston, IL: Early Childhood Professional Development Project, National-Louis University.

Bolman, L.G., & T.E. Deal. 1991. *Reframing organizations: Artistry, choice, and leadership.* San Francisco: Jossey-Bass.

Boyatzis, R.E. 1982. *The competent manager: A model for effective performance.* New York: Wiley-Interscience.

Burns, J.M. 1978. *Leadership.* New York: Harper & Row.

Collins, J.E., & J.I. Porras. 1994. *Built to last: Successful habits of visionary companies.* New York: Harper Business.

Deal, T.E., & K.D. Peterson. 1994. *The leadership paradox: Balancing logic and artistry in schools.* San Francisco: Jossey-Bass.

Decker, C.A., & J. Decker. 1984. *Planning and administering early childhood programs.* Columbus, OH: Merrill.

Deming, W.E. 1986. *Out of the crisis.* New York: Cambridge University Press.

De Pree, M. 1987. *Leadership is an art.* Lansing: Michigan State University.

Drucker, P. 1966. *The effective executive.* New York: Harper & Row.

Drucker, P. 1974. *Management tasks, responsibilities, practices.* New York: Harper & Row.

Drucker, P. 1990. *Managing the nonprofit organization: Principles and practices.* New York: Harper Collins.

Drucker, P. 1993. *Post capitalist society.* Oxford: Butterworth Heinemann.

Francis, D., & D. Young. 1979. *Improving work groups: A practical manual for team building.* San Diego, CA: University Associates.

Frank, L.K. 1962. The beginnings of child development and family life education. *Merrill Palmer Quarterly* 8 (4): 7–28.

Freeman, R.E. 1984. *Strategic management: A stakeholder approach.* Boston: Pitman.

Graves, C. 1966. Deterioration of work standards. *Harvard Business Review* 50 (3): 117–19.

Greenman, J.T., & R. Fuqua, eds. 1984. *Making day care better.* New York: Teachers College Press.

Heifetz, R.A. 1994. *Leadership without easy answers.* Cambridge, MA: Belknap of Harvard University Press.

Hennig, M., & A. Jardin. 1976. *The managerial woman.* New York: Pocket Books.

Hesselbein, F., M. Goldsmith, & R. Beckhard, eds. 1997. *The leaders of the future.* Drucker Foundation Future Series. San Francisco: Jossey-Bass.

Jentz, B.C., & J.W. Wofford. 1979. *Leadership and learning: Personal change in a professional setting.* New York: McGraw-Hill.

Jones, E.W., Jr. 1986. Black managers: The dream deferred. *Harvard Business Review* 67 (3): 84–93.

Kagan, S.L., A.M. Rivera, N. Brigham, & S. Rosenblum. 1992. *Collaboration: Cornerstone of an early childhood system.* New Haven, CT: Bush Center in Child Development and Social Policy.

Kanter, R.M. 1983. *The change masters.* New York: Simon & Schuster.

Kelley, R. 1991. *The power of followership: How to create leaders people want to follow and followers who lead themselves.* New York: Doubleday.

Kinney, J. 1992. New thoughts on child care administration and leadership involving emerging information on the psychology of women. Paper presented at the Annual Conference of NAEYC, November, New Orleans.

Kotter, J. 1985. *Power and influence.* New York: Free Press.

Lawler, E.E., S.A. Mohrman, & G.E. Ledford Jr. 1992. *Employee involvement and total quality management.* San Francisco: Jossey-Bass.

Maslow, A. [1954] 1987. *Motivation and personality.* New York: Harper & Row.

McClelland, D.C. 1994. Testing for competence rather than for intelligence. In *Competency assessment methods: History and state of the art,* eds. L.M. Spencer Jr., D.C. McClelland, & S.M. Spencer. Boston: Hay/McBer Research Press.

McGregor, D. 1958. *The human side of enterprise.* New York: McGraw-Hill.

Micklethwait, J., & A. Wooldridge. 1996. *The witch doctors: Making sense of the management gurus.* New York: Random House.

Mintzberg, H. 1973. *The nature of managerial work.* New York: Harper & Row.

Mintzberg, H. 1983. *Power in and around organizations.* Englewood Cliffs, NJ: Prentice-Hall.

Mintzberg, H. 1994. The fall and rise of strategic planning. *Harvard Business Review* 72 (1): 107–14.

Mintzberg, H. 1995. *The rise and fall of strategic planning.* New York: Free Press.

Morgan, G. 1995. Collaborative models of service integration. *Child Welfare* 72 (6): 1329–42.

Morrison, A.M. 1992. *The new leaders: Guidelines on leadership diversity in America.* San Francisco: Jossey-Bass.

NAEYC. 1996. *Guidelines for preparation of early childhood professionals.* Washington, DC: Author.

Peters, T., & R.H. Waterman. 1982. *In search of excellence: Learning from America's best-run companies.* New York: Harper & Row.

Rodd, J. 1994. *Leadership in early childhood: The pathway to professionalism.* New York: Teachers College Press.

Rowan, B. 1994. Comparing teachers' work with work in other occupations: Notes on the professional status of teaching. *Educational Researcher* 23 (6): 17–21.

Schein, E.H. 1980. *Organizational psychology.* 3d ed. Englewood Cliffs, NJ: Prentice-Hall.

Schein, E.H. 1987. *Process consultation, Vol. 2.* Reading, MA: Addison-Wesley.

Schein, E.H. 1993. How can organizations learn faster? The challenge of entering the green room. *Sloan Management Review* 34 (2): 85–92.

Schorr, L.B.. 1992. Community support for student success. In *Ensuring student success through collaboration.* Washington, DC: Council of Chief State School Officers.

Seeley, D. 1981. *Education through partnership.* Cambridge, MA: Ballinger.

Selznick, P. 1957. *Leadership in administration: A sociological interpretation.* New York: Harper & Row.

Senge, P.M. 1990. *The fifth discipline: The art and practice of the learning organization.* New York: Doubleday.

Sennett, R. 1980. *Authority.* New York: Knopf.

Siu. R.G.H. 1979. *The craft of power.* New York: John Wiley & Sons.

Spencer, L.M., Jr., D.C. McClelland, & S.M. Spencer, eds. 1994. *Competency assessment methods: History and state of the art.* Boston: Hay/McBer Research Press.

Spenner, K.I. 1990. Meaning, methods, and measures. *Work and Occupations* 17: 399–421.

Tichy, N.M., & M.A. Devanna. 1986. *The transformational leader.* New York: John Wiley.

VanderVen, K. 1992. Preparing practitioners for professionalism in early childhood education: Premises and proposals. Paper presented at NAEYC National Institute for Professional Development Conference, June, Los Angeles.

Waldrop, M.M. 1992. *Complexity: The emerging science at the edge of order and chaos.* New York: Simon & Schuster.

Woodcock, M., & D. Francis. 1981. *Organizational development through team building: Planning a cost effective strategy.* New York: John Wiley.

Five Faces of Leadership

SECTION **2**

Chapter 3

Pedagogical Leadership

Lilian G. Katz

The central mission of early childhood programs is to ensure that the quality of the day-to-day lives of the participating children supports and enhances their growth, development, and learning. The pedagogical function of early childhood programs addresses the role and responsibilities of caregivers and teachers with respect to what they intend children to learn and when and how knowledge and skills are best learned.

During my 25 years as director of the ERIC (Educational Resources Information Center) Clearinghouse on Elementary and Early Childhood Education, based at the University of Illinois in Urbana, and during my professorial duties, I have had ample opportunity to observe trends and shifts in pedagogical ideas and practices; to participate in local, national, and international events and organizations concerned with pedagogical issues; and to work alongside many leaders in the field. Three aspects of pedagogical leadership, based on my view of the field as derived from this experience, are discussed in this chapter. The first aspect involves the essentially ideological nature of education in general and early childhood education in particular. Second, pedagogical leaders are discussed as interpreters of research and practice to those involved in both of these activities. And third, leadership in setting the pedagogical agenda of the field is examined.

Pedagogical leadership and ideology

Pedagogical theories and methods are only two of the many complex determinants of the quality of children's experiences in early childhood settings. Such theories, and the methods based on or associated with them, have been the focus of frequent debate and dissension for as long as the field has existed. Indeed, one of the most salient aspects of education, or pedagogy in general and early childhood pedagogy in particular, is its embeddedness and involvement in ideological assumptions and commitments concerning the nature of childhood, what is worth learning, and how it is best learned. In other words, pedagogical orientations in early childhood education as well as in the later grades are often based on ideological positions about which advocates and detractors have strong feelings.

The nature and function of ideologies

The term *ideology* generally refers to strongly held ideas and values about which there is no hard evidence and that are personally important to their advocates (see Katz 1995). Ideologies are also related to an ideal conception of humanity and the "good life." Although the term sometimes carries with it derogatory connotations, ideologies serve important functions and are probably indispensable.

A basic assumption here is that in any field in which the database is weak, contradictory, or inconclusive, a vacuum is created that is filled by ideologies. Early childhood education is especially susceptible to data weakness for several reasons. First, because the target of investigation—the young child—is, by definition, immature and undergoing rapid growth, the testing and interpretation of observed changes is difficult. Second, conducting definitive experiments that might settle important pedagogical questions would be unethical. As long as we have any reason to believe that something is good for children, it is unethical to withhold it from them just for the sake of the advancement of science or to test theories and methods.

A number of acrimonious debates concerning teaching and curriculum methods cannot be settled by the rigid experimental paradigms borrowed from the natural sciences. Furthermore, many of the main arguments about appropriate pedagogy are related to assumptions about the long-range effects of early experience that are notoriously difficult to follow up and confirm or disconfirm with confidence. While the experimental methods of natural science constitute a problem for all social scientists, they are especially problematic for our field. First, as already suggested, the organism under investigation is in a period of rapid growth. Second, studies of the long-term effects we wish to learn about necessarily take years to conduct, and the intervening period between early experience and later functioning is subject to multiple, often unknowable, influences that are extremely difficult to as certain.

An example is the debate on the National Association for the Education of Young Children's position statement on developmentally appropriate practice, which has evoked heated discussion since it was published in 1987. In such discussions it has been difficult to disentangle ideological commitment from pedagogical rationale with respect to issues ranging from early education's goals and methods to the role of culture. Even when researchers present evidence on the outcomes of developmentally appropriate practice (e.g., Hyson, Hirsch-Pasek, & Rescorla 1990; Charlesworth et al. 1993), these findings are often applauded or attacked on ideological rather than empirical grounds. A revised position statement, which appears in the new edition of *Developmentally Appropriate Practice in Early Childhood Programs* (Bredekamp & Copple 1997), strives to respond to the key issues raised by critics from various ideological perspectives, but inevitably this new position too will be critiqued—and advocated—on ideological grounds.

Similarly, as noted by Smagorinsky (1995), Vygotsky's work, particularly the concept of the zone of proximal development, has been "invoked to account for the success of theoretically incompatible pedagogical approaches" (p. 193), such as a whole-language approach that minimizes teacher direction or reciprocal teaching in which the teacher takes a far more directive role. As Cazden (1996) points out, most readings of Vygotsky are selective, revealing more about the appropriators than they do about Vygotsky's psychological theories.

Open discussion and exchange

The only recourse for professions facing such constraints on their knowledge base is for their leaders to present their views, positions, and arguments to their colleagues via public forums and documents. In this way, critics as well as supporters can examine, question, and debate in light of the best available knowledge and analysis. One of the important functions of our professional associations, such as NAEYC, is to provide forums for advocates and adversaries to come together and develop consensus on the major contentious issues that members confront.

The inevitability of ideological considerations in pedagogical issues suggests that leaders are likely to be effective when they make explicit their ideological assumptions, strive for openness to counter-evidence, and explicate their views with appropriate qualifiers as to the sources of their convictions. The ideological nature of the field also places special burdens and responsibilities on leaders to be clear about the bases on which they advocate pedagogical practices and about what is known with what measure of certainty, remaining open to alternative interpretations and positions on the main issues. No matter how carefully our pedagogical theories and methods may be developed, their implementation and evaluation occur in contexts of sometimes passionate and often bitter ideological controversies—a fact of life that the expert and leader must learn to accept with understanding, insight, and forbearance.

Pedagogical leadership as interpretation

Like most professions, the early childhood field can be thought of as consisting of at least two subcultures: practitioners working on the "front line" (in daily contact with children) and social scientists engaging in research and producing new knowledge, typically in research centers in higher education settings (see Katz 1994).

These two groups do not always readily understand each other. By virtue of their familiarity with the knowledge base and with the daily frontline challenges, many directors, principals, curriculum specialists, education coordinators, and trainers serve as interpreters of research and theory to teachers. Ideally, people in these leadership positions are both knowledgeable and effective at helping teachers understand and put into action principles and practices derived from the knowledge base. But many are not so knowledgeable or effective, and even when they are, a substantial gulf remains between researchers and practitioners.

I myself have been involved, through my role as director of the ERIC Clearinghouse, in the ongoing effort to help researchers and practitioners understand and appreciate the other's potential contribution to our common ultimate goal of improving the life chances of all our children, especially with respect to pedagogical practices. Fulfillment of this function requires understanding that each group has its own professional and occupational pressures, customs, and hazards. For example, for the social scientist, skepticism about the knowledge base is both functional and desirable; on the other hand, the pedagogical practitioner cannot function effectively in a continual state of skepticism and doubt. A balance of skepticism and conviction seems to be required for the practitioner, although it is often difficult to sustain against intense and constant pressures for accountability. For the researcher, emphasis must be on the conceptual and theoretical soundness of ideas and methods; for the practitioner, emphasis must be on what works—typically, on "what works for me"—even when there is little theory or relevant data to back up the practice.

Interpreting each of these groups to the other, and being fluent in both their "languages," is no simple task. It requires genuine respect and understanding of each group's knowledge base, methods, needs, concerns, and temptations. Successful leadership depends also on being able to achieve and maintain credibility in both groups.

In the interest of strengthening the links between early childhood knowledge-producers and practitioners, the ERIC Clearinghouse, in cooperation with NAEYC, launched the *Early Childhood Research Quarterly* (*ECRQ*), for which I served as editor-in-chief in its first six years. At the initiation of *ECRQ*, no other research journal was devoted exclusively to the field. Now in its 12th year, *ECRQ* is devoted to publishing original studies, as well as analyses and syntheses of research on current topics in the field, and to stimulating integrative reviews of its large and growing database.

Interpreting the field to outsiders

Added to the within-profession interpretive role, pedagogical leadership also includes responsibility to interpret the knowledge bases and views of practitioners and researchers to many interested parties, including parents, school boards, and others involved in making pedagogical decisions. Thus, leadership requires not only a within-field bicultural and bilingual proficiency (i.e., communicating with practitioners and researchers). It actually requires the kind of "multicultural and multilingual" competence that makes possible genuine interpretation and communication between and among those outside the field who also have a stake in early care and education.

Shaping the agenda for discussions of pedagogy

One of the main roles leaders play in their spheres is setting the agenda of issues on which discussions and literature become focused, as well as participating in both of those activities. Fulfilling this role involves a variety of activities and strategies. First and most important is maintaining awareness of the concerns of practitioners and how they define the pedagogical predicaments and choices they regularly encounter. On the basis of such awareness a leader is then in a position to assist in reflection and perhaps redefinition and reinterpretation of the problems at hand.

For example, in my own early experience, I had several encounters in which caregivers and teachers raised questions that could not be settled on the basis of either regulations or available research evidence. Reflection on their concerns made me aware that many situations frequently faced by teachers—including those involving pedagogical choices—involve ethical and moral dilemmas that cannot be settled on the basis of pedagogical or developmental theory and research. After extensive discussions with practitioners around the country over a period of a year or so, I wrote "Ethical Issues in Working with Young Children," which was published by NAEYC in 1977 (see Katz 1995). Subsequently, under the leadership of Stephanie Feeney of the University of Hawaii, NAEYC developed and adopted a code of ethics for its members that addresses most of the issues raised in the original paper and other ethical issues as well (Feeney & Kipnis 1992).

Sometimes a leader shapes discussion at the national, local, or even program level by reinterpreting a perennial issue or perhaps by rediscovering a practice from the past and revisiting it in the light of new evidence. One such experience in my own work arose in the course of working with preschools in the People's Republic of China in the mid-1980s. Educators were struggling with the challenges created by the very high proportion of "only" children and the way these children's behavior diverged from traditional Chinese childhood patterns and expectations. In response to the questions they raised concerning how to address the new behavior patterns, I suggested placing children in mixed-age groups, thereby giving them simulated sibling experiences.

The enthusiasm with which my Chinese colleagues greeted this proposal led, upon my return to the University of Illinois, to my examination of the literature on mixed-age grouping. I soon learned that mixed-age grouping is a pedagogical strategy that has been advocated in the United States approximately every 25 years in this century, only to fade away within a decade each time. However, in the course of reexamining the issues, my colleagues and I were able to incorporate contemporary research on cross-age interaction that had not been available to our predecessors (Katz, Evangelou, & Hartman 1990). More than 20,000 copies of our summary, published by NAEYC, have been distributed, helping to spark interest in mixed-age grouping. This interest has intensified and spread—for a variety of reasons, such as a trend toward humanizing school environments and the desire to minimize grade retention. The number of books, newsletters, computer-based discussion groups, conference presentations, seminars, and workshops on the topic of mixed- or multi-age grouping continues to grow at a rapid pace.

Disseminating news of developments in pedagogical practices

Leadership in setting the field's agenda also involves identifying new developments of potential value in inspiring fresh thinking about pedagogical practices. A notable example is American educators' interest in the Reggio Emilia approach and its implications for early childhood programs in this country. Beginning in the early 1980s, Rebecca New, Carolyn Edwards, George Forman, and others visited schools in the northern Italian city and were struck by the extraordinary quality of children's visual representation of their experiences, theories, and ideas (New 1990; Edwards, Gandini, & Forman 1993). Intrigued by what I heard from them, I too began to visit the schools of Reggio Emilia, returning again and again (Katz & Cesarone 1994). As each of us shared our observations and interpretations of the philosophy and practices with groups of early childhood educators throughout the United States and other countries, the impact on early childhood programs outside Italy began to grow. Reports of practitioners around the United States attempting to incorporate ideas gleaned from the Reggio Emilia story continue to accumulate rapidly.

Although many of the examples in this chapter relate to pedagogical leadership at the national or international level, such leadership occurs at all levels. Program directors and teachers, for example, may evolve innovative teaching practices for working with the children in the program and may share these with practitioners.

Conclusion

Leadership in pedagogical theory and practice in early childhood care and education takes many forms. Through the examples outlined briefly in this chapter, I hope to encourage readers to put their views and proposals out for examination and cross-examination in this highly ideological field, to make explicit the bases of their assumptions, and to base their positions on the best available evidence—acknowledging its limitations. As in all other language learning, proficiency, understanding, comprehension, and appreciation of the languages of both the knowledge-producers and the practitioners in our field requires frequent interaction between members of each of the two groups.

References

Bredekamp, S., & C. Copple, eds. [1987] 1997. *Developmentally appropriate practice in early childhood programs*. Rev. ed. Washington, DC: NAEYC.

Cazden, C.B. 1996. Selective traditions: Readings of Vygotsky in writing pedagogy. In *Discourse, learning, and pedagogy*, ed. D. Hicks. Cambridge: Cambridge University Press.

Charlesworth, R., C.H. Hart, D.C. Burts, R.H. Thomasson, J. Mosley, & P.O. Fleege. 1993. Measuring the developmental appropriateness of kindergarten teachers' beliefs and practices. *Early Childhood Research Quarterly* 8 (3): 255–76.

Edwards, C.P., L. Gandini, & G. Forman, eds. 1993. *The hundred languages of children: The Reggio Emilia approach to early childhood education*. Norwood, NJ: Ablex.

Feeney, S., & K. Kipnis. 1992. *Code of ethical conduct & statement of commitment*. Washington, DC: NAEYC.

Hyson, M.C., K. Hirsch-Pasek, & L. Rescorla. 1990. The classroom practices inventory: An observational instrument based on NAEYC's guidelines for developmentally appropriate practices for 4- and 5-year-old children. *Early Childhood Research Quarterly* 5 (4): 475–94.

Katz, L.G. 1994. Information dissemination in early childhood education. *Knowledge and Policy: The International Journal of Knowledge Transfer and Utilization* 7 (4): 115–27.

Katz, L.G. 1995. Ethical issues in working with young children. In *Talks with teachers of young children: A collection*, ed. L.G. Katz. Norwood, NJ: Ablex.

Katz, L.G., & B. Cesarone. 1994. *Reflections on the Reggio Emilia approach*. Urbana, IL: ERIC Clearinghouse on Elementary and Early Childhood Education.

Katz, L.G., D. Evangelou, & J.A. Hartman. 1990. *The case for mixed-age grouping in early childhood*. Washington, DC: NAEYC.

New, R. 1990. Excellent early education: A city in Italy has it. *Young Children* 45 (5): 4–10.

Smagorinsky, P. 1995. The social construction of data: Methodological problems of investigating learning in the zone of proximal development. *Review of Educational Research* 65 (3): 191–212.

Commentary

by Maurice R. Sykes

Lilian Katz seeks to establish a framework to examine how leaders decide what children should learn and the best context for these learnings. What she seems to overlook in her discussion is the importance of the social, political, and economic context in which pedagogical leadership is nurtured.

Some pedagogical "leadership" springs from nagging social/political questions such as what can we do to raise the level of reading acquisition among young "disadvantaged" children. One pedagogical response, for better or for worse, was the creation of the DISTAR reading program. Other examples of the social/political context shaping pedagogical leadership are the state of Georgia's attempted ban on developmentally appropriate practices and antibias curriculum and, according to a recent *Education Week* article, another community's concern regarding single-sex toilets for young children.

I believe there is a real danger in creating an artificial dichotomy between practitioners and researchers. The truth of the matter is that practitioners are researchers. Each day teachers and other practitioners, through a series of planned and spontaneous interactions with young children, form hypotheses and conduct action research, usually without the technical tools employed by social scientists. Although teachers may be excellent at developing and testing hypotheses about children's behavior and learning, they are operating on the basis of intuition; nothing in their training prepares or credentials them to perform the role of practitioner/researcher/pedagogical leader.

With notable exceptions, the established research community has offered too little to early care and education. Most field-initiated research explores esoteric questions that offer little guidance and assistance to the practitioner. Research is often published in scholarly journals that are not read by most practitioners. Furthermore, the research community often fails to articulate the implications of the research and application to practice. In some instances researchers may need to work collaboratively with teachers to develop guidelines and suggestions for applying research findings to classroom settings.

And while I agree that young children are a challenging group to study, some perennial research questions are worthy of pursuing—such as how to develop social competence in young children and how an understanding of language acquisition helps us to better facilitate the teaching of reading to young children. The basic data for answering these queries reside in the minds and anecdotal records of thousands of teachers of young children. We should seek these teachers out, especially those who are engaging in cutting-edge pedagogy such as the Reggio Emilia approach or looping.

I can envision two ways that the officially recognized research community can offer guidance and assistance to early care and education practitioners. First, the research community can engage practitioners in discussions around nagging questions of practice that they would like to pursue and serve as *true* co-principal investigators in a research project, coaching the practitioner in the technical aspects of research. Researchers also can work to expand opportunities for research to reach the realm of practice by publishing in trade journals frequently read by practitioners and by providing forums in which practitioners and researchers can discuss current and emerging research interests.

The real pedagogical leaders provide care and education on a daily basis. And because leaders are made and not born, we must nurture and develop these interests in practitioners; we should help them to become consciously skilled in their craft of practitioner/researcher.

Chapter 4

Administrative Leadership

Mary L. Culkin

$\mathbf{M}$anaging a care and education institution today entails maintaining a business organization that provides services to children, families, and other consumers. The administrator must pay attention to the bottom line, provide for ongoing learning for staff, direct child and family services, and build internal and external communication networks that support the organization's work toward its goals. The organization, while being true to its mission, must adapt to internal and external changes, including staff and parent strengths and interests. Some people see this type of organization as a dynamic community in which staff and clients (families and others) work and learn together, accepting the challenges of constant change. And in a central position in all this activity is the person responsible for managing the program, the director.[1]

The scope of the early care and education manager's task

Managers in early care and education settings such as preschools, child care centers, and schools are in fact operating small businesses that deliver a complex set of services to children and families. They have much responsibility and, typically, little preparation for assuming that trust (Larkin 1992). Whether one thinks of a program as a complex system, a community, a business, or some combination of these three, there is a lot of work to be done. Early childhood managers work in the areas of personnel, budget, pedagogy, adult education and staff development, families, outreach to community, communication, planning, and overall attention to the internal and external values, mission, and goals of the program. The job is complex and challenging, requiring more than knowledge and successful classroom experience and,

to perform at an optimal level, more than the one or two courses in administration that some states require.

By learning management skills that approach programs as organizations and stress team building to provide good-quality services, the program manager gains a framework for increasing knowledge and skills to meet organizational goals. While the role of the director is gaining increased interest and value in the early childhood field, the lack of consensus about the character and parameters of the role, the lack of accessible management training and educational experiences in community or higher education settings, and the fiscal realities of the field make it a challenge to determine how to develop well-trained, competent managers.

Why are managers important in early childhood programs?

Research indicates that managers/directors play an important part in the production of quality services. Bloom and Sheerer (1992) found that providing leadership training to a group of directors had a pronounced effect on the quality of teaching practice at their centers. The managers reported an increased sense of competence and improvements in curriculum, teacher-child interactions, use of physical space, and health and safety practice. The Cost, Quality, and Child Outcomes Study Team (1995) found that directors at high-quality centers had more experience and more education than directors of low-quality centers. Directors of higher quality centers also were viewed by staff as more involved in curriculum planning. Similarly, Bredekamp (1989) reported that in the National Association for the Education of Young Children (NAEYC) accreditation process the director was the strongest indicator of overall program quality. Since directors are managers of service quality, a better understanding of their role, along with increased attention to their professional preparation, is a promising means to improve the quality of services for young children and their families.

Managing or leading?

Effective early care and education managers of good-quality programs must accomplish many things as they move through an active day—for example, attend a teachers' meeting about an individual child's development within the center's curriculum, explain the program to parents or local community leaders, phone the center bookkeeper about the monthly payroll and financial report, develop a collaborative fundraising project with other directors, and engage in the myriad other management details. Managing a program is demanding, and the quality of services provided by managers and their teams varies. Not all managers are skilled in their jobs. Further, not all managers are leaders. (See Mitchell, pp. 86–87.)

Management is one responsibility of an administrator; leadership, another. Rodd (1994) notes that while *managers* in early childhood settings focus on the specific details of daily practice, early childhood *leaders* spend more time in reflective, dynamic, value-based planning and organizing. This definition of management is grounded within the phrase *to succeed in accomplishing*. And there is no doubt that directors have a great deal to accomplish in managing their programs and are able to do their jobs more effectively if they become competent managers of their organization's human and financial resources. On the other hand, leaders provide vision and are a source of inspiration, as well as structure and direction, to their colleagues. Though management and leadership often go together, the two have separate meanings, and in this discussion the work of management is considered a central leadership task. Thus, one can consider the management of human and financial resources in an early childhood organization as only a part of the leader's job. The term *leader* implies a deeper and more far-reaching developmental relationship between persons within and outside the organization. As early care and education managers become more skilled at their jobs, and as their understanding of management deepens, it is appropriate to expect they may continue their professional development, mastering both management and leadership skills. In such a sequence of training and professional experience (Conger 1992; Leithwood 1992; Morrison 1992), the development of leadership skills is one component in the process of developing competence in management (Bolman & Deal 1991).

Is this the time for early care and education leaders to join with policymakers to make management training, in conjunction with leadership experiences, a more stable, comprehensive, and supported aspect of the preparation of directors and other managers for our field? If so, what issues apply? And what special considerations are appropriate for comprehensive management training for practitioners who seek successful entry into the domain of management, and ultimately leadership, in the early care and education field?

The early care and education organization

Early care and education managers direct organizations. Strictly speaking, managers are "vested with the formal authority over an organizational unit" (Mintzberg 1989, 15), and their work concerns the overall climate and culture of the organization—the details of the daily service patterns that keep the program functioning and moving toward its goals and mission. Central to the internal system in the early childhood organization is the interaction between manager, teachers, and other staff. Effective directors of good-quality programs support the staff through an approach that honors the individuals' interconnectedness and the necessary or natural links between the program components of environment, people, structure, processes, culture, and outcomes (Bloom 1991). A first step in considering how directors manage is to examine the ways their programs are subject to the principles affecting all organizations.

Organizational culture

Through the action of its founders, administrators, and staff, in interactions within the internal and external environment, an early care and education organization, like other organizations, develops a unique organizational culture. This culture consists of the assumptions—frequently unconscious—that underlie group behavior (Schein 1991). Ultimately, members of the organization express cultural meanings through the group's activities. Groups hold assumptions about such things as human nature (idealistic or practical, altruistic or selfish) and whether an authoritarian, democratic, or collegial approach is most effective. These assumptions, developed over time, provide stability and predictability. They also play a part both in major decisions such as hiring, budgeting, and collaboration with other groups and in less complex day-to-day decisions such as ordering supplies and equipment, writing menus, or organizing a parent cleanup day.

Further, as the assumptions are made and goals defined, individuals in organizations face internal and external adaptations and integration tasks (Schein 1991). Internally, organizations must establish consensus on a common language and group boundaries, the criteria for assignment of status, authority and power, friendship, and rewards and punishments. Organizations are thought to be more effective if the group is aware of culture, values, and plans on a more conscious level. The early care and education organization's culture underlies all aspects of its provision of services to children and families, and the manager represents that culture. With a combination of knowledge and skills in management and early childhood development and pedagogy, practitioners can address the complex challenges that are a part of day-to-day practice.

Competencies required of managers

Although the manager's title and specific responsibilities may differ depending on the sponsoring organization and the program's mission and purpose, a look at textbooks in early childhood program administration indicates that there are broad, generally agreed-upon areas of responsibility for the manager. These areas include planning, implementing, and evaluating the program; complying with regulations and policies; managing personnel; ensuring facility and equipment needs; financing and budgeting; planning activities; providing for nutrition, health, and safety; assessing and reporting children's development; working with parents; and contributing to the profession (Travis & Perreault 1981; Hildebrand 1984; Seaver & Cartwright 1986; Decker & Decker 1988; Bloom 1989a; Sciarra & Dorsey 1990; Morgan 1993).

The manager's role comprises competence in several areas. The following set of seven competencies, first outlined by Morgan (1993), provides an overview of the manager's areas of responsibility and delineates some specific tasks.[2] When one considers the personal investment required to master the listed competencies, the complexity of the manager's role becomes apparent. Frequently, administrators utilize these competencies in combination, integrating knowledge to manage the components of the program. In interviews with directors of highly rated centers and with experts on early childhood administration, a former director said,

> She [the director] is the point person between all these different perspectives, and she has to be able to translate. I see her more as an interpreter. A director helps the teachers understand the parents' point of view, she helps the church [or other sponsor] understand the board's point of view. . . . [It is as if] there's the teacher

who speaks Russian and the parents who speak French and the board who speaks something else. The director is the trilingual person who moves around. (Culkin 1994, 128–29)

The following review of competencies underlines the complexity and dynamism of the management task. The first competency area has to do with the context in which management occurs—the organization.

Competency 1: Develop and maintain an effective organization

This area includes legal and regulatory processes, development of a mission statement, and management strategies based on teamwork, ongoing evaluation, and strategic planning.

Seeing organizations as a system of components. In an early childhood organization, whatever its auspices, a director uses her skills to manage and lead the organization. Whether she inherits the organization and culture or establishes it as a founder, developing the organization requires meeting the regulations and legal requirements that apply to the chosen organizational and program parameters. Bloom (1991) uses a systems theory perspective to frame the manager's role as at the center of a dynamic organization in which the parts of the whole are constantly interactive. She posits six interactive system components for an early childhood program:

- **environment**—including the sponsoring agency;

- **people**—including teachers, parents, other staff, clients, local community, government, and economic and business influences;

- **structure**—the legal structure, size, policy orientation, job descriptions, financial systems, budget, payroll, accounting, mission, and written curriculum;

- **processes**—such as communication networks, including conflict resolution, planning and evaluation, socialization and teaching practices, and supervisory and training processes;

- **culture**—the shared values and beliefs, history, traditions, and ethics; and

- **outcomes**—such as the reputation of the center, staff competence, tenure and job satisfaction, and the children's social and cognitive competence.

Maintaining equilibrium between program components. The systems model, incorporating the legal, evaluative, and planning process, is a framework for a director or other manager to use in allocating and balancing resources with heightened understanding of the underlying relationships between the components. The manager has the central role of assessing and conserving equilibrium between system components to preserve balance and harmony underlying the various aspects of serving children and families and to support continued organizational vitality and variability.

It is critical for an organization to clearly define the mission, goals, and functions of its components, and some aspects of the functioning are always open to change. However, once clear policies and procedures are established, the manager uses the structure of the interactive components to understand, manage, and track organizational functioning and to address organizational goals. Managers complete much of their work in ongoing interactions with staff, clients, and the external community. A director of a large public center described a supervision process in which she coached a teacher over time. She helped the teacher learn to effectively address the center's vision for work with parents. In this process, organizational goals are more than dry abstractions. They serve as criteria for this manager's activities with a specific teacher toward a specific goal, such as effective family-teacher communication. The director explained,

You [the director] have a goal in mind, too. You have a vision there in mind, of how you would like the relationships [to be] between the teachers and parents. . . . I'm picturing you sitting working with a teacher, say over a two- or three-month period. [The] teacher has a problem and you have something in mind, but you're helping the teacher move toward what you would perceive to be a more effective way of working with families and children in care. (Culkin 1994, 120)

Another former director described how her center's vision of curriculum served as the impetus for a participatory planning process. People, structure, process, culture, and outcomes—all components of the organization—became part of the activity.

We had a real team approach. We met every single day. . . . We had a whole list of principles and assumptions. . . . We were studying whole language and preschoolers. We had staff developers coming in and documenting it in a way with those people. . . . [We were] evaluating ourselves, having meetings about it . . . we continued it during the week where we included the families in the process. (Culkin 1994, 129)

Evaluation processes enable organizations to use current experience as the basis for future plans.

Looking ahead. With flexible plans in place, a manager can respond to crises as well as to the routine issues that emerge as staff work toward the organization's mission. Management is sometimes characterized as the process of looking ahead, and a manager may need to work quickly, resolving crises, organizing work, and performing regular duties. Successful managers improvise, have a diverse web of contacts both inside and outside the organization, and seem to manage affairs well despite constant demands

on their time and energy (Peters & Waterman 1982; Mintzberg 1987; Bennis 1989; Sayles 1989). Further, Peters and Waterman (1982) say an effective manager uses "management by wandering around" or establishing "informal control through regular casual communication" (p. 51) to deal with the human, technical, resource, and theoretical networks that make up her business. As a result, although the program environment may appear chaotic and not deliberate, it evolves from a dynamic framework in which the manager encourages each individual to contribute most productively to the organization (Peters & Waterman 1982; Albrecht 1991a, 1991b).

Competency 2: Plan and implement administrative systems that effectively carry out the program's mission, goals, and objectives

This area involves organization of tasks and the team's decisionmaking process, facilities, and systems. It includes all program components for children, families, and community, such as individualized developmental curriculum, communication with parents, health and nutrition, recruitment and enrollment, and social services.

Authority is given to the manager (who often work in collaboration with other individuals in the sponsoring organization) to develop and maintain administrative systems. In contemporary organizations the authority of the manager is frequently negotiated as well as delegated. This means that to address individual goals and shared collaborative goals, managers must build teams and close-knit crews of colleagues inside and outside the organization. Within those teams, authority for shared work is established through negotiation. These negotiations, along with more formal agreements and planning processes, are the foundation for the provision of services. As one management specialist explained,

In modern organizations, the person who is responsible for tasks almost never has the authority to carry them out. Almost all management is by negotiation. Further, a lot of the tasks that you have to carry out are with people who are not technically within your organization. You have to deal a lot with the environment. More and more a lot of that isn't being seen as the environment anymore. This border between what is the organization and what is the place where it meets the environment keeps changing. (Culkin 1994, 162)

A skilled manager learns to successfully organize staff to complete shared responsibilities for achieving organizational goals.

If teams are to provide good-quality services, clear goals and purposes that are understood (and are renewable) are essential. According to a leadership consultant,

What really needs to happen in an organization . . . is that at least the leader and the senior staff need to sit down and really work through "Why are we here? What do we want to accomplish and how are we going to do it?" If you can't articulate that in very simple terms and have everyone agree to support it, [the program cannot accomplish its goals]. You don't have to like it—you want consensus. But everyone agrees that is why we're here. You can just tell when you're in an organization and they're clearing the line [reaching their goals] and when they're not. You're successful in spite of yourself. (Culkin 1994, 121–22)

Teachers also need clarity in their goals. "[Teachers] have a purpose. They're real clear. Everything they do keeps going back to that [purpose]" (Culkin 1994, 120). Implicit in current prototypes of management is the setting of clear goals and expectations, based on strongly held values and adapted to the changing needs of the community served. Goal setting requires a heightened awareness of the importance of each team member's part in the provision of care and education services. Thus, the systems of the organization work through the relationships developed in staff members' day-to-day work.

Organizational systems operate through relationships. Self-awareness and relationship with staff are central to the early care and education manager's competence and the organization's functioning. Neugebauer (1990) advocates the development of effective, people-oriented managers who value influencing staff as a means of improving the organization. Neugebauer maintains that these managers will focus on a solid sense of delegation, goal setting, organizational identity, communication, consistency, objective feedback, and facilitation. The manager's concern for the staff in relationship to the organizational effort will be greater than his need to be liked. Exercising self-awareness and personal reflection as a part of planning for children is a long-held and valued approach to early childhood practice (Bowman 1989), and self-reflection is part of managing as well.

Teacher mentorships and collaborative team efforts are two areas in which early childhood practitioners and specialists more consciously link the self-reflection techniques, often intuitive, that have been common in early care and education practice with management practices used by the business world. This is a complex and potentially very productive approach but not a simple one. Schon (1983) points out that in addition to applying theory, managers learn to be effective through extensive practice with analysis, problem solving, and dealing with uncertainty. This marriage of the art and science of management has particular meaning for those who want to understand and use what Schon calls *reflective practice*.[3] Trust is fundamental to building the rela-

tionships that are the foundation for teamwork, for solving problems, and for achieving a sense of community. As a former director insisted, "One of the major factors in effective administration is to create and build and nurture a sense of trust in the environment—safety and trust for families, staff, and the environment—which is no small thing given the constraints and obstacles" (Culkin 1994, 127). Another administrator, who coordinates an early childhood program, commented, "Actually I develop their confidence . . . more than that, most basically their trust" (p. 127). For systems to work toward the achievement of goals, ongoing, consistent attention to detail is important. The director plays a facilitating role for the teaching staff. As the founder and director of a program put it,

It's a support system—managers getting everything in order, just as the teachers are the ones who set up the classrooms. They make sure the toothpicks are there and the Q-tips, paint, scissors, so their children can be independent and learn. . . . The director does the same thing. The director enables the teacher to teach. (Culkin 1994, 135)

Competency 3: Effectively administer a program of personnel management and staff development

Competency in this area includes gathering information from staff and parents; hiring and firing and developing or implementing personnel policies; facilitating community among parents, children, staff, and boards; and maintaining confidence and stability in self. It also includes providing support for teachers' professional development by observing and giving feedback, communicating expectations, supervising, and modeling appropriate behavior with children, families, and staff.

Early childhood programs can be viewed as communities. Clear expectations and policies support a dynamic learning community.

Clear personnel policies are fundamental. By creating and maintaining written policies and procedures, a manager presents a stable picture of the program to participants and potential members of the community. One director described how she uses her center's policies and why she established them.

I give them [teacher applicants] the policies and procedures manual and ask them to read it carefully so they can make a decision. . . . I think that [writing a manual] is real important—you can't expect someone to . . . read your mind. We did consensus building [around planning developmentally appropriate curriculum, using drafts of the manual]. I wrote it down. [Before we did this] we had this sort of mystery. (Culkin interview 1, lines 240–303)[4]

Managers design approaches to support teachers' professional development. Mentorships, collaborations, and supervision are three ways early childhood managers work with their staff to improve the quality of services through professional development. Teacher mentorships have been described as relationships for learning. They draw from a variety of professional traditions and are characterized by reflection, collaboration, and regularity (Fenichel 1992). In early care and education practice in child care centers, mentorships are designed to promote professional growth as well as to link training opportunities to increased pay (Whitebook & Sakai 1995). For the administrator, this approach links the three major management goals: (1) the production of good-quality services, (2) increased staff education linked to credit, and (3) increased staff remuneration linked to education.

In business management literature, mentoring is sometimes called coaching and involves "management by wandering around" (Peters & Waterman 1982). A researcher talked about the central role of a center director in managing her team's professional development:

We found [in a national study of early care and education training] that when people talk about the kind of training they have, they cited conferences and workshops and the director in their own center as being the primary sources of training. This was an interesting thing. . . . The directors are overtly and covertly charged with that responsibility. You asked me what the quality thing is: the director is a mentor, a teacher, a leader. The director is working with whatever the staff configuration is to make sure there is some strong philosophy—how do you approach curriculum? How do you approach all of that? . . . My corollary to that would be that directors need to be involved in some very important training themselves. They need to be going to director support groups, to be involved in whatever training there is—or create it. (Culkin 1994, 135, 136)

Whatever the approach, managing the professional development of staff requires a director to forge links to the external community to access training resources in the form of consultants, collaborations, financial support, or access to higher education opportunities. These types of activities put the director in touch with the larger community—that larger external community in which there are other opportunities for the director.

Competency 4: Foster good community relations and influence the child care policy that affects the program

This area involves gaining knowledge of community services and functions, such as child care resource-and-referral organizations and other child care programs, and includes establishing a personal relationship to the administrators. A competent manager knows health services, social services, vendors of needed services, policies, and legislative processes, as well as how to use media resources. He or she builds networks and coalitions through effective communication skills, including the ability to do public speaking and to produce written materials for internal and external use.

Internal and external communities. Managers work in both the internal and the external communities, negotiating between several subcommunities—teachers, families, sponsoring agencies, advocates, and others. Increasingly, work that was previously thought external to the organization is now part of a director's management responsibilities. Strong communication skills are a must. Routine conversations and written communication with the internal communities of families, children, teachers, and sponsoring agencies are part of daily responsibilities. Families are an important part of the community, and intentional communication with families is ongoing. One director said,

Every day the assisting teachers make sure they let the parents know in a concise manner how the [children's] day was, and [they are] careful in how they use their words. If a parent walks in and you go, "Well, [the child] had a rough day," you have to be careful how you say that, because you have not a clue as to what the parent's day was like. (Culkin 1994, 123)

Communication with external communities of other agencies, resource-and-referral agencies, possible funders, and others may require the manager to develop new skills for interagency negotiation, presentations, proposal writing, and media work. One director, who worked with her supervisor to meet the planning and process challenges that expansion places on both the frontline staff and the sponsoring organization, realized,

As we continue to grow and get involved with collaborations of all sorts, not only with . . . [our program's] dollars, but [with] other agencies coming in . . . she [the supervisor] is aware of that and that the whole structure needs to start changing. . . . We need to start looking at a five-year plan which we're putting together. With all this growth, what does that mean for our program? (Culkin 1994, 134, 135)

Working in and between communities is not simple. It requires clear goals, negotiation skills, a capacity for varied types of communication, and the capacity for thoughtful planning on the organization's mission and goals.

Competency 5: Maintain and develop the facility

A competent manager establishes and maintains procedures to monitor and correct any building problems to comply with all codes, such as fire and zoning; maintains all equipment safely; establishes and maintains security practices; and works with teachers to ensure that center design and organization of space support children's learning and development.

The facility both symbolizes and houses the community. The facility is important not only as the housing for the learning spaces for children and families but also as a means of expressing some of the program values in a meaningful and visual manner to the public, families that might enroll their children, and staff. Here again, the manager's competence and vision in one area support her efforts in another area. An executive pointed out,

> A part of the community is the physical building. The director needs to be in charge, at least leading that charge of making sure that it's a livable place, that the physical playground and building is as good as we can make it—as pleasant and as functional, as appropriate for what we do here. So we deal with it when the dishwasher doesn't work, when the furnace is making it too hot or too cold—all of those things. (Culkin interview 1, lines 298–308)

The executive director of a university-based center recalled how she has needed to negotiate with members of the university maintenance staff, who had initial resistance to cleaning rooms where children play with messy sensory-motor activities. She explained that such negotiation is all part of the manager's job of maintaining the physical environment to meet program goals.

Particularly when a facility is first being developed or is substantially modified, the manager must master a set of responsibilities that involve law, zoning, insurance and other aspects of business. Facility development is an area in which early childhood managers often use a team approach. Teachers, parents, and community volunteers can make some important contributions to the facility with the guidance of a manager who has a vision of the learning environment appropriate for their staff, children, and client families.

Competency 6: Have the legal knowledge necessary for effective management

This area involves gaining a general knowledge of regulations and the ability to work with legal counsel on policies and practices relating to child care custody issues, confidentiality laws, labor laws, antidiscrimination laws, liability issues, health rules, and the basics of contracts.

Legal structures underlie the organization. Because a child care center is an organization and a business, the manager must be informed about a variety of applicable laws and lead the organization in complying with them. Laws pertaining to regulations, child welfare, personnel issues, taxes, facility development, and contracts are relevant to child care settings. Risk implications and other liability issues are important and ongoing. Here, as in other areas, carefully designed systems organized around a preventive approach proactively protect the organization's interests and capital. This is the nature of business management areas such as law and finance—they underlie and are the base for operations. Planning is central to dealing with legal issues, especially when they involve major organizational issues. Regarding a new facility plan, a Head Start director said, "I have these Plan A, B, C kind of things" (Culkin 1994, 137).

Directors often learn about legal issues on the job, some through consultation with a board member or representative of a sponsoring agency and others through an early care and education administration course. One director/founder commented on several areas in which knowledge of legal procedure is crucial, especially in the technicalities of workers' compensation and for child abuse reporting. She then went on to say,

> Somebody has to prepare the 1040s. . . . [The director is the person] who is going to put together the benefit package and talk with all those insurance agents and figure out what they're saying—even just learn the terminology for starters. (Culkin interview 3, lines 384, 385, 388–91)

This director also said she wished there was recognition of the breadth of the director's business management responsibilities. As she put it,

> I don't think the director is a glorified teacher. I think the director is a wholly different animal who should probably have been a teacher at one point. . . . That's one-fourth of it. We're talking about the other three-fourths, which is the bottom of the iceberg. (Culkin interview 3, lines 414–19)

Competency 7: Have financial management skills

A competent manager takes responsibility for the center's financial management and directs others in financial planning and reporting; mobilizes needed resources; and maintains accurate records. She or he uses financial tools such as budget planning, cash-flow projection, and break-even analysis; knows marketing concepts; sets fee policies; and develops a compensation system that rewards the staff for increased knowledge and skills.

Financial planning is essential. The budget expresses the business plan for the center. It is central to planning and monitoring operations. An experienced manager said, "If I had to look at one thing, if somebody was writing me a proposal [a project plan including a budget] . . . the one thing I would look at above everything else is how realistic are they in forecasting what they think is going to happen in the next two or three years" (Culkin interview 5, lines 869–74). Or as a current manager put it, "If your program is not structured well and is not financially viable, it's not going to survive" (Culkin 1994, 126).

Managers can benefit from training in financial management and planning. Research suggests that centers typically have weak organizational structure and directors have particularly weak financial management ability, demonstrating little capacity to adapt to the dynamics of the marketplace and very limited skills in long-term planning or market assessment (Greenman & Johnson 1993). Greenman and Johnson recommend that administrators join forces in a consortium or other organization to support development of new legal and financial management skills. Directors themselves express concern about financial management and indicate they are not prepared for the stresses of fiscal uncertainty (Bloom 1992).

Fiscal and related tasks take a large proportion (almost 50% according to the Cost, Quality, & Child Outcomes Study Team [1995]) of directors' time. And yet, while these administrative tasks are central, they need to run so smoothly as to be almost imperceptible to the central service providers, the teachers. One director described it this way:

> The best thing is for the teachers to do their job and wonder, once a week, what is she doing down there in the office? But not really think about it very much. But know that there are supplies in the supply closet, the first-aid kit is up to date, that all the parent files are current, that the licensing is current, that the insurance is paid. (Culkin 1994, 125)

Some directors stress that while they, as the managers, have responsibility for the budget, it is also important to involve staff in the process. The first director primarily involves staff in decisions about the use of budgeted staff development funds: "Here's how much we have been allotted for staff development this year. So should we have everybody go to [the state AEYC annual conference] or to another meeting?" (Culkin 1994, 125). The second routinely discusses the financial report with the teachers. She said, "I used to hand out the financials every quarter. . . . They said, 'Would you look at that—this line. We did better here.' Or 'We gotta concentrate on this.' . . . So you know where the money comes from and where it goes" (Culkin interview 3, lines 441, 442, 444–48). This director would have liked more formal course work in management, especially in relation to early care and education settings, as well as more opportunities for working with a mentor. She, like others, observed that despite the importance of management expertise, training in how to be a skillful manager is hard to come by in the early childhood field.

Professional preparation for managers

Generally, directors are promoted to a management role from a teaching position (Bloom 1989; Larkin 1992; Cost Quality, & Child Outcomes Study Team 1995), and while some value the opportunity to learn their management skills on the job (Buckner 1988; Larkin 1992), others express an increased interest in management and leadership training as a part of professional preparation. With an increased recognition of the complex and wide-ranging set of competencies that a director must either have or be able to mobilize through teamwork, most directors assume their responsibilities with little preparation (Buckner 1988; Bloom 1989; Larkin 1992; Morgan et al. 1993; Culkin 1994). And while professional literature and administrative coursework present aspiring and practicing administrators with necessary fundamental information, more is needed for management expertise to become a routine and substantive part of the provision of good-quality programs. Research findings point to the need for more management training.

Current training opportunities are inconsistent and limited

In a national study of current training requirements (Morgan et al. 1993), researchers reviewed management-training requirements. They found inconsistent management-training requirements across the states, with most having a mix of preservice and on-the-job training. Most significantly, they reported that

> Informants in all but six states identified a lack of management training to meet the specific needs of administrators in early care and education as a critical issue. Many informants pinpointed management training for administrators as the largest unmet need in the field, describing the process of learning to be an administrator as a "seat of the pants" experience in most states. (p. 54)

Similarly, Bloom (1989) found when directors identified their training needs, they highlighted management issues. At the start of a professional development process, these directors felt most competent in the areas of child development, implementation of a developmentally appropriate curriculum, organization of children's school records, and communication with parents and the community. They expressed the least confidence in the area of organizational theory and leadership and legal and fiscal issues, and they expressed concern about their competence for responsibilities as adult educators for staff. Other researchers stress the need for directors to understand a broader range of market and community issues if they are to deal successfully with the current dynamic child care environment (Greenman & Johnson 1993) and note the importance of sophisticated external as well as internal communications skills (Buckner 1988). Specific training needs emerge from the research.

The team at the Center for Career Development in Early Care and Education (Morgan et al. 1993) presented recommendations for training. Their suggestions regarding management and related issues are summarized as follows:

1. Offer administrators training in supervision, personnel administration, and financial management.

2. Emphasize salary scales that reward training and longevity, assuring that administrators emphasize teamwork, participatory decisionmaking, and empowerment of staff, rather than hierarchical supervisory structures.

3. Broaden the scope of programs offered in the higher education system.

4. Prepare students for both advanced teaching and leadership roles—e.g., as master teachers and directors.

5. Offer training for a broader array of roles in the field—e.g., as resource-and-referral specialist, trainer, or policy researcher.

6. Provide degree-level concentrations in those areas that are not linked to kindergarten and primary teacher certification—e.g., in school-age child care, infant/toddler studies, family child care, and administration (Morgan et al. 1993, 107–08).

The implementation of some of these recommendations is under way in a scattering of management and leadership training efforts around the country. The inclusion of some recommendations within particular state professional development plans (or other venues such as universities and resource-and-referral agencies) would potentially improve program management, quality level, and organizational functioning.

While there are some excellent preparation programs, many administrators assume management responsibilities without preparation (Bloom 1989; Larkin 1992; Culkin 1994). Whether they succeed in learning what they need to know is dependent on their circumstances (e.g., the local resources available and the individual's personal learning style) and their drive. But lacking the guidance and support that can come from clearly held professional practice principles and standards, many fall short of the solid competence required. Besides providing inadequate preparation in specific skills such as budget and personnel management, current training also neglects the psychological growth involved in assuming the management role. Larkin (1992) suggests it may be more difficult to learn communication and human resource management skills than to master the financial planning and legal aspects of the work. Most

challenging is internal growth related to leadership ability. Larkin writes,

> The more difficult hurdles are internal: the tension between being an authority and providing support, the psychological isolation of being at the top, and being able to conceptualize and articulate a clear philosophy to parents and teachers. These are areas where learning and growth are facilitated by role models and mentors who can influence the evolving leader at a deeply personal level—both intellectually and emotionally. (p. 125)

Clearly, as we recognize the importance of managers in the provision of good-quality care and education services, we see that new professional development strategies are needed.

Future strategies

The field can consider several approaches to provide directors with management training. One possibility is *mediated entry,* in which a fledgling administrator learns management by working with a mentor or supervisor and gradually assumes new responsibilities (Larkin 1992). Other possibilities include *director credentialing,* which could take place under a variety of sponsoring organizations, and *higher education* toward differentiated levels of management credentials at the associate, baccalaureate, master's, or doctoral degree levels. Experimentation and exploration with several of these possibilities is under way. As the field explores, redefines, and develops a clearer view of the roles of the manager, it will be important to explore the strengths and weaknesses of these and other models. Communication among approaches and sharing of insights gained from field practice will not only publicize successful innovations but also will serve to guide and support a process of strengthening the management function. It seems likely that a combination of these approaches—and others that may evolve—will provide new managers with flexibility in terms of needed practice skills and a comprehensive knowledge base.

All three approaches could utilize what Larkin (1992) suggests—that is, mediated entry to administrative positions as a means for administrators to begin their management experience with limited part-time or assistant director responsibilities. This would enable the directors to build their new skills on the base of their development and pedagogical skills. They would also be able to combine initial management experience with access to a mentor or other guide. Here again, learning through a mentoring relationship is proposed as a means for new administrators to develop new skills in the context of a professional setting with a more experienced, knowledgeable, and available expert. (The current development of director support groups around the country is also promising, potentially linking new and experienced managers in mediated entry partnerships.) The mentoring experience provided by mediated entry seems to be an approach that could be built into existing and developing professional development training delivery systems. Any approach to training will have to be based on available and developing research concerning early care and education managers.

If managers are to be well prepared, more research regarding early care and education management and the provision of quality-level services is needed. Studies are needed to

1. further delineate the relationship between quality level, measures of quality level, and management competence in early care and education programs;
2. identify management competencies that are critical to the provision of quality programs;
3. define and pilot management strategies that link early childhood emphasis on developmental and reflective practice with business insights into systems and learning environments;
4. determine the economic impacts of competent managers on their programs;
5. determine any impact of competent managers on program outcomes for children, teachers, and families;
6. develop an understanding of how much management training is effective and how continuing education in the form of formal or informal support and information can be built into the system; and
7. examine other management roles in the early childhood field, such as management in resource-and-referral programs, higher education, and family child care organizations.

Kagan (1994) has pointed out that leadership approaches historically prevalent in the early childhood field resemble the new leadership approaches now espoused in the larger business community. In early childhood that commitment to concepts and techniques such as the emphasis on teamwork and the importance of values, participatory management, and shared decisionmaking is substantial and long-standing, but the resources and the training opportunities to develop these skills may be lacking. While such models may be valued and appreciated in the field, with early childhood managers and leaders typically working at collaborative, team, and participatory approaches, their successful implementation requires the commitment of human and financial resources (Kagan 1994; Bloom 1995).

In today's more complex and expanded early care and education market, small, intimate organizations may face larger challenges. Some managers stretch either within their corporate structure or in collaborations launched as a means to access financial or other resources for the field. In this new environment, management techniques based on long-held values may need to be relearned in a more systematic and comprehensive manner. And early care and education practitioners and their associates in higher education can turn to allies in the corporate world, higher education, and business practice to master at a deeper level the skills of facilitating communication and individual development, managing resources, and practicing self-reflection as a part of successful professional practice.

Notes

1. The topic of early childhood management is again engaging the attention of planners, practitioners, policymakers, and academics. Knowledge of the work of the manager in early care and education programs has developed over the last 25 years, but there are many gaps in our understanding of such managers and of the preparation they need for their jobs (Buckner 1988; Bloom 1989; Larkin 1992; Culkin 1994). In *Day Care Administration* (U.S. Department of Health and Human Services undated [circa 1970]), a plan for developing a day care center, the authors provide no discussion of the role of the director and assign such management tasks as budget and personnel to a board of directors. In this model of service delivery, one assumes that the board takes active responsibility for tasks such as staff evaluation and planning. Finance and budget planning appear to be left to their pro bono efforts. There is no mention of a manager or administrator. Yet, even at that point (the 1970s), the role of program manager, leader, and director was being reported, analyzed, and supported in *Child Care Exchange* magazine and at programs to prepare administrators, such as those at Wheelock College.

2. Management competencies can be organized in many ways. The director credential of the National Child Care Association is organized in a set of nine competencies: (1) developing and maintaining the organization, (2) developing ways to carry out your goals, (3) marketing the program, (4) handling personnel management and staff development, (5) maintaining the facility, (6) having legal knowledge, (7) promoting community relations, (8) managing finances, and (9) ensuring self-development. Current discussion in the field concerning the role of the program director as manager involves developing a clearer consensus about the parameters of the knowledge base for early childhood management and leadership activities.

3. Schon (1983) notes that some management ability (especially in the less experienced manager) may be on a more intuitive level—what he calls *knowing in practice,* or reflecting on and learning from their actions, in response to different conditions of uncertainty and opportunity. Schon points out that awareness of one's intuitive reflection-in-practice experience develops out of the articulation of intuitions to others. Without the experience of articulating in relationship to another person or experience, the managerial strategy or ability stays at an intuitive level and cannot be communicated to others.

4. Some quotes are from the transcripts of my interviews with directors and experts.

References

Albrecht, K. 1991a. Helping teachers grow: Talking with parents. *Child Care Information Exchange* 82: 45–47.

Albrecht, K. 1991b. Managing teacher performance by walking around. *Child Care Information Exchange* 78: 21–22.

Bennis, W. 1989. *On becoming a leader.* New York: Addison Wesley.

Bloom, P.J. 1989. *The Illinois director's study: A report to the Illinois Department of Children and Family Services.* Evanston, IL: Early Childhood Professional Development Project, National College of Education.

Bloom, P.J. 1991. Child care centers as organizations: A social systems perspective. *Child and Youth Care Forum* 20 (5): 313–33.

Bloom, P.J. 1992. The child care center director: A critical component of program quality. *Educational Horizons,* Spring: 138–45.

Bloom, P.J. 1995. Shared decisionmaking: The centerpiece of participatory management. *Young Children* 50 (4): 55–60.

Bloom, P.J., & M. Sheerer. 1992. The effect of leadership training on child care program quality. *Early Childhood Research Quarterly* 7: 579–94.

Bolman, L.G., & T.E. Deal. 1991. *Reframing organizations: Artistry, choice and leadership.* San Francisco: Jossey-Bass.

Bowman, B.T. 1989. Self-reflection as a element of professionalism. In *The care and education of young children: Expanding contexts, sharpening focus*, eds. F.O. Rust & L.R. Williams, 108–15. New York: Teachers College Press.

Bredekamp, S. 1989. *Regulating child care quality: Evidence from NAEYC's accreditation system.* Washington, DC: NAEYC.

Buckner, L.M. 1988. Supervising with communicative competence in early childhood centers: Sociopolitical implications of the legitimation deficit in administrator preparation. Unpublished Ph.D. dissertation, San Francisco University (UMI Abstracts International, #8820727).

Conger, J.A. 1992. *Learning to lead: The art of transforming managers into leaders.* San Francisco: Jossey-Bass.

Cost, Quality, & Child Outcomes Study Team. 1995. *Cost, quality, and child outcomes in child care center. Public report.* 2d ed. Denver: Economics Department, University of Colorado at Denver.

Culkin, M.L. 1994. The administrator/leader in early care and education settings: A qualitative study with implications for theory and practice. Unpublished Ph.D. dissertation, The Union Institute (UMI Abstracts International, #9502953).

Decker, C.A., & J.R. Decker. 1988. *Planning and administering early childhood programs.* 4th ed. Columbus, OH: Merrill.

Fenichel, E., ed. 1992. *Learning through supervision and mentorship: A source book.* Washington, DC: Zero to Three.

Greenman, J., & N. Johnson. 1993. *Child care center management.* Minneapolis: Greater Minneapolis Day Care Association.

Hildebrand, V. 1984. *Management of child development centers.* New York: Macmillan.

Kagan, S.L. 1994. Leadership: Rethinking it—making it happen. *Young Children* 49 (5): 50–54.

Larkin, L. 1992. The preschool administrator: Perspectives in early childhood education. Unpublished Ph.D. dissertation, Harvard University, Cambridge (UMI Dissertation Services, Ann Arbor: #9219109).

Leithwood, K. 1992. The move toward transformational leadership. *Educational Leadership* 49: 8–12.

Mintzberg, H. 1987. Managerial work: Analysis from observation. In *The great writings in management and organizational behavior*, eds. L.E. Boone & D.D. Bowen. New York: McGraw-Hill.

Mintzberg, H. 1989. *Mintzberg on management.* New York: Free Press.

Morgan G. 1993. Competencies of child care center directors: Draft for discussion. Background materials for the 1993 conference of the National Institute for Early Childhood Professional Development. Washington, DC: NAEYC.

Morgan, G., S.L. Azer, J.B. Costley, A. Genser, I.F. Goodman, J. Lombardi, & B. McGimsey. 1993. *Making a career of it: The state of the states report on career development in early care and education.* Boston: Center for Career Development in Early Care and Education, Wheelock College.

Morrison, A.M. 1992. *The new leaders: Guidelines on leadership diversity in America.* San Francisco: Jossey-Bass.

Neugebauer, R. 1990. Being a boss. In *On being a leader: The best of exchange: Reprint collection no. 5*, ed. R. Neugebauer. Redmond, WA: Exchange Press.

Peters, T., & R.H. Waterman. 1982. *Excellence.* New York: Warner.

Rodd, J. 1994. *Leadership in early childhood: The pathway to professionalism.* New York: Teachers College Press.

Sayles, L.R. 1989. *Leadership: Managing in real organizations.* New York: McGraw-Hill.

Schein, E.H. 1991. What is culture? In *Reframing organizational culture*, eds. P.J. Frost, L.F. Moore, M.R. Louis, & J. Martin. Newbury Park: Sage.

Schon, D.A. 1983. *The reflective practitioner: How professionals think in action.* New York: Basic.

Sciarra, D.J., & A.G. Dorsey. 1990. *Developing and administering a child care center*, 2d ed. Albany, NY: Delmar.

Seaver, J.W., & C.A. Cartwright. 1986. *Child care administration.* Belmont, CA: Wadsworth.

Travis, N.E., & J. Perreault. 1981. *The effective day care director: A discussion of the role and its responsibilities.* Atlanta: Save the Children/Child Care Support Center.

U.S. Department of Health and Human Services. (Undated). *Day care administration.* Washington, DC: Author.

Whitebook, M., & L. Sakai. 1995. *The potential of mentoring: An assessment of the California early childhood mentor teacher program.* Washington, DC: Center for the Early Childhood Work Force.

Commentary

by Paula Jorde Bloom

Anyone who has chased the shadow of a center director for even a brief time knows that an effective administrator wears many hats—from that of budget analyst to nutritionist to fundraiser. The list is long and varied. While administrating an early childhood program has never been easy, the director's job has become increasingly complex and more difficult in recent years.

When veteran directors reflect on the changing scope and nature of their jobs, they point out that funding and regulatory agencies now require more paperwork and documentation of program activities. They comment that the changing nature of the American family has created a host of issues that make meeting the needs of children and their parents more challenging. And directors report that they now spend considerably more time on personnel issues, particularly recruiting and hiring staff. The pool of talented, eager, and highly qualified teachers they once drew from has diminished dramatically. In addition, directors must now deal with complex legal issues relating to child abuse, infectious disease control, and insurance liability that they did not confront a decade ago.

Culkin does a thorough job of delineating the many competencies required to effectively administrate an early childhood program in this era of increased expectations and shrinking resources. She is right on target when she stresses that the tasks that consume a director's day require a unique blend of leadership and management expertise. In this commentary, I would like to expand the discussion in four areas. First, I will elaborate on the subtle but important distinction between the two key concepts of leadership and management as they relate to the director's role in the early childhood context. Second, I will raise some questions about how we define and measure director competence. Third, I will propose a hierarchical framework for viewing different levels of director competence. Finally, I will discuss the implications of this framework for director training and credentialing.

Clarifying the leadership and management functions of the director

The organizational literature from business and industry often differentiates between leadership functions and managerial functions. *Leadership functions,* we are told, relate to the broad view of helping an organization clarify and affirm values, set goals, articulate a vision, and chart a course of action to achieve that vision. Like an artist, the leader paints the picture, creating the images of what an organization could be. The leader's job is to create a healthy tension between current reality and an imagined ideal. *Managerial functions,* on the other hand, relate to the actual orchestration of tasks and setting up systems to accomplish a vision. Some organizational theorists define this distinction between leadership and managerial functions as the difference between effectiveness and efficiency—leaders do the right things; managers do things right (Bennis 1989; Covey 1991).

The implied message in much of the organizational literature is that leadership functions are not only distinctly different from management functions but that they are also more important or lofty. This conceptualization is reinforced by our culture's abundant images of elder statesman and CEOs at the pinnacle of power delegating the business of the day to dutiful managers.

Because of the relatively flat organizational structure of most early childhood centers, the tidy distinction between leadership and management functions that might be possible in other organizational settings seldom exists. Effective center directors are both leaders—providing vision and inspiration—and managers, orchestrating the way that policies and procedures are implemented. These two functions, therefore, are just different sides of the same coin. One is not necessarily subordinate to or less important than the other; both are essential for optimum program functioning.

How do we define director competence?

In an era when high-quality child care is in such short supply and state standards for director qualifications are so dismally poor, it is tempting to advocate that every director of every center demonstrate proficiency in every competency delineated by Culkin before the key to the front door is handed over. That goal is not only unrealistic but also somewhat foolhardy. It rests on a rather simplistic notion that a competent director is one who has merely accumulated a number of different knowledge and skill competencies.

Defining competence as it relates to the multiplicity of roles the director assumes each day is a thorny task. It is thorny in part because as a field we have not defined precisely what we mean by the terms *competence, compe-*

tent, and *competency.* As Short (1984) points out, these terms are overused and misused in our well-intentioned attempts to improve educational practice.

Many educators embrace a definition of competence similar to the one put forth by Fenichel and Eggbeer (1990). They believe that competence is "the ability to do the right thing, at the right time, for the right reasons." Fenichel and Eggbeer add that "Competence involves the capacity to analyze a situation, consider alternative approaches . . . evaluate the outcome, and articulate the rationale for each step of the process" (p. 13). Though definitions of this kind are appealing, they rest on qualitative judgments that are value laden. *The right thing* or *the right reasons* are highly subjective terms open to multiple interpretations. How does one begin to measure competence using this kind of yardstick?

Competence is clearly context specific. The repertoire of competencies needed to effectively carry out the director's role varies by the age and background of the children enrolled, the range of services provided, the philosophical orientation of the program, and the legal sponsorship of the center. The size of the program, as well, certainly affects the scope and complexity of the administrative role. Directors of small programs may have few administrative tasks and serve as classroom teachers for part of the day, whereas directors of large programs may have multiple sites, multiple funding sources, and a large, diverse staff to coordinate. Thus, directing different types of programs requires varying levels of administrative sophistication.

Another problem with current discussions of director competence is that they tend to frame the issue in dichotomous terms. But competency isn't like the chicken pox—either you have it or you don't. Rather, proficiency in various competencies must be viewed on a continuum. A director may be highly proficient in one competency but only moderately so in another.

A conceptualization of competence must include three components: (1) *knowledge competency,* which includes knowledge in such areas as group dynamics, organizational theories, child development, teaching strategies, and family systems; (2) *skill competency,* which includes the technical, human, and conceptual skills needed to perform different tasks (e.g., develop a budget, motivate staff, or solve problems); and (3) *attitude competency,* which includes beliefs, values, dispositions, and emotional responses that support optimum performance.

Isenberg (1979) cautions that competence must be viewed as a synthesis rather than a collection of knowledge, skills, and attitudes. In other words, it is an *integrative* rather than an *additive* process. Attitude competency, for example, is integral to both knowledge and skill competency. As Katz and Raths (1985) point out, it is possible to have a particular professional skill in one's repertoire but not use it. The disposition to use one's knowledge or skills in a way that promotes desired outcomes is an essential ingredient in the competency equation.

Culkin's list of competencies seems to imply a conceptualization of competence as a command of knowledge and skill and demonstrated behaviors. Conceptualizing competence in this way implies choosing and knowing why one does what one chooses to do. The problem with this conceptualization is that it does not address the degree or level of capability deemed to be sufficient. Culkin's list also includes many competencies that are simply too complex to be measured.

It is not surprising that the list of competencies delineated by Culkin falls predominantly in the knowledge and skill domains. This is to be expected. Knowledge and skill competency areas are easier both to describe and to operationalize. Attitudes, which are also essential for optimal performance, are far more difficult to assess. Some attitude competencies can be inferred from behavior (performance). For example, a director who values reflective analysis and consensus building in decisionmaking will be more inclined to use coalition building and participatory management. As the field moves toward a clearer definition of director competence and a refinement of desired director competencies, the attitudes and dispositions for optimal performance in early childhood settings must be included.

A hierarchy of leadership and management competencies

One way to begin to define levels of competence is to categorize the myriad knowledge and skill areas needed for effective program administration and then prioritize them with respect to essential elements of program functioning. The work of Sergiovanni (1984), further developed by Hayden (1996), provides a convenient springboard for this type of analysis. Sergiovanni describes the distinguishing features of competent (good) schools versus outstanding (exemplary) schools. Hayden builds on Sergiovanni's hierarchy of management forces by providing corresponding functions that relate to early childhood educational settings. Her model can easily be applied to the knowledge and skill competencies developed by Morgan (1993) and described in Culkin's chapter.

Figure 1 provides a graphic representation of a hierarchy of knowledge and skill competency areas. The five ascending areas are technical, staff relations, educational programming, public relations, and symbolic competencies.

Technical competency areas include those tasks that relate to the operations of the center–budgeting, record keeping, facilities management, scheduling, and developing policies and procedures to meet state and local regulations pertaining to the health and safety of children and the delivery of services. *Staff relations competency* relates to those knowledge and skill areas needed to cultivate positive interpersonal relations and motivate staff to high levels of performance. The core of this human relations competency

Figure 1. Hierarchy of Competency Areas

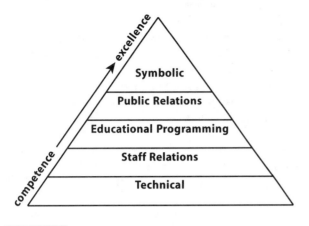

Adapted from Sergiovanna 1984 and Hayden 1996.

cluster is skill in effective communication. Specific competencies include supervision, mentoring, team building, professional development, and performance appraisal. *Educational programming knowledge and skill competency* relates to all the client-oriented functions of the center—dealing with children and their families, curriculum planning, and overseeing the implementation of developmentally appropriate classroom teaching practices and assessment. *Public relations competency* involves community outreach and advocacy, networking, dealing with regulatory agencies and professional organizations, marketing, fundraising, and special events. *Symbolic competency* relates to the director's ability to serve as a symbol for the collective identity of the group by articulating a vision, clarifying and affirming values, promoting reflection and introspection, and creating and sustaining a culture built on norms of continuous improvement and ethical conduct.

From competence to excellence

Effective management at the technical and staff relations levels can be viewed as a repertoire of generic knowledge and skills that are needed for essential program operations. They are generic because most of the specific competencies that fall in these categories can be achieved by anyone with a good business and/or management background. Tasks that fall into the technical and staff relations areas *must* be addressed before there can be lasting success at the upper levels of the hierarchy. In other words, these lower two levels of the hierarchy represent the foundation upon which upper levels can thrive. While it is assumed that many of the tasks included in these areas will be delegated to others to carry out, the director is usually responsible for the overall coordination of the work to be performed.

Hayden (1996) believes that budgets, filing systems, record keeping, scheduling, and other issues that fall within the technical area should be the central focus of management activity until they are running smoothly. Then the director can concentrate on the human aspects of administrating a center, such as developing a team, dealing with conflict, and promoting professional growth. Effective directors who have achieved competency in staff and human relations know how to motivate and energize others to pursue common aims. They are empathic listeners, sensitive to differing points of view, and they appreciate diversity as an organizational asset.

When systems are in place to ensure that the human aspects of management are addressed, directors will be more successful in the next layer of the hierarchy, the client-oriented functions of the center, educational programming. Most directors come to their jobs with a strong background in child development theory and a solid repertoire of teaching strategies (Bloom 1990). But just because they have been identified as good teachers does not mean they will automatically succeed in implementing an exemplary educational program centerwide. Success in this third level of the hierarchy rests squarely on the level of competence achieved at the preceding staff relations level.

Likewise, a director would not be wise to focus attention on community and public relations without having addressed the more basic issues that are lower in the hierarchy. Successful public relations could result in an increased demand that the center might not be able to meet if the basic systems for the delivery of services were not in place. There is not much value in promoting a service when the center cannot follow up on inquiries or when application forms get lost because of a poor filing system or lack of adequate staffing (Hayden 1996).

As directors achieve the knowledge and skill competency at the higher levels of the hierarchy, they move from a state of *minimum competence* to a state of *excellence*. Competent directors have mastered the skills necessary at the technical, staff, and educational programming levels of the hierarchy. The difference between a competent director and a master director lies in the upper levels of the hierarchy. The tasks performance areas at the lower levels are typically those associated with management functions. Those at the upper levels are those that are more often associated with leadership functions.

Directors of exemplary centers are trend watchers; they seek out and sort out pertinent data that is important to the future of their organization. They focus on the present and the future simultaneously. They know how to define problems, weigh creative alternatives in solving those problems, and then take appropriate and timely action to implement needed changes. And they know how to set up evaluation systems to monitor personal and organizational performance.

Implications for training and credentialing

The competency areas delineated by Culkin and the hierarchical framework presented in this commentary have implications for director training and credentialing. They may provide some structure to the content and sequence of training and help frame the way credentialing efforts are conceptualized. The ultimate goal of both training and credentialing is to create a system to screen out incompetence, guarantee competence, and promote excellence.

Administrative training should prepare directors for both the management and the leadership functions inherent in their role. This dual training need presents a special problem for trainers, however. Traditional management topics (those typically located at the bottom of the hierarchy) lend themselves readily to short-term training; they are focused, skill based, easily packaged, and easy to evaluate. On the other hand, topics traditionally associated with leadership functions (those at the top of the hierarchy) take longer because they involve fundamental changes in the way people view their role and the overarching principles that guide their behavior. Training in these areas is not easily packaged and does not lend itself to clean, precise methods of evaluation. The professional development of early childhood directors must provide a delicate balance of both management and leadership training.

Initial training for directors should focus on policies, budgeting, regulations, and other topics that are part of the technical level of knowledge and skill competency. Ideally, training in these topics should be taken as a prerequisite for assuming the position of director. Training in these topics could be delivered at the prebaccalaureate level either as part of a degree program or through workshops. As one moves up the hierarchy of competency areas, the content of training embraces more abstract theoretical topics that depend on a deeper level of conceptual thinking. Training at the community relations and symbolic levels is best suited for the graduate level and only after the director has had some experience in an administrative role. More detailed recommendations regarding the content, structure, and delivery of training of directors is provided elsewhere (Bloom & Rafanello 1995).

As director credential efforts evolve in different states, it will be interesting to explore the desirability and feasibility of a credential that specifies different degrees of competence in each of the competency clusters. If the hierarchical model is applied to developing a credential, a director's level of competency at each level would be assessed on a continuum from weak to strong or on some other scale.

This added dimension to the paradigm may be difficult to put in practice, but it is important because it legitimizes the different levels of training and expertise that already exist in the field. For example, in the fiscal management of programs, a director can now take either course work providing a basic and rudimentary understanding of accounting concepts and procedures or advanced computer programming classes for more sophisticated analysis of financial statements. Recognizing and valuing the varying degrees of proficiency at each level would reinforce the idea that true professionalism is an ongoing process of competency building.

Conclusion

We now have ample research demonstrating that sound management practices improve the quality of work life for staff, decrease teacher turnover, increase respect and status for the profession, and significantly influence the quality of program services. As Culkin has so forcefully argued, there is mounting consensus that the administration of child care centers needs to be recognized as a specialized area of expertise in early care and education, separate from teaching. This will come about, though, only by a concerted effort within the field to expand the availability of and access to specialized training, create a director credential, increase the number of director resource networks, and promote greater recognition and rewards for the role. Continuing the discussion about how we define director competence and clarifying specific and measurable competencies is an important first step.

References

Bennis, W. 1989. *On becoming a leader.* New York: Addison-Wesley.

Bloom, P.J. 1990. The early childhood center director: Policy perspectives on increasing requisite qualifications. *Early Education and Development* 1 (3): 185–204.

Bloom, P.J., & D. Rafanello. 1995. The professional development of early childhood center directors: Key elements of effective training models. *Journal of Early Childhood Teacher Education* 16 (Winter): 3–8.

Covey, S. 1991. *Principle-centered leadership.* New York: Fireside.

Fenichel, E.S., & L. Eggbeer. 1990. *Preparing practitioners to work with infants, toddlers, and their families: Issues and recommendations for educators and trainers.* Arlington, VA: National Center for Clinical Infant Programs.

Hayden, J. 1996. *Management of early childhood services: An Australian perspective.* Wentworth Falls, NSW: Social Science Press.

Isenberg, J. 1979. *Requisite competencies for the early childhood educator.* ERIC, ED 182 009.

Katz, L., & J. Raths. 1985. Dispositions as goals for teacher education. *Teaching & Teacher Education* 1 (4): 301–07.

Morgan, G. 1993. Competencies of child care center directors. Unpublished manuscript, Wheelock College, Boston.

Sergiovanni, T. 1984. Leadership and excellence in schooling. *Educational Leadership* (February): 5–13.

Short, E.C., ed. 1984. *Competence: Inquiries into its meaning and acquisition in educational settings.* Lanham, MD: University Press of America.

Chapter 5

Advocacy Leadership

Helen K. Blank

Strong leadership and advocacy by the early care and education community within both the public and private sectors has helped improve the landscape for children and families. The elements viewed by the field as the essential underpinnings of a system of early care and education—support for staff training and credentialing, accreditation, strong licensing standards, decent salaries, resource-and-referral services, and affordable care—are more prevalent today than a decade ago as the direct result of nothing less than forceful advocacy and leadership. Leaders from the Head Start and child care communities have worked together to put in place the building blocks essential to a strong child care system. While we have a long way to go to ensure that every child is in a supportive and nurturing early childhood environment, significant progress has been made over the past two decades to increase investments in and support for early care and education.

In an ideal world, many of the activities described in this chapter would not be necessary. Policymakers and the public would understand that investing in children—our most viable resource—is truly cost effective and productive for the society as a whole. We would value and care for children because they are our most precious resource. However, until this common sense value is embraced by the policymakers and the American public, creative and determined leadership must put in place, step by step, the building blocks for an early care and education system that meets the needs of children and their families.

Working together, advocates have demonstrated a range of traits that characterize effective leadership. They have utilized their leadership skills to influence both federal and state early care and education policies as well as private sector investments in child care. Having devoted a good part of my career to advocacy for early care and education

policies that support children and families, I am interested in what makes leaders effective as they advocate for children and families. This chapter examines those leadership characteristics.

Having a vision, planning for the long term, and moving beyond the press of everyday responsibilities

Early care and education leaders display forward thinking not only in shaping federal and state policies but also in understanding the potential role that the private sector plays in improving the quality of child care. But effective leaders also must have a vision or agenda for what they believe children need to grow and thrive. While leaders must be able to compromise and make tough decisions, their work must be fueled by an ultimate vision of what early care and education should look like. They must be able to share and communicate this vision with a broader community.

In the mid-1980s, child care advocates worked together to build that vision as they planned the campaign to pass comprehensive child care legislation. Advocates realized in the spring of 1986 that the time would soon be ripe for the passage of federal child care legislation. Demographics had changed radically and women with young children were working in record numbers. The media were constantly discussing families' unmet child care needs, and Congress was interested in moving a child care bill. However, advocates knew that they had to step back from the press of their everyday responsibilities to lay the groundwork if such an initiative was to be successful. They faced a formidable task. They had to build a broad-based coalition that would involve more than their typical early care and education allies, stay united to develop a vision that all could agree on, and move quickly enough that the vision could be incorporated into a bill that could move through Congress in 1988 and make child care a pivotal issue in the 1988 presidential campaign.

Advocates placed a great deal of their effort on the front end of this campaign. Planning ahead, they met for more than a year to draft a bill that met the needs of children and families and reflected the expertise of the field. A small group of national experts met during the summer of 1986 to discuss the outlines of a bill. This meeting was followed by a much larger gathering during the NAEYC Annual Conference in Washington. Summaries of that meeting were sent to advocates around the country for their input. Several small meetings then tackled unresolved issues such as infant care, salaries, the role of schools and child care, welfare reform and child care, and family child care. Advocates built a national, broad-based coalition to support the bill and organized state alliances for better child care that had the capacity and the will to direct grassroots efforts to pass the legislation.

This longer-term thinking, crucial in passing federal legislation, has also helped spur the growth of private-sector investments in child care. In the early 1980s child care advocates, realizing that public funds would never by themselves solve the child care crisis, began publicizing early private-sector investments in child care. They systematically sought expanded private support for child care and also developed tools for advocates to use in their own communities with their local employers. Advocates quickly realized that investments in a single company's workforce would not provide the funding necessary to strengthen the child care infrastructure. They convinced several key employers that investments in community resource-and-referral programs, training, family child care recruitment campaigns, and other programs would be beneficial not only to their own workforce but also to the broader community's economic well-being.

At the state level, child care leaders in North Carolina understood that their state was ready for major changes in early care and education. Working together, they conceived a vision that encompassed a comprehensive approach to meeting each community's child care needs. They then approached Governor James B. Hunt Jr. about the idea, and he made it an integral component of his children's agenda. The initiative, which was called Smart Start, brings community representatives together to design their own vision for strengthening their early care and education system. Unlike many other planning efforts, Smart Start also brings state dollars to local communities to implement the plan. Today, thanks to the visionary leadership of North Carolina's children's advocates, Smart Start operates in more than 40 counties.

Reaching out and working with people and organizations beyond familiar colleagues

The face of early care and education will not be changed in this country solely through the efforts of the field. Good leaders move beyond their own colleagues to convince others of the importance of their cause. Without new allies, child care providers and others in the field are too easily characterized by policymakers as "self-interested." Child advocates have a history of reaching out to new constituencies.

In the early 1980s child care leaders set the stage for the successful effort to pass the Child Care and Development Block Grant by developing strong relationships with a wide range of national organizations. They joined forces with women's organizations to convince the Internal Revenue Service to place a line on the short tax form for the Dependent Care Tax Credit, making it more accessible to lower-income taxpayers. Following this success, child care and women's organizations reached out to elderly groups in a unique coalition, the Multigenerational Coalition on Dependent Care. This group, which included the American Association of Retired Persons and the National Council of Senior Citizens, lobbied to make the Dependent Care Credit refundable and to expand the amounts available to lower- and lower-middle-income families. Coalition members testified at congressional hearings, paid joint visits to members of Congress, and briefed congressional staff about the importance of dependent care both for families with young children and for those with aging family members. While the coalition's efforts came close, it did not succeed in improving the credit. However, in the midst of this campaign, coalition members discovered another issue that they had in common. The need for increased funding for the Title XX Social Services Block Grant also cut across intergenerational lines, as Title XX was a critical source of funding for child care as well as services for the elderly. The group joined with the National Association of Counties, the American Public Welfare Association, and labor unions in a major push to restore Title XX funds that built on their efforts with legislators around the Dependent Care Credit. They were successful in winning a significant increase in funds.

The campaign to pass the Act for Better Child Care (ABC), which evolved into the Child Care and Development Block Grant, was a success because it followed up on the relationship forged with many new allies in the early 1980s and involved a broad-based coalition that included not only children's organizations but also key women's organizations, labor unions, religious organizations, representatives of minority groups, professional organizations such as the American Academy of Pediatrics, and others. Organizations such as the National Governors' Association, the National Association of State Legislatures, the American Public Welfare Association, and the National Association of Counties also worked for the passage of child care legislation. The diversity of support for a new child care initiative was evident not only in the membership of the ABC coalition but also in the day-to-day leadership of the campaign, which included representatives of children's organizations, labor unions, and women's organizations. While leadership from the early care and education community across the country was essential to the success of many of the actions that finally led to the bill's passage, these efforts would not have been successful without the support of the broader coalition.

After the passage of the bill, when the Bush administration issued regulations that not only would have compromised the quality of child care but also would have limited state flexibility to invest in and support high-quality child care, the expanded coalition was critically important. Child care advocates already had the relationships established and were able to join forces with governors, state legislators, state child care administrators, and county officials to convince the Bush administration to change some of the most limiting and damaging features of the regulations.

Similarly, efforts to expand Head Start have been buttressed by a broader coalition, including the strong support of the business community. Support has ranged from official pronouncements in favor of full funding from organizations such as the Business Round Table, to testimony by key CEOs at congressional hearings, to appearances by business leaders in films about Head Start. In addition, Primerica (now Travelers Inc.) supported advertisements, public service announcements, and a grassroots campaign that encouraged its employees to support Head Start.

State and local advocates also developed new constituencies to support increased investments in child care. In Indiana, state and local crime officials helped pass a bill that increased funds for school-age child care. Advocates in Colorado, Minnesota, Kansas City, and many other localities have worked closely with business leaders to expand support for significant new investments in child care.

Scanning the environment to seize strategic opportunities to move an issue forward

To help move an issue forward or to prevent implementation of a bad policy, leaders must find vehicles for addressing the issues. Federal-level advocacy around Head Start has involved a number of cases in which advocates took advantage of new op-

portunities to ensure the quality of the program and protect features such as the Child Development Associate Program (CDA). Their efforts have had ramifications for the entire field of early care and education. For example, training is a key component of a good early care and education system. The congressional dialogue about training began with Head Start; funds earmarked for Head Start training set the precedent for the concept of investing federal dollars in training for child care.

However sound the concept of training is and whatever linkages it has to better teacher-child interactions, the path to winning support for training dollars was not smooth. The training system, so integral to Head Start and welcome by child care centers that partner with the program, was not an accepted component of the program in 1983. That year, the Reagan administration concluded that since Head Start was a mature program, its then $25 million training budget could be slashed in half. Advocates faced a dilemma. The Head Start program was not up for reauthorization, so they could not address this issue in the core Head Start bill. Efforts to convince the administration to reverse its course failed, so advocates turned to the congressional appropriators responsible for funding Head Start. There was no line item for Head Start training at that time. Funding levels for training were determined by the Department of Health and Human Services (DHHS) without congressional guidance. Arguing the linkages between training and program quality, advocates prevented the cutback by convincing members of the House and Senate Appropriations Committees to direct the DHHS secretary to maintain Head Start's training funds at $25 million.

Head Start was up for reauthorization in 1984. This offered another opportunity to address several key program issues. Concerned that the Reagan administration would emphasize expansion of services at the risk of quality, advocates worked with Congress to design a reauthorization bill that would protect its key features. This battle not only brought training again to the fore but also addressed the future of the CDA (credentialing) concept. The administration was in the process of eliminating funding for such an organization. This decision would have had ramifications far beyond the Head Start community. The field was alarmed. Without federal support for a credentialing body, the costs of CDA would have likely doubled, making the credential out of reach for the majority of child care providers who—unlike Head Start staff—had no access to subsidies for CDA training and certification. Dr. Edward Zigler, who had developed the CDA while heading the Office of Child Development, quickly came to its defense. He arrived in Washington to lead a briefing for congressional staff about the importance of the CDA to the quality of not only Head Start programs but child care as well.

The advocates' hard work paid off. Language in the bill made permanent the concept of spending at least a fixed amount of the Head Start budget for training, ensured that the program's performance standards could not be made less comprehensive, preserved the system for training staff to work with children with special needs, and, perhaps most significantly for the early care and education field, preserved federal funding for a national body to handle the CDA credential. The 1984 Head Start reauthorization also included a step forward for child care. Leaders encouraged members of Congress to attach authorization for a very modest new program that provided start-up funds for school-age and resource-and-referral programs. This initiative helped spotlight these two critical issues around the country and laid the groundwork for future expansion of these programs.

In 1992, Head Start leaders once again sought a legislative route to strengthen the program. Head Start was not up for reauthorization, and Congress typically did not pass legislation affecting the program unless it was dealing with a reauthorization bill. However, the lack of adequate facilities was hampering the growth of the program and keeping children in environments not conducive to their sound growth and development. Many grantees who did not own their buildings restored classrooms only to lose their leases shortly after work was complete. Advocates convinced Congress to pass the Head Start Improvement Act, which allowed Head Start programs to purchase facilities. The act also addressed the issue of the CDA national credentialing body. The Bush administration had announced that it was phasing out support for such a body, and the field again had responded by claiming that the costs of the credential would double. The Head Start Improvement Act made permanent the federal funding for a national body to administer the CDA, and the House and Senate Appropriations Committees earmarked more than $800,000 to ensure its funding.

Advocates at the state level have also been able to take advantage of strategic opportunities to build a stronger early care and education system. For example, as governors and legislators become interested in funding state prekindergarten programs to ensure that every child entered school ready to succeed, many state advocates helped design initiatives that included the option of full-day, full-year services. This ensured not only that new investments would continue to be made in prekindergarten programs but also that these investments would support services that met the needs of working parents. California advocates used another tack that centered on the pre-K

agenda. When the governor proposed an increase in the state's prekindergarten program, they worked to have half the funds targeted to full-day child care services funded through the state's child care subsidy program.

Making strategic use of data and expert support

Leaders understand the role of well-timed reports and data, as well as the value of experts in promoting their cause. Much of the progress made in the field of early care and education has been fueled by data indicating the need to move ahead in areas ranging from affordability to quality. In some cases, leaders have taken advantage of relevant studies that happened to be released in the midst of their campaign. In other cases, leaders have actually initiated data-collection efforts for a report that they knew would help to change the climate of opinion around a specific issue. Such data were incorporated in reports that were released to the public and the press at opportune times. A report, even if it includes the best possible information, is not helpful to a campaign if the information is not timely or if it does not reach the right hands.

There are abundant examples of leaders in both Head Start and child care using reports to move their issues forward. While President Bush had made expanding Head Start one of his key goals, less and less attention was being paid to grantees' requests for support to maintain the quality of the program. The National Head Start Association (NHSA), working with other early childhood leaders and members of Congress, developed a reauthorization bill in 1990 that addressed new and familiar concerns alike. The bill set aside funds for hiring new staff, purchasing equipment and materials, and making other quality improvements. Half of the funds was directed to improving salaries. Concerned that Head Start was growing rapidly and that training funds were not adequate to meet this growth, Congress set aside increased funds for training. In addition, over the objections of the Bush administration, a provision ensured that every classroom would have at least one teacher with a CDA or equivalent credential by 1995. Grantees were also encouraged to provide full-day, full-year services. Understanding that their proposals would fare better if backed up by well-documented materials, NHSA assembled a panel of experts to produce *A Silver Ribbon Panel Report on Head Start,* which laid out many of the issues that needed to be addressed both to improve Head Start's quality and to make the program more responsive to children and families. The report was a useful tool; it provided advocates an opportunity to schedule briefing sessions with congressional staff and members about the issues that had to be tackled to strengthen the program.

The lobbying campaign of the Multigenerational Coalition on Dependent Care received a boost from a Children's Defense Fund (CDF) study released in the early fall of 1983 just before the final push to expand Title XX. The study focused on states' child care cutbacks as a result of a 20% reduction in Title XX's funding in 1981. The study was distributed to all members of Congress and was the subject of many briefings on Capitol Hill.

When President Clinton proposed to fully fund Head Start, the program became the object of renewed controversy. Some critics argued that Head Start should not grow substantially until its quality was improved. However, the president, unlike his predecessors, supported expanded funding not only for serving additional children but also for quality improvements to ensure that resources would be forthcoming to help programs strengthen their services. Early childhood professionals stepped forward to help improve, defend, and expand Head Start. Fearful that Congress would listen to critics of the president's budget and be reluctant to expand Head Start, a number of renowned early childhood academicians cosigned a letter to every member of Congress. The letter detailed the success that Head Start had in working with our poorest children and families and described why the program must be expanded. The scholars' leadership and support were essential in convincing Congress that the research community had a firm grasp on the program and its history and was 100% behind an expansion of Head Start.

Experts also made their voices heard throughout the 1986–90 campaign to pass the Act for Better Child Care (ABC). They joined a panel of early care and education academicians to provide advice and input, appeared as witnesses at congressional hearings, and communicated with their members of Congress. When House leaders were hesitant to schedule a vote on the bill, a letter coauthored by Sheila Kamerman and Alfred Kahn and signed by more than 200 colleagues stressed the importance of the legislation and the need for its immediate passage.

Developing new approaches to reach the public and policymakers

Leaders strive to develop new ways to get their message across. Advocates have become increasingly sophisticated about working with the media. For example, as the 1984 congressional session was drawing to a close, advocates were distressed that the Senate still had not voted on the then landmark Head Start bill. The Children's Defense Fund (CDF) used a technique that had been pioneered that summer during the consideration of Medicaid expansion. CDF placed a *Washington Post* ad that proclaimed, "400,000 Head Start Children Need One Good Senator." A number of key senators were moved by the ad and helped bring the bill to the Senate floor and to conference with the House of Representatives just before Congress adjourned for the 1984 elections.

Ads also were used at strategic times during the campaign to pass the Act for Better Child Care. They were placed in *Roll Call*, a newspaper for members of Congress, as well as in *USA Today* and the *Washington Post*. In preparation for a possible presidential veto, advocates contacted thousands of individuals opposed to such a veto and made plans to publish their names in a two-page ad in the *Washington Post*. In addition, in strategic locations around the country, leaders of the ABC campaign broadcast radio messages about the importance of good child care. Leaders also briefed reporters and editors, appeared on countless television and radio interviews, and helped local advocates and opinion makers develop op-ed articles and other stories for their local press.

State child care advocates also use unique strategies to make their case. In Florida, for example, advocates rolled the waiting list of the more than 25,000 families who needed child care assistance down the steps of the state capitol building to indicate the magnitude of the need for help in paying for child care. Wisconsin advocates forged a coalition with elderly groups to fight the governor's welfare reform plan that would significantly limit parents' choices of high-quality child care. A poster highlighting their joint opposition to the plan was placed in the statehouse bathrooms within easy sight of legislators. In Utah when the governor and legislators refused to heed pleas for increased funds to help more families with child care costs, JEDI Women, an organization of low-income mothers, staged an all-night sit-in and a press conference at the governor's office. They used a large key that symbolized child care as the key to staying off welfare. The result was more money for child care and the elimination of a long waiting list.

In Colorado, life-size dolls with messages about individual children's needs were placed on the chairs of state legislators. The doll campaign helped win millions of dollars in new investments for services to children and families. Building on the success of this effort, child care advocates brought similar dolls to the National Association of Child Care Resource and Referral Conference in February 1995. And when Congress prepared to make major cutbacks in federal child care programs, dolls appeared at congressional sessions, at a rally and press conference on the steps of the Capitol, and in members' offices. They were eventually banned from the Capitol because of the significant impact they were making.

Child Watch is a CDF project that invites policy-makers, business leaders, and others in the community to visit local programs both to see the type of support that children need to grow and thrive and to witness the conditions of vulnerable children and families. The project technique has been used by many early care and education advocates. After Child Watch visits, during which they play games on the floor with young children in a child care center, business leaders have increased their investments in their community's child care programs. This see-for-yourself approach helps them understand the importance of good child care to children's sound development.

Pennsylvania advocates staged community dialogues that brought together business leaders, media representatives, policymakers, and others to hear parents, caregivers, and business leaders describe how gaps in child care affect their lives. Minnesota advocates helped make the case for a $16 million increase in their state's child care assistance program for low-income families by interviewing families on waiting lists for child care assistance and publishing a moving report on the strains and stresses that these families faced. Using the report strategically, advocates briefed legislators, the media, and the business community about the need for increased funds for child care.

Making tough decisions and risking being unpopular

Advocates must decide not only how to use our resources and time most effectively but also where our efforts will be the most successful. Working with Congress or state legislatures, we must make tough decisions about which investments will provide the biggest payoff for children and which will provide the strongest base on which to build in the future. We cannot support every program or initiative with the same level of effort and commitment. We often must decide which pieces of the agenda are the most necessary and the most worth fighting for. These decisions can mean putting some issues on the back burner or even totally abandoning efforts around certain smaller initiatives. The decisions may not please everyone in the field, but to succeed and be productive, they must be made.

For example, in 1995 when Congress proposed a multitude of changes in federal supports to children and families, it was important for advocates to save as much of the child care infrastructure as possible. Child care leaders were compelled to focus on two or three key issues in order to preserve as much as possible for children and families. Increased funds for child care was a top priority. Welfare reform would generate a sig-

nificant new demand for child care assistance for families on welfare who had to meet stiff new work requirements. Without additional child care dollars, states would be more likely to cut back child care assistance for low-income working families and also reduce investments in improving quality. Once funding increases were in place, advocates moved on to place greater emphasis on specific provisions concerning quality.

Advocates also placed a great deal of emphasis on the Child and Adult Care Food Program (CACFP) since it offers open-ended entitlement funding to child care and Head Start centers and family child care homes. Without these funds, many programs could not stay in business. Losing a guaranteed source of funds to feed young children would have had major ramifications on the healthy development of young children and the health of the child care industry in general. Therefore, advocates made CACFP's continued existence a top priority.

Sometimes leaders have the luxury of making tough decisions at the front end of a battle. Often, however, they must be ready to make a tough decision on the spot. In all cases, they must be willing to bear the consequences of their decisions and stand up for their actions. In the midst of a vote on an amendment concerning child care, legislators may come to advocates and ask them to make an instantaneous choice about which way to go. Good leaders must be ready to make this choice because they have the facts at hand and the presence of mind to decide what they believe is the best for children and families.

Hanging tough, being relentless, and continually developing new approaches to highlight the issues

Effecting change for children is not an easy task. Leaders understand that being a leader means that they occasionally will be seen as thorns in others' sides. Leaders are willing to stick to an issue and stay on course until they win as much as they can. They do not give up when the going gets tough.

Child care advocates worked for four years to pass the Child Care and Development Block Grant. They were willing to try strategy after strategy, both new and old, until they won. Those who worked on the campaign remember a string of advocacy techniques, such as tying up the phone lines of the congressional leadership. They also recall mustering their creative energies to employ a plethora of new strategies during the closing months of the campaign. The push to the finish line began by making thousands of miles of paper chains that provided the backdrop for a number of local rallies for the ABC bill. The chains were then sent to Washington, where they were used on numerous other occasions, including at a rally for children and families held across from the White House; at a national press conference of mayors, women's leaders, governors, religious leaders, and others in front of the Capitol; at a press conference of mothers and grandmothers whose children were injured or who had died in child care; and at a rally in which supporters stretched the chains from the Capitol to the White House and delivered a mock-up of the bill to the president. After the final rally, members of Congress were urged to hang the chains on their doors to express support for the legislation.

Other strategies were also employed during the home stretch of the ABC bill. An advertisement insisting that children who needed child care had been abandoned by Congress was placed in *USA Today*. A Labor Day release of a report on the status of state efforts to protect children in child care also drew a great deal of press attention to the issue.

Knowing how and when to compromise

Each step toward a strong early care and education system requires compromise. Unfortunately, no final bill, regulation, or administrative decision is constructed exactly as advocates would design it. We must know when to compromise and accept victory, understanding that change often occurs by taking smaller steps toward an ultimate goal.

For example, the original Act for Better Child Care contained federal standards for all child care. Advocates realized that a bill containing federal standards would generate a filibuster in the Senate and that it would not be possible to generate the necessary 60 votes for cloture. Therefore, they worked out a compromise, discussing what might be a reasonable position with Senate staff, who then met with representatives of the National Governors' Association to garner their views. A version passed by the House and Senate required states to have standards in certain key areas. The final version endorsed by the Bush administration simply required that all providers (except certain relatives) meet minimum health and safety standards related to training, physical premise safety, and health (including immunizations). While this was a far cry from the original version of the bill, the health and safety language made a significant difference in many state approaches to protecting children in exempt child care settings that receive federal funds— child care that is not required to be regulated by the state. Equally important, by being willing to compromise, leaders were able to unlock significant new funds for early care and education. If advocates had held out for federal child care standards, it is highly possible that the bill would never have been enacted, and communities would have lost billions of dollars provided by the Child Care and Development Block Grant.

Inspiring and supporting new leaders and collaborating with colleagues

Finally, leaders who advocate for children understand the importance of working with colleagues and supporting new leaders as they help make the case for better early care and education opportunities for children and families. No one leader makes change alone. Many leaders across the country worked in concert to pass the Child Care and Development Block Grant and stave off some of the most onerous changes proposed by Congress in 1995. Similarly, leaders have come together to build and strengthen the Head Start program over the past 30 years. Leaders understand the value of working in collaboration with others. They also understand the importance of new leadership, and they recognize the vitality, creativity, energy, and fresh ideas that it can bring. A leader always works to help others to move into leadership positions so the strongest possible team is on board for children and families.

Leaders are individuals who keep their focus on their true constituency. They never forget that they are working for children. They also understand that people with different perspectives may share their goals for children and families, and they do not hesitate to build bridges with varied organizations and individuals. As they move forward, leaders understand the importance of taking small steps to put in place the foundation for a more comprehensive child care system. They understand that more modest initiatives not only seed an issue but also offer an opportunity to educate policymakers about the importance of good child care.

The next decade will bring new challenges for leaders committed to ensuring that all families have access to high-quality early care and education opportunities. With welfare changes, governors and legislators are increasing investments in child care. However, they are simultaneously implementing policies that threaten the progress that has been made in building a strong early care and education infrastructure. Many of their decisions could force families to choose the lowest quality, most inexpensive child care. Pressures on the federal budget, reflected in proposed cuts in Head Start and other critical children's services, threaten Head Start's ability to provide the comprehensive services that children and their families need. Leaders will have to draw upon all of their best resources and muster their colleagues to ensure that the nation continues to move forward toward the vision of a sound and supportive early care and education experience for all children.

Commentary

by Susan Muenchow

As the Children's Defense Fund's premier lobbyist for child care, Helen Blank illustrates the importance of having a long-term vision, forming coalitions, taking advantage of strategic opportunities, making timely use of data, finding new approaches to reach out to the media, being willing to compromise, and, most important, being persistent. Her insights in this chapter are particularly informative about how these strategies have contributed to major victories at the federal level. Having been the key player in many of these victories, Blank knows whereof she speaks. She points out how the same lessons apply to state child care advocates.

From my experience working at the state level, I would like to expand on Blank's strategies to promote better state policy on child care. In the wake of welfare reform and block grants, state-level advocacy takes on new importance. It is imperative that state advocates become as sophisticated in their understanding of the state legislative process as are federal advocates of the congressional process.

Focus on appropriations

There are three keys to mastering the state legislative process: budget, budget, and budget. Those who understand the state budget and the various decision points involved in assembling it stand by far the best opportunity to make positive changes for children. Advocates too often devote the bulk of their energies trying to secure substantive legislation to create a new program without working on the appropriations necessary to fund the program. As a result, state statutes are full of good ideas that are never fully implemented. In my state, for example, a wonderful piece of legislation establishes a continuum of prevention and early intervention services, but the only pieces implemented are those programs on which advocates have focused systematically on the funding (such as for Healthy Start or child care).

The first step in influencing the state budget is to find out the time schedule for the appropriations process. By the time the legislative committees meet formally to discuss appropriations, advocates have already lost much of their opportunity to influence the process. To be most effective, advocates should find out when the state agencies involved in early care and education submit their funding requests to the governor and when the governor's office submits its recommendations to the legislature.

Advocates should first meet with the agency level staff charged with developing budget recommendations, then with the governor's budget office staff overseeing the same policy area. Rarely does a state legislature appropriate more funds for a program than the governor has requested. Thus, it is extremely important to secure the governor's support for a budget issue. The governor's staff budget and policy coordinators frequently look for new ideas and information to develop budget recommendations. The advocate who can supply this information accurately and in a timely manner may well find an appreciative ear in the governor's budget office. For example, one of the keys to winning support from Florida's governor for a $60 million child care expansion was providing information that showed the child care supply was large enough to accommodate the planned expansion.

The spokesperson selected to meet with the governor's staff must be someone who has the time to do the required homework. The representative must be familiar with the current level of funding for the program, the unmet need, and the costs and benefits of meeting that need. An advocate with this type of knowledge may be accompanied by a person with more practical experience working in the program.

While working to secure support from the governor's office, advocates should also get to know the key legislators and staff on the appropriations committees. Legislators may come and go, but staff with knowledge of appropriations tend to remain. Developing credibility with the right appropriations committee staff member may be just as important as getting to know the committee chair.

Once advocates have done this background work with the state agencies, the governor's office, and the appropriations committees, the next step is to closely follow the work of the House and Senate appropriations committees. Advocates should have a representative at every committee meeting. During the final hours of conference negotiations to work out differences in House and Senate appropriations bills, it is frequently important to assign someone, whether it be a professional lobbyist or a volunteer, to basically "live" at the statehouse until a budget agreement is reached.

Consider the audience

Anyone familiar with early care and education knows that quality programs have multiple benefits. Evidence shows that quality early childhood programs help children enter school ready to learn, prevent or minimize disabilities, protect children from abuse and neglect, allow parents to enter and remain in the workforce, and even contribute to a reduction in crime. When preparing a policy briefing paper, it is important to frame the arguments in the manner most likely to be understood. In other words, the paper should emphasize the early childhood benefits that relate best to the issues foremost on that year's legislative agenda, whether they be crime prevention, education, or welfare reform.

As state legislatures turn their sights to welfare reform, many advocates believe they are losing ground with the usual arguments about the benefits of quality child care. While a growing number of legislators agree that child care is one of the keys to welfare reform, very few seem to understand the importance of quality care. Arguments about the long-term savings related to investments in quality preschool may not work with a legislator concerned about meeting next year's welfare-to-work requirement. For example, during a recent debate on the child care needed to support welfare reform in Florida, one key legislator, without apology, announced, "We're not into quality care. We're into quantity."

A lengthy defense of programs accredited by the National Association for the Education of Young Children may not be effective with such a legislator. However, the same legislator might be interested in research from California's GAIN program indicating that former welfare mothers are most apt to remain employed when their children are in NAEYC-accredited programs. As we enter a new era of advocacy, it will be important to hone our message to address new concerns.

Localize and personalize the message

A message, however appropriate, is more effective when it includes information specific to the district of the legislator one is trying to persuade. The advocate who can remind a state senator how many children are on the waiting list for child care in his or her district will be more effective than one who just gives a state overview. A visit to the legislator by one or two mothers on the waiting list is even better.

Putting a face on the issue for which one is advocating is as important as good, timely data. That is why, as Helen Blank points out, it is so important to develop new strategies such as Colorado's doll campaign or Florida's rolling out the waiting list for subsidized care on the Capitol steps.

The importance of "up close and personal" was never more vivid than in an effort to convince a prominent state legislator not to relax the staff-child ratio for infants. This legislator had been hearing from a few providers that the key to solving the state's child care problems was to suspend a requirement that no more than four infants be in the care of one adult. However, after advocates invited the legislator to visit a local center, and he had the experience of trying to hold and pay attention to all the babies and toddlers who wanted his attention, he became one of the state's most reliable advocates for investments in quality care.

Choose the right messenger

It is important not only to localize and personalize the message but also to choose the right messenger. Frequently, as Helen Blank points out, the best messenger is not an advocate in any traditional sense. Just as Head Start enlisted the business community to help make its case, so too will advocates need to look for new allies to expand and preserve state investments in prekindergarten, child care training, and protective licensing regulations.

Recent success stories at the state level include mobilizing employers to defend state investments in child care resource-and-referral services. Legislators are likely to dismiss the arguments of staff trying to preserve their own jobs working in resource-and-referral agencies. However, when an employer points out that he or she relies on this community service to help employees locate appropriate child care, legislators listen. Similarly, in Florida, the sugar industry regularly helps make the case for investments in subsidized child care for the children of migrant workers.

Given all the obstacles and the overall climate unsympathetic to public investments in social services, advocates have done a good job of making the case for child care at the federal level. Now we must devote similar attention to state-level battles. Only by having leaders with the dedication and skill of Helen Blank will we have any chance of success.

Chapter 6

Community Leadership

Dwayne A. Crompton

In the early care and education arena, a real leader is an agent of change. Much more than being a good administrator—merely keeping an organization afloat in an age of declining resources—an effective leader transforms a vision of what should be into reality.

The leader who makes a difference is not a sit-at-your-desk kind of person. This individual is out in the community educating others about important community issues in a way that mobilizes them to action. For the early care and education professional, this means helping the community to understand—on both an intellectual and visceral level—why early care is crucial to the health and welfare of children and families. It means communicating a story so compelling that the power brokers in your city or state make improving early care and education a major community priority.

The best leader in the early care field

• demonstrates to the community that early care and education is a watershed issue that determines to a great extent the future success of children in school and in life.

• persuades local power brokers to put improved early care at or near the top of the community's agenda.

• functions as the community's early care and education expert in a way that influences early care policymaking on a community-wide basis. This includes defining what needs to be done—e.g., providing more caregiver training, securing increased resources, or offering better programming—to create early childhood programs that give children the care and support they need to thrive.

• plays a key role in securing or leveraging the kind of substantial public and private human and financial resources required to improve early care and education programming in all parts of the community.

But, having recognized the important functions of community leadership in the early care and education field, how do you begin to develop a leadership role in your own community? Many steps are involved in getting from teaching in or running your own early care program to becoming a catalyst for changing the face of early care and education on a neighborhood or community-wide basis.

This chapter outlines the primary steps or strategies required to bring early care issues to the attention of the public. Also discussed is the critical *how* portion of the leadership challenge—the personal attributes and professional skills it takes to become a leader and catalyst for change in the early care and education field. These strategies and characteristics apply to virtually every kind and level of early care and education leadership, from the academic who teaches early childhood theory to the director who runs a center or home program to the executive director who manages an agency.

Leadership strategies

No more business as usual

Probably the most important first step is acknowledging that you can't do business as usual anymore. You can't afford to be invisible, to stay in your office concentrating solely on program, if you want the community to know who you are and what you have to say about early care and education. You have to stop being a one-issue person and become involved in a wide variety of social and civic concerns. You have to learn how to relate to the funders and other power brokers in your community. Stop whining because they don't seem to understand the importance of early care and education; it's your job to make them understand.

Visibility: Getting noticed

No matter how skilled you are in the field of early care and education, you will never possess the credibility you need to influence funders and other power brokers until you are recognized as a positive force in the greater community. To achieve this, you must care about and participate in community issues and concerns.

For example, my initial foray into community activism focused on my neighborhood association. I worked hard to ensure that we had decent, safe neighborhoods. I was eventually elected president of the group, and once people saw that I was willing to work hard for a community cause unrelated to my profession, I was invited to join the boards of several human service agencies. There was nothing phony about my involvement in these activities. I still belong to many of these organizations, and I vigorously support their goals. At the same time, however, my activism gives me a bully pulpit for early care and education issues. While working on community projects, I've had many opportunities to talk about early childhood care—to influence elected officials and civic leaders who one day might be in a position to improve, through legislation or philanthropic support, the early care system in my community.

Don't be intimidated if you are not accustomed to participating in community activities outside the contexts of your agency or center. Start small. Join a local church or neighborhood group that works to improve the quality of life in the community. Although you should let the other participants know where you work and what you do, your initial goal is to support the efforts of the group. Be a dependable member and complete all assigned tasks. Over time, you will be recognized as a valuable group member and people will listen when you talk about the needs of the children and families served by your early care program.

Plugging into the community's power source

In the late 1980s I was a frustrated executive director looking for the resources I needed to improve early care programs for low-income families. My agency, the KCMC Child Development Corporation, had been serving the urban core of Kansas City, Missouri, for some 18 years. By almost any measure, we were doing a great job. We had the best possible programming we could offer, given the limited amount of resources we had (primarily Head Start dollars and state funding). We had a successful track record. Our work was widely respected nationally, at least in early care and education circles.

But in my own community, our agency was the best-kept secret in town. As a result, funders had little interest in talking to me, much less in writing a check for the agency's programming. I shared my frustration with a colleague in another field who was familiar with most of the decisionmakers in our community. She immediately understood my problem. "You lack access to community leaders," she said. "If you can gain access and tell your story, I'm sure you'll get what you want."

Over the next few years, I came to understand the importance of her message. Early care professionals rarely have access to the inner circle of community decisionmakers because, in an environment of scarce resources, we tend to devote all of our energy to program management. As a result, we're not out in the community telling the early care and education story. This is a costly mistake.

Not long after the "lack of access" conversation, I had an opportunity to meet some of the power brokers in my community. I was invited to a public forum to help the local community foundation, one of the city's largest foundations, establish funding priorities. I would later learn the reason for my invitation: Several key leaders from the community groups I was involved in had described me as an "emerging community leader" and an "honest and dependable person" to the president of the community foundation. All those years of community activism were beginning to pay off. Broader opportunities to get out the message of early care and education were coming my way.

In addition, the timing was right for early care and education to receive the attention it deserved. The entire country was focused on improving education, specifically on "school readiness." Locally, the community foundation had been told by experts that early care and education was the place to begin.

Telling the early care and education story

Relishing the opportunity to tell my early care story, I told a variation of it at every subsequent priority-setting meeting I attended. I talked about the poor quality of the community's early care and education system. I explained in simple, human terms what happens to a child who receives inadequate early care—whether that means little Mary sitting in front of the television during most of her waking hours or baby Johnny turned over to caregivers who lack the training to provide nurturing, developmentally appropriate care.

I looked into the eyes of the people sitting around that meeting table and told them that until the community got serious about early care issues, we would produce more and more "kindergarten dropouts," children ill prepared to handle the demands of a formal education. Within a few months after entering school, such children begin withdrawing mentally and emotionally from the educational process. They become frustrated and even humiliated when they can't perform some of the simple tasks that their peers seem to master so easily. They get labeled early: slow learners. And while kindergarten dropouts don't literally quit school at the age of 5, they do tend to adopt an attitude of failure that prevents them from overcoming problems and pursuing academic excellence. These are the kids who are most likely to leave school before high school graduation and who, too frequently, are doomed to a life of low-paying jobs and/or dependence on public assistance.

Of course, early care and education professionals already know this. I'm detailing the theme and some of actual words of my presentation because—as I would later learn—it was the power of my story that appealed to funders and other community leaders. "He was so passionate about the issue of early childhood care that we had to listen to him," said one community foundation board member. This woman later became one of my agency's staunchest supporters, spearheading a capital campaign that netted nearly $3 million for our new family and child development center.

Making meaning

What I did instinctively in relaying my early care and education story is what the Center for Creative Leadership defines as *making meaning,* or connecting with what people already have in their minds and hearts (Drath & Palus 1994). A leader who can make meaning, who can demonstrate how an idea or point of view coincides with the values of the majority, will find it much easier to win the support of the community.

The ideal way to make meaning is to define your vision—your *what is*—in a way that most of the community can embrace. Rather than saying, "We need to improve the quality of early care and education" or "We need more and better training programs for caregivers," you might begin with a much simpler, more universal statement: "All children should have a safe, healthy, loving environment." Who would disagree? Then you can explain the relationship between a proper environment for children and quality early care and education.

The next step in making meaning is to show the contrast between the what-is vision and *what exists,* in essence, the relatively dismal state of your community's early care system. One way to make your case is by documenting how many children in your neighborhood or city participate in early care programs that neither protect them from harm nor provide the kind of enriching experiences that prepare children for school. Part of the what-exists story is answering the *so-what* question. What happens to the thousands of children who are exposed on a regular basis to substandard early care?

Also emphasize the outcomes for children who have access to quality early care and education. I like to do that because it gives me a chance to focus on my agency and what we are doing in the community. In my experience, it is useful to present simple but meaningful research data that demonstrate that children who participate in quality early care programs are more likely to graduate from high school, enroll in college, and be employed than children who do not. Buttress these facts with anecdotes, success stories about children enrolled in your program.

Take the time to research one or two outstanding success stories that clearly convey the importance of early care and, at the same time, demonstrate the efficacy of your program. For example, I might talk about Don and Robert, two young brothers who dealt with conflict by shoving and hitting other children. Rather than demeaning the boys and making them feel bad about themselves—as the poorly trained caregivers in some centers might do—our staff taught the boys how to communicate their wishes with words rather than fists. The staff also worked closely with the boys' mother and assisted her in providing more consistent discipline at home. Today Don and Robert know how to play cooperatively and communicate effectively with other children. They are poised to succeed in school because they are not hampered by negative labels such as "behavior problem" or "learning disabled."

The final step in making meaning is the *what-is-important* message: What can we as a community do to ensure that all children receive the kind of early care and education they need to thrive? Once the community understands what the vision is and how far the community is from that vision, it can rally around an action plan, whether that involves buying playground equipment for a center, establishing better caregiver-training programs, or lobbying for more rigorous licensing statutes.

Collaborating with community power brokers

My attempts to make meaning by telling the early care story at the community foundation's priority-setting sessions paid off. Several months after I met the president of the community foundation, she approached me with an irresistible question: What could the foundation do to improve early care and education? Over the next few years, we worked together on several projects that began changing, in some very fundamental ways, the face of early care and education in metropolitan Kansas City.

The first project, known as New Start, extended Head Start to the children of working parents who require child care services on a full-day, year-round basis. The program was initially operated by our agency but has since been expanded to other early care and education programs in the central city. Our agency also partnered with the community foundation, the federal government, and our local community college in the design of a citywide training program for caregivers with little or no early childhood expertise. Today, the Francis Institute is one of the most innovative caregiver-training models in the nation. It addresses the real needs of caregivers, showing them how to turn theory into practice so they can implement tomorrow what they learn in training today.

Our agency does not operate this training program, although we had an opportunity to do so during the planning process. The goal was to make sure that all early care and education providers—including the early care staff at KCMC—had access to meaningful, ongoing training opportunities.

And therein lies a basic lesson in leadership. If you are to be viewed by your community's power brokers as a leader in your field, you must lend your support to all important early care projects, not just those that you will manage or those that will result in funds for your agency.

Forging community partnerships and collaborations

New Start and the Francis Institute substantially enhanced the quality of early care and education in Kansas City. And my involvement in these initiatives helped cement KCMC's reputation as a cutting-edge early care provider, as well as my standing as an early childhood leader and expert. This opened many doors for other early care partnerships and collaborations with a variety of funders, the business community, the public sector, and other not-for-profit agencies. Two particularly noteworthy affiliations resulted in wonderful benefits for the children we serve. Blue Cross and Blue Shield agreed to provide health care for children not covered by Medicaid or a private insurer, and the city's largest public health care clinic provided space on its new campus for a state-of-the-art family and child development center.

Such partnerships and collaborations are essential in early care since it is almost impossible for one person acting alone—no matter how skilled and charismatic—to spur meaningful change within the field. It is essential that you join any early care and education council or consortium in your community. If there isn't one, start one by networking with the early care professionals that you already know. Once your group has a clear mission that the community can support, gradually bring in other public- and private-sector leaders. Concentrate on people who might have the resources and/or influence to help your group accomplish its goals.

Adapting to the private sector

One of the biggest mistakes early care and education professionals make is in assuming that the private sector will meet our needs on our terms. The fact is, our terms are often appalling to funders and business executives, who are successful primarily because they manage lean, efficient, productive organizations. They do not understand and frequently will not tolerate

• long, rambling presentations or funding proposals that never adequately explain the needs of young children or how a specific early care program will make a difference;

• vague program budgets that do not detail and adequately explain program costs; or

• a communication style that is based on the lingo of our field. (Our goal is not to create within the private sector a master's level understanding of early childhood principles; rather, it is our responsibility to explain in simple, ordinary terms the purpose and value of early care and education.)

Early care and education professionals must learn to adapt to the expectations of the private sector. You must demonstrate to funders that you understand the fiscal and management aspects of running an early care program. Prepare a business plan for your program or agency that (1) identifies your clients—both children and parents, (2) outlines their needs, (3) provides a brief synopsis of how your program will address those needs, and (4) includes a detailed budget breakdown as well as an analysis of your funding needs.

If you want to capture the attention of the private sector, you cannot write convoluted 10- to 20-page proposals and community reports that confuse and bore people. Concentrate on your story—how your program makes a difference in the lives of children—rather than cluttering documents with a lot of professional jargon and grandiose notions. You must master the art of condensing your story into two or three pages containing a concise, well-organized message that virtually anyone can understand.

Leadership characteristics

In the summer of 1995, as I wrote this chapter, I surveyed pivotal funders and other power brokers in Kansas City about what, in their view, constitutes a leader in the early care and education field. Their responses were remarkably similar. They expect early care leaders to utilize the basic leadership strategies previously outlined. But they also insist that the early care leaders they invest in be both credible human beings and competent early childhood experts.

For clarity, I divide the characteristics of leadership into two broad categories: personal attributes and professional skills. In my experience, those individuals who possess most of the traits from both categories inevitably become leaders. They will be leaders whether they are in a small rural town, running an early care program for disadvantaged children, or in the nation's capital, advising the president about early care and education policies.

It is important to note the difference between leadership characteristics and leadership styles. For our purposes, leadership characteristics refer to the specific personal attributes and professional skills listed below. A leadership style, however, might best be described as a manner of presentation. For example, one leader may have a flamboyant style, while another might be more restrained. Leadership styles are a matter of disposition and taste, but leadership characteristics are a matter of necessity.

Personal attributes

Character. Your character is the unspoken message you send to people about who you are. It is revealed both by your behavior and by your attitude—by what you do and say, how you treat people, and how you respond to conflict and a host of other situations. In the early care and education field, where leadership must be earned, a strong moral character is essential. It was the aspect of leadership mentioned by every community power broker surveyed. The respondents said two interesting things: Virtue counts and it cannot easily be imitated. One prominent civic leader said she decided to support my agency in part because I was a "principled man who could be trusted."

Passion. Funders and other decisionmakers in Kansas City who have come to support the notion of quality early care tell me that one of the things that influenced them early on was my fervor for children and families. "He is passionate about child care, and his concern and caring for children permeates his being," explained one high-profile early care advocate.

Passion is a spontaneous response, not something you can manufacture on cue. The truth is, I believe so strongly in meeting the needs of children that my underlying passion and enthusiasm seep through my words. I am like a defense attorney fervently advocating for clients. Making life better for children, especially disadvantaged children, is like a ministry to me. If what you are advocating is part of your heart's desire, then people will instinctively know.

Passion for an idea has many forms. I have an intense personality and an animated speaking style, but many effective early care leaders have a more reserved demeanor and a softer speaking style. They are just as influential as I am because they speak from their hearts, and everyone in the room can feel it.

Optimism. A number of very decent folks are ardent, knowledgeable early care advocates and yet have little impact in their communities. Although these individuals may take on leadership roles at one time or another, they are rarely recognized as community leaders because they lack the optimism—the enthusiastic spirit—to inspire and lead the public. They are so busy beating their early-care-is-horrendous drum that they never applaud the incremental changes in the field. This kind of negativity deters many potential supporters, who want to believe they can help to make things better.

The optimist, on the other hand, views early care as a work in progress. He or she encourages supporters to celebrate every small and large victory, from acquiring a new piece of equipment for a child care home to enacting of a state law making early care and education safer for children.

Professional skills and accomplishments

No matter how fine your character, the measure of your leadership ultimately will be determined by what you do in the community. To become a leader, you must possess the skills to define and implement your vision. Part imagination, part common sense, vision involves finding a realistic way to achieve a worthy goal. My personal vision, for example, is that all children be raised in safe, healthy, loving environments. My strategy for achieving my vision is improving the quality of early care and education, which I have attempted to do through activities outlined elsewhere in this chapter.

Communicating your vision. Telling your story in a way that makes sense to the average person is an essential skill. The early care professionals most likely to realize their vision are those who have learned to make meaning. They are able to demonstrate how their vision of what should be coincides with what people want in their hearts (See the discussion of making meaning on p. 51).

Honestly assess your oral and written communication skills. Always use the skill that serves you best. For example, if you speak well, try to communicate your early care issues in person. If you think you fall flat in public forums but know you can write a good report or letter, use the mail for effective communication.

Of course, you can always upgrade deficient communication skills. For example, consider taking a basic writing course at your local community college. Tell your professor you want to learn how to write an organized, persuasive document, such as a fundraising letter or brief funding proposal. By the end of the course, you should have a finished product that can be used, with minor adjustments, in a variety of situations. Or take a public speaking course.

Professional knowledge and experience. This is a basic yet often overlooked skill in the early care professional. One reason I was able to help shape programs that tremendously improved early care in my community is because I had a good balance of theory and practice. Funders are often leery of academics who seem to be mired in theory or research that seems to relate to the laboratory but not the real world. But funders are also reluctant to invest in programs recommended by practitioners whose primary knowledge base consists *only* of what they have learned working on the frontline in an early care program.

Those of you with lots of experience but little education need to take advantage of both formal and informal opportunities for professional development. These include classes at your local university or community college, as well as short-term workshops and seminars. Select courses and training sessions that will help you better understand child development fundamentals so you can explain to parents and other people in the community what children need and why.

Unwavering commitment. Effective leaders are willing to do whatever must be done—educating the community, talking to funders, meeting with legislators—to improve the quality of early care and education. You should go anywhere that you are invited to talk about the needs of children and families and your vision of quality early care. You must be prepared to address a variety of groups, from powerful business leaders at a civic event to a few neighbors in a church basement.

Take advantage of every opportunity to tell the story of high-quality early care and education. And don't wait for formal invitations. Attend and speak out about early care at public meetings concerning social service issues. Send editorials to your local newspaper and policy papers to your legislators. You never know where you're going to find an early care advocate. After my state senator received an opinion paper I had written, he told me he liked what I said, and he asked me to analyze his early care and education bills on a regular basis.

The only thing you have to lose is time. I realize that most of us work 10-plus hours a day just trying to operate a quality program. One of our biggest challenges as early care professionals is striking a balance between managing and leading. We've got to do both if we want children to have access to better early care and education. The truth is, if we aspire to be effective leaders, we must be prepared to lose some sleep.

Presenting a strong track record. Of course, without a credible track record, it doesn't matter how much time and effort we spend. Funders, civic leaders, and other power brokers invest in people as much as they do projects. They are looking for individuals who operate financially responsible programs that make a difference.

It behooves any early care administrator to learn how to document the impact of the program—how it makes a difference. This means demonstrating how the children served by the program are improving their social and thinking skills and/or how well they are performing in school, as compared to peers who are not in quality early care environments.

One way to demonstrate the efficacy of your early care program is by inviting funders and other interested parties to evaluate your home, center, or agency. Don't just tell current and potential supporters how you make a difference; show them. Let them see your program in action. Then document the long-term value of quality early care by providing anecdotal and statistical information about the ongoing academic and personal progress of children previously served by your program. This means you have to get serious about tracking children and their families.

Our agency has cooperated in several independent evaluations, and this has enabled us to prove beyond a doubt the efficacy of our early care and education services. It also helps us garner support from funders and other community leaders who value our willingness to be put under the microscope.

Taking risks—and choosing your battles. Risk takers speak out for what they believe in, even if their convictions ruffle some feathers. They are prepared to lay their reputations on the line—and perhaps lose something they value, such as funding and/

or personal credibility and influence—for a chance to sway the community to act in a way that will improve the quality of early care and education.

For example, several years ago a local politician running for office took a position that, in my opinion, was not good public policy for children and families. After some soul searching, I spoke publicly about my views on what constituted sound public policy related to children and families in general and quality early care and education in particular. The politician was elected. And my agency subsequently paid the price—the funding we received from the political body he served was terminated.

At the same time, however, my reputation as an early care community leader with integrity was enhanced. When word got out that my public position had resulted in a loss of funding, private funders quickly made up the difference.

If you are going to be a successful leader, you not only must be willing to take risks, but you also must develop a sense of when and how to take those risks. For example, learn to choose your fights. Don't make waves about nonessential policy or program concerns. Focus your energies on the big issues that make a difference to early care and education. And remember, every disagreement does not have to be public. I have many times contacted a funder or other community leader by phone or in person to dissuade him or her from supporting an initiative that I did not believe was in the best interests of children and families. When I explained the facts—and spoke from my heart—more often than not the person would change her or his position or at least agree to further investigate the issue.

Sharing the credit. An important objective of any community leader is to build a corps of community advocates to champion your cause. You can't do this by being the sole architect of all ideas or taking credit for all the successes that occur. There are several reasons to share the accolades: You make people feel good and, ultimately, you increase their commitment to work for quality early care.

Conclusion

In the early care and education field, an effective leader is someone who can mobilize the entire community to improve the quality of care that children receive. In most cases, this requires a change in attitude and a change in strategy. Early childhood professionals can no longer be encapsulated in our educational institutions or agencies, preoccupied solely with the day-to-day problems of teaching or program management. We must go into the community and tell the early care story, explaining in ways that people can understand the critical relationship between quality care and a child's future success in school and in life. We must maintain our integrity and develop other personal and professional skills necessary to earn the respect of funders and other community power brokers. We must demonstrate that our agencies operate efficient, productive programs that make a discernible difference in the lives of children and families. We must forge partnerships with other institutions both within and outside the early care field to generate the resources and broad public support needed to change the face of early care and education in our communities.

The kind of leadership I am describing is not an overnight phenomenon, a sudden flash of brilliance manifested by someone with no track record or no history in the community. True leadership—which is rooted in the high regard the community has for a man or woman who has been an articulate, thoughtful, and effective advocate for a cause—is built over many years. In essence, our success as leaders is tied to who we are (personal attributes), our professional skills, and how we use these (strategies) to further the cause of early care and education.

Reference

Drath, W.H., & C.J. Palus. 1994. *Making common sense: Leadership as meaning-making in a community of practice.* Greensboro, NC: Center for Creative Leadership.

Commentary

by Marce Verzaro-O'Brien

In his chapter, Dwayne Crompton identifies an important and often-missing dynamic in the literature on early childhood leadership: the extension of our knowledge and skills from those communities served by our program to broader venues. My own experience in developing advocacy skills for high-quality early care and education parallels that of Crompton. Circumstances also forced me to wrestle with knowledge and skills development. During my shaping experiences as a Head Start administrator in New York state—a challenging arena and in many ways a microcosm for the country—I found it puzzling and frustrating that so few early care and education professionals engaged in dialogue with local, regional, and state power brokers.

For me, examining our typical education and training paradigms proved instructive. First, I speculated that we may be attracted to the early childhood profession because we are most comfortable in settings that value flexibility, spontaneity, and creativity. Many early childhood leaders may feel that systematic data analysis, followed by distillation of complex information into succinct presentations, is best left to those in the "hard sciences." During our formal training, we learn how to work with young children and become very good at fostering social competence in a variety of settings over which we have some (or even a great deal of) control.

When opportunities to move into managing other adults and/or organizations become available, we depend on our shared commitment to young children and our commonality of profession to frame this new experience of being in positions of power vis-a-vis other adults. As we survey the wider community, it seems as if others value neither our work nor the information we have about promoting healthy development for children and their families. Even when early childhood programs receive additional funding, we often are not able to see this as an outcome of our own activity but rather as the work of larger political forces beyond our control. And underlying our uncertainty about participating in community endeavors and advocacy is our deeply held belief that because our cause is just and right—that quality care and education for young children has positive short- and long-term benefits for children and families—early childhood priorities and programs will triumph on their own merits.

Lacking a knowledge and experiential base and burdened by the loss of self-confidence that comes with feeling powerless, we early care and education professionals have often been uncomfortable venturing into the uncharted waters of our local, state, and national communities. As Crompton well knows, circumstances now are forcing us to take the plunge. Faced with competing demands for ever-scarcer funds, politicians are questioning the need for early care and education of high quality. Why can't one caregiver take care of 9 or 10 babies; after all, they need to be fed and diapered only once in a while! Even some businesspersons who acknowledge a relationship between employee productivity and comprehensive child and family services see the solution as resting with individual families. Others with firmly held beliefs about both the primacy of the family and the necessity to teach a narrowly proscribed set of learnings to young children question the validity of what, to us, is commonly accepted practice in our field. You and I have important information and experiences that need to be shared in these discussions! How then can we develop or enhance our capacity to become leaders in the wide community?

Those of us who have engaged in these adventures find several strategies to be useful. They include the following:

• Set a professional goal to develop a message about which you not only feel passionately but also have theoretical and practical knowledge. You are not going to be "preaching to the converted," so make sure you have facts and that they are accurate. Businesspeople and politicians have at least 20 other issues that are as important as early care and education, so make sure your message can be effectively distilled into five minutes, which will include the specific strategies, actions, or policies that you want considered. Once I had five minutes to convince an incoming county executive that investing dollars in child care should be a priority for his administration. I knew he was serious when he set a timer and told me, "You child care folks ramble on too much and you bore people!"

• Practice delivering that message with colleagues who will give you honest and constructive feedback. If speaking, even in a quasi-social situation, is uncomfortable for you, consider joining a local Toastmasters Club or taking an adult education public-speaking class.

• Arm yourself with statistical data and evaluation information, about both your own program and the research in our field. Remember that the cost-effectiveness research of the High/Scope Foundation has been a powerful persuader to those considering the long-term merits of investing in quality early care and education. If your training is deficient in these areas, you could seek additional education. But consider forging a collaboration with other human service agencies or public school systems that do have research offices and might want to engage in a joint evaluation project. If a college or university is nearby, seek out a professor to help you design a study that would engage her students as well as your staff.

• Make sure your message also contains powerful anecdotes about the impact of your work with a child or family. In the past, these experiential data were all that we offered to the community. Now, in our zeal to be more convincing, we often are leaving out these testimonies. Don't! Merge them with your other data. To be most effective, however, these stories need to show long-term effects, and this means following up on the later life events of the children and families we serve. If you don't have a plan for staying in touch, work with your staff to develop those ongoing linkages with families.

• Carefully consider what you do best and where you feel most comfortable. This advice may seem contradictory to our earlier message that everyone needs to be a community leader, but it is not. The new NAEYC Advocacy Lattice (*Be a Children's Champion* brochure 1995) reminds us of the many ways to impact on a community, and each way is valid, valued, and important. Choose your target audience, venue, and delivery strategy. And respect and recognize the efforts of your colleagues. Too often, we tend to admire the contributions of someone who testifies at the state legislature and we never acknowledge the person who works diligently on a school board committee to revise the assessment process. Both are leaders. Another example of local leadership could be advising a Girl Scout or Boy Scout troop about skills needed for effective volunteering in child care centers or babysitting with young children. Working closely with the local adult education or vocational system to ensure that meaningful and accessible training opportunities are available for early care and education staff could be a critical leadership contribution. The message is that leadership takes many forms and often begins with seemingly small steps.

• Reflect on your professional preparation and training to be an early childhood educator. Determine what knowledge and skills you wish had been provided to you so you could be an active community leader. Then share those thoughts with the professionals in your community who are responsible for training the next generation of leaders. This may be the faculty at the local junior college or the staff at the local resource-and-referral agency. Make it your business to ensure that those coming behind us have the tools they need to be spokespersons in any venue.

• Consider your personal responsibility to pass on to someone else what you know and now are learning. Those of us who became early childhood educators in the 1960s and 1970s entered a rapidly expanding field that had many opportunities for leadership. Many of us had invaluable opportunities to shape our profession early in our careers and in simpler times. Yet, years later, we still are filling leadership positions, and the next generation is queuing up behind us. The discussions about the succession to the British throne come to mind! Now is the time for us to pass on what we have learned to those in the wings, to provide the guided opportunities for leadership that many of us never had.

Mentoring the next generation is a critical issue in our profession. One of my deepest professional regrets is that I did not pass on to my colleagues in Buffalo the very specific information and skills that I had developed as the Head Start administrator. Truly, we do have unique and special information tucked away in the recesses of our minds! The Head Start Mentor Teacher Initiative is but one example of our recognition that passing the torch should be a deliberate and well-considered process.

While Crompton identifies the challenge of our moving into a broader community arena, there is homework that needs to be done, either first or simultaneously, within our own profession. We as early childhood educators have unspoken conflicts with one another. In our own community, child care providers may be envious that Head Start staff are better paid than others and continue to get salary increases. Or Head Start staff may perceive that public school and private preschool teachers have a stranglehold on leadership of the local NAEYC Affiliate and do not welcome new input. Family child care providers may not even see themselves and their work as part of a larger community of educators. Local organizations that represent these separate constituencies find it difficult to engage in joint planning or sponsorship of initiatives. But if we cannot come together around common cause, how can we be effective leaders in the broader community, where our perceived divisions quickly dilute our message?

Those of us in leadership positions must honestly analyze our local situation, our part in creating and maintaining that reality, and whether changes need to be made so that all of us can reach the wider world with a joint and powerful message. My most instructive experience was the opportunity, as a Head Start state association president, to begin negotiations with representatives from a statewide pre-K teachers' organization and a statewide child care organization to create legislation that would allocate state early childhood dollars in a fair and productive way. I have painful memories of each group "staking out" its positions in rigid terms during our early meetings. And yet I warmly recall the final compromise, reached once everyone understood that money is finite, that each of us was there to stay, and that each sector of our field has special and important gifts to offer young children and families.

The early childhood educator as community leader provides us with a challenging yet rewarding opportunity to test our knowledge and skills in new arenas. It also affords us the opportunity to complete the circle of responsibility to the young children and families we serve. Multiple entry points allow each of us to find our own developmentally appropriate niche. Our capacities to make meaning of our own and others' early care and education experiences surely are rich enough that we can join Crompton and others in making a difference for America's most important resource—its young children.

Chapter 7

Conceptual Leadership

Sharon L. Kagan and Michelle J. Neuman

*Of all the civil rights for which the world
has struggled and fought for 5000 years, the right
to learn is undoubtedly the most fundamental.*

—W.E.B. DuBois
From *W.E.B. DuBois Speaks* (1970)

Throughout the course of social history, new learnings emerge, replacing old ideas and theories. If the new learnings—scientific, technological, or theoretical—are sound and if we are lucky, some are transformed into action for social good. However sound and however applicable, few such learnings are as critical to advancing our social life as *human learnings*—those that unleash the human spirit and create the momentum of possibility. Human learnings are the moral, ethical, and interactional learnings that enable people and communities of people to be the best they can be, to use their values, passions, and talents to do what they care most about and, in so doing, make contributions to each other and to society.

This chapter is about human learnings and the early childhood community. It is about how we think about ourselves and how we unleash our individual and collective possibilities. It is about how we conceptualize our field and how we envision its future and the future of the world today's children will inherit.

The chapters up to this point advance our thinking about the domains and functions of early childhood leaders. Collectively, the chapters suggest that there are multiple opportunities for leadership, that leadership may take many forms, and that leadership exists irrespective of job title or classification. In discussing conceptual leadership, we support this orientation. We also suggest that if the field (as opposed to a single organization) is to move forward, another kind of leadership—one far more intangible—is necessary. For the purposes of this discussion, we call it *conceptual leadership*. This is not a term that appears in the literature or in our everyday vocabulary;

it is not a term that can be identified with any particular role, nor can it be identified with any precise body of knowledge, as is the case with a pedagogical leader who must possess an understanding of child development and learning theory or an advocacy leader who must know the legislative process. Conceptual leadership is more about how we think together about the field's destiny and the role that early care and education must play in a democratic society.

What is conceptual leadership?

Webster defines a concept as an "idea or thought, especially a generalized idea or class of ideas." Hence, this notion of conceptual leadership revolves around the creation of new ideas. In using this term, we mean to suggest that for a field to advance, individuals in the field must be open to new ways and processes of thinking, willing to challenge conventional assumptions, and prepared to think forward and to think broadly.

In the early childhood field, conceptual leadership means getting beyond thinking about individual programs and having a sense of the field as a whole. As a colleague in New Mexico says, "We are sick and tired of being funded, governed, and treated like 'projects.' We want to be a profession!" In addition to this thinking about the field as a whole, conceptual leadership means thinking together—early childhood educators (the "we" in the above quotation) contributing our diverse perspectives and experiences to a common "think." Conceptual leadership also means thinking long term—having an eye toward the future and imbuing these ideas with a sense of what might be, of possibility. It is breakthrough thinking. Conceptual leadership also means creating these possibilities within the context of a vision of a just society. Conceptual leaders, then, may be recognized by at least five characteristics: They (1) think in terms of the whole field; (2) are responsive to diverse perspectives; (3) think long term; (4) push the what-is to the what-might-be—thinking possibility, invention, and vision; and (5) seek to impact the social good.

Visionary leadership

Conceptual leadership, as we are defining it, has elements in common with the "visionary" leadership described in the literature. Examining this literature will be useful both for elucidating conceptual leadership and for clarifying how it differs from visionary leadership.

According to most leadership scholars, vision is an essential dimension of successful leadership (see Bennis & Nanus 1985; Senge 1990; Koestenbaum 1991; Nanus 1992; Lynch 1993). For some theorists, vision is the essence of leadership (Nanus 1992; Lynch 1993); for others, it is just one necessary ingredient for success (Gray 1989; Senge 1990; Terry 1993). The first group views visionary leadership as a unique leadership type; the second group places visionary capacities within broader characterizations of leadership. An example of each approach is illustrative.

A vocal proponent of the view that vision is the essence of leadership, often called content visionary theory, Nanus (1992) suggests that the role of a visionary leader is to define a positive, credible, and feasible future for a constantly changing organization. "For leadership to succeed, it needs both form and function, both process and purpose, and that all starts with a clearly articulated vision of the future of the organization" (p. 15). By creating a vision or statement of what the organization will be like in the future, leaders inspire the creativity of their people and give them a sense of what the organization could become (Lynch 1993).

Content visionary theory argues that vision enables leaders to call forth skills, talents, and resources to make the future happen. A visionary leader helps people establish goals for daily action and inspires proactive behavior. Nanus (1992) gives examples of individuals such as Martin Luther King Jr., Bill Gates, Betty Friedan, and Walt Disney who, inspired by a powerful vision, marshaled resources and organized a constituency to make their vision a reality. What these leaders share is "a desperate sense of dissatisfaction with the present and a muffled cry for

hope for a better future" (Nanus 1992, 187), which alerts them to the need for change and calls them to action. Even in this view, visionary leadership is not restricted to titular or upper-level leaders; it guides individuals at every level of an organization.

Exemplifying those who believe that vision is one of many leadership traits, Koestenbaum (1991) suggests by contrast that there are four ways in which leaders express greatness; vision is a component, among others, of leadership. By vision, Koestenbaum means that leaders always see the larger perspective, thinking big and new. Visioning in this sense is not a noun but a verb. It is not what one thinks, but how one thinks; the process, not the content, matters. Extending this idea, Lynch (1993) cites proactive thinking and behavior as essential characteristics of creative, effective leadership. Visionary leaders replace the we-can't-do-that mentality with the how-can-we-do-that? necessary to pursue vision and effect change. Vision means moving away from micromanagement and allowing oneself and others the space to be creative. Lynch notes that visionary leaders must lift their "gaze from the dusty road of the standard operating procedure and keep [their] eyes on the horizon" (1993, 16).

A variation of the process perspective is some theorists' assertion that sharing the vision is an essential dimension of visionary leadership. They suggest that visionary leadership is deficient unless the vision itself is shared with others within the organization. Senge (1990), for example, emphasizes the importance of building a shared vision connected to personal visions throughout an organization. Senge considers shared vision a means to creating learning organizations in which "people continually expand their capacity to create the results they truly desire, where new and expansive patterns of thinking are nurtured, where collective aspiration is set free, and where people are continually learning how to learn together" (p. 3). In this construct, by definition, visionary leadership is collaborative and necessitates thinking about collective ideas of governance values, purpose, and vision.

In a similar vein, Gray (1989) notes that visionary leadership must recognize the need for problem solving through collaboration. Collaboration offers parties with different perspectives on a problem the opportunity to constructively explore their differences and search for solutions beyond their own limited visions of what can be achieved.

Conceptual leadership and visionary leadership: Similarities and differences

Visionary leadership clearly shares many elements with conceptual leadership, as it is being discussed here. These include a focus on (1) broad thinking; (2) inclusion of diverse perspectives in a collaborative vein; (3) thinking long term; and (4) pushing the what-is to the what-might-be. Indeed, the motto of much visionary leadership seems to be embodied in the optimism of Walt Disney, who noted, "If you can *dream* it, you can *do* it."

The question at hand is, what is the *it*? In much of the literature on visionary leadership, the *it* is the *organization*. Note, for example, this quote from Nanus, an architect of the visionary leadership construct: "There is no more powerful engine driving an organization toward excellence and long-range success than an attractive, worthwhile, and achievable vision of the future, widely shared" (1992, 3). Visionary leadership, as it has been conceptualized in much of the business literature, focuses on organizations as the units for change.

This orientation is not unique to the business literature. Indeed, one of the finest volumes on leadership in early childhood education adopts essentially the same organizational focus. Writing from an Australian perspective, Rodd (1994) notes that the purpose of leadership in early care and education is ensuring quality services. She suggests that leaders of early childhood *programs* must articulate a clear vision of the program's future and a general plan of action for getting there. Noting that leaders can be center directors, classroom teachers, or those responsible for the administration of the service or program, Rodd asserts that these individuals show leadership in their organizing of ideas and ideals, not just in their organizing of day-to-day activities and tasks. Rodd recommends that individuals in such positions develop vision in the form of a program (or classroom) philosophy. This philosophy should be created by the leader in conjunction with others involved in the center or class, including staff and parents, and should be based on shared values and goals. Although Rodd acknowledges the importance of collaboration and research and their contributions to broad-based thinking, this concept of leadership, like many others, focuses on a single organization, such as the center, not on the field as a whole.

One critical difference, then, between visionary leadership and conceptual leadership, as presented here, is a focus that transcends any single organization or program. Conceptual leadership focuses less *within* organizations than it does *between and across* them. Inherent in this construct of conceptual leadership is a decided de-emphasis on any single program, funding stream, or service. Similarly, conceptual leadership is less concerned with the development of any single curriculum, policy, or strategy. Rather, it is concerned with the cumulative effects of such discrete efforts, with how they interact and fit together. Conceptual leadership considers, for example, how policy advances in one segment of the field may affect other segments. Different from the construct of visionary leadership that is often organizationally bound, conceptual leadership for early care and education visions the entire field as its domain of work. In other words, conceptual leaders consider how individuals and organizations with very different roles and responsibilities mesh to create what is understood as the early care and education field.

A second distinct element of conceptual leadership builds upon and extends the first. Conceptual leadership not only regards early care and education as a target for change but also considers this reform within the context of broader social change. At the national, state, and local levels, conceptual leaders approach early care and education as inextricably linked to educational reform, health care reform, community development, and welfare reform. They acknowledge that early care and education is not an isolated service, discrete from the social fabric of communities, but is inextricably woven throughout society. Conceptual leaders understand that what happens as a result of welfare or health reform may have as much, if not greater, impact on children than specific child care legislation. Conceptual leaders see with wide-angle vision, so they tend to think about not only how contextual factors—political, social, and economic—may affect and be affected by the early care and education world, but also how these efforts will yield a more just, democratic, and well-functioning community and society. This broad perspective includes understanding the current status of the early care and education field and other fields, as well as what children's services might look like in a future in which social conditions for all are improved.

A third element that distinguishes conceptual from visionary leadership is that conceptual leadership cultivates a large and diverse audience. Instead of focusing efforts on members of a particular agency or organization, conceptual leaders target early childhood workers as well as policymakers, media, business and civic community members, parents, children, and other groups and institutions. Conceptual leaders in our field do not ignore plaguing concerns of early childhood practitioners; indeed, they are profoundly interested in issues of pay and compensation, appropriate training, and pedagogical support. But the concerns of the conceptual leader do not stop here. Conceptual leaders are also eager to provide policymakers with a better understanding of what the major issues are, how they fit together, and where the field should be going—knowledge that can be incorporated into legislation. Conceptual leaders recognize the importance of cultivating links with power sources in the community—

media, corporate, philanthropic, and community leaders. They encourage parents to become better consumers and advocates for their children. Children experience the direct results of any movement toward the vision at the core of the conceptual leader's efforts. Finally, the way in which conceptual leaders think about and approach early care and education is within the context of many community institutions; they understand that early care and education is one critical piece of the bedrock upon which children's development rests. Conceptual early care and education leaders are often deeply enmeshed in the life of their communities, advancing early care and education along with a host of child and family issues.

In sum, conceptual leadership in early care and education is distinguished from conventional visionary leadership theory in that it is not limited by a single organizational focus; rather, it is characterized by concern with many institutions that impact child and family life. Key to conceptual leadership are concern about broader social issues—advancing the way early care and education contributes to the broader community and social good—and attention to diverse audiences, including institutions not regularly considered part of the early childhood community.

Conceptual leadership in action

The history of early childhood education is studded with examples of conceptual leadership. In contemporary history, we have only to look back at the formation of the Head Start Program. At the time Head Start was conceptualized, there was little formal governmental involvement in early childhood education. Early planners, concerned about the needs of low-income children, developed a comprehensive program with a strong commitment to parents, which was visionary at the time. Not limiting the impact to the Head Start program alone, its early leaders embarked on a series of rich research and demonstration efforts, the results of which were designed to inform and upgrade the nation's services to young children. More than a single program, Head Start was designed to spearhead invention in all early care and education (Zigler 1979).

The development of the National Association for the Education of Young Children's accreditation system is another example of effective conceptual leadership. Noting that the establishment of federal regulations was unlikely and recognizing the need to increase the quality of care and early education in the nation's services to young children, NAEYC embarked on a landmark effort to establish consensually agreed-upon criteria of quality (NAEYC [1984] 1991). Using these criteria as the basis for an inventive self-appraisal process, centers of all types could elect to embark on the process toward accreditation. The accreditation initiative has revolutionized our understandings of quality through an important by-product, the delineation of "developmentally appropriate practices." It has also brought about higher levels of quality early care and education through a voluntary accreditation process that has served as a model for other accreditation programs. When a leader or leaders indentify a problem and construct solutions that evolve over time, as was the case with the launching of accreditation, conceptual leadership is evident. Not limited to any single group, the process was explicitly constructed to engage the field and to provide a rich alternative to regulation as a means of achieving quality in early childhood programs.

The growth of resource-and-referral agencies is another example of conceptual leadership. Leaders understood parents' needs and that solutions transcend single programs. Resource-and-referral agencies have spawned some of the finest community planning efforts in the nation, serving as models for how collaborative planning and capacity building can take hold. Collaborations, community planning efforts, state advocacy organizations, and state and community councils are all examples of how the early care and education community is reconstructing its role and adopting a new and vigorous leadership stance. Broad-based, national planning projects that deal with systemic reform in early care and education are another illustration of how the field is rethinking its future directions. These and hundreds more examples constitute a new approach to, and a new function of, leadership, which we have termed conceptual leadership.

In each of these cases, leaders cut across programmatic and institutional boundaries, they dared to conceive a long-term vision, they worked collaboratively with others, and they were not afraid to take risks. Moreover, each of these efforts contributed to the social good either by advancing the state of young children and their families or by altering understandings of participatory democracy. These, then, are key elements of active conceptual leadership.

Challenges to conceptual leadership

Conceptual leadership is hard and often unrecognized work. First, because we have never had a term for this kind of leadership, it often occurred unnoticed or as part and parcel of a set of actions that evolved over time. In other words, the idea of conceptual leadership did not exist, so even though it was being done, it had no label, no identity.

Second and more pragmatically, conceptual leadership is tough because of the few rewards and many risks. Individuals or groups of individuals who embark on efforts that are truly generative are often dubbed mavericks, critics, fools, or dreamers. These terms connote being out of touch with reality, a condition that may disengage leaders from ongoing thinking or mainstream work. The risks of being a conceptual leader are high in terms of professional sanctions; incentives are few and rewards are oblique, often accruing more to a group or organization than to the individual or individuals who spearheaded the effort.

Third, limited opportunities exist for many early care and education workers to contribute in this way. In part, such limitations exist because the financing of early care and education is so inadequate and irregular that leaders have to spend time commandeering and maintaining scarce resources, giving them little time or energy for ahead-of-the-curve thinking. Further, the structure of the field, with its diverse funding streams, regulations, and limited forums for interactions, has done little—until recently—to nourish broad across-the-field thinking where advance planning can take place. Though beginning to change now with the emergence of numerous collaborations, these alliances are difficult to develop and sustain.

Fourth, conceptual leadership is difficult to achieve because of a lack of training for it. In fact, few courses in overall leadership development in the early childhood field exist, much less a course in conceptual leadership. While the shortage of training for conceptual leadership is in part linked to the overall inattention to leadership in general in the early childhood field, another contributing factor is that we have done little to define the characteristics, skills, and related training for such conceptual leaders. To integrate conceptual leadership into training programs for early childhood leaders, we must further explore what ingredients are necessary to cultivate this form of leadership.

Fifth, in times of crisis (e.g., war, natural disaster, health crisis, or fiscal failure)—arguably, when conceptual leadership is most needed—such leadership is often skimped upon, in favor of direct services or more expenditures designed to curtail the disaster. For example, during a health crisis, we correctly pour in dollars to limit the spread of the disease (e.g., polio or AIDS), but we invest too little in preventing the disaster. Although it is an ongoing set of services and not a temporary "disaster," American early care and education responds in the same way. Dollars are invested in direct services to children to meet immediate needs (as should be the case), but there is little simultaneous investment in long-term infrastructure development. Moreover, when funding is limited, an emphasis on long-term planning and quality enhancement is often the first priority to be curtailed. Without a sustained capacity that solidifies forums and mechanisms for dealing with the long-term future of the field, conceptual leadership will be fragmented and episodic, as will durable advancement of early care and education.

Next steps

Several types of next steps need to be taken to promote conceptual leadership: attitudinal, behavioral, and structural.

Attitudinal next steps

The early care and education field must recognize that it offers more than a set of services to children and families; rather, that high-quality early childhood education is a social imperative deserving a permanent place on the social agenda. All our actions must take place within a context that views early care and education as a social necessity, as essential to a democracy, and not merely as an ancillary fringe. To achieve this, our "think" (be it in legislative, quality enhancement, or service delivery efforts) must transcend individual programs and projects; we must conceptualize ourselves as a unified field and profession. Given the social need for early childhood education, we must acknowledge that direct services without viable infrastructure are insufficient to this effort. Like other essential undertakings, early care and education needs to develop a system of structural supports.

Behavioral next steps

Changes in attitudes will not occur throughout the field unless there is a training apparatus to support them. All individuals entering early care and education need to engage in training that creates the skills necessary to work with children and families and that enables them to be conceptual leaders, training that enables individuals to see and experience the diversity of programs and services that constitute early care and education. All those in the field need to see their work as both service and leadership—service to children and families and leadership to the field and the nation.

Training for such leadership is necessary, but only after the skills and attributes of leaders in general and conceptual leaders in particular are more clearly defined. At a minimum, such leadership development must include a fundamental knowledge of children and of child and human development. Beyond this knowledge, conceptual leaders should learn the history of the field and the current status of working conditions, programs, and legislation. Ideally, they should have opportunities to work in allied fields to participate in transdisciplinary training. Conceptual leaders must be trained in problem solving and creative decisionmaking; moreover, they must learn to bring out the best in colleagues.

Structural next steps

In addition to defining and creating the training necessary to support conceptual leadership, we need durable structures in which such conceptual work can flourish. To date, these structures have taken the form of task forces, commissions, and other short-term entities. The products of these efforts often overlap one another and are sufficiently remote from political realities to gain implementation. What is needed are several durable entities to carry out such ahead-of-the-curve work. These entities can take the form of new organizations or they may be arms or components of existing organizations. For example, subcommittees of boards can do this work, so long as their target for change is not limited to the organization itself but to issues that transcend a single organization. To this end, teams from organizations can do this collaboratively; the April 19th Group was one such effort. In short, conceptual leadership needs collaborative forums and structures; it is not likely to take root by an individual operating separate from a durable structure.

Building on the need for durable collaborative forums and structures, another important structural next step is for the field to consider the wide range of positions in which early care and education professionals can influence issues related to children and families. Individuals may exercise conceptual leadership in positions that are outside what is traditionally viewed as early care and education. These positions may exist in foundations, government agencies, corporations, and the media, or in fields such as welfare reform, social and human services, and the public school system. For conceptual leadership to flourish, strategies to capitalize on such previously untapped leadership opportunities must be identified and pursued. Expanding conceptual leadership possibilities can enable the field to achieve its dreams for the future of early care and education.

* * *

In *Listen! The Children Speak* (World Organization for Early Childhood Education 1979) is the story of 4-year-old Liza, who was afraid to paint. With gradual encouragement from her teachers throughout the year, Liza finally approached the easel in January. As she did, one teacher overheard her saying, as if to encourage herself, "I know painting is easy. First, you need to think your thoughts. Then, you need to paint your think!"

This chapter has been about the same challenges that Liza encountered—notably, thinking new thoughts and painting a "think." Though somewhat embryonic, the "conceptual leadership think" suggests that leadership is first and fundamentally about generating new learnings—new *human* learnings. Second, it is about applying new human learnings not to serve the status quo, not to perpetuate a democracy that accords primary value to external possessions, but to create a nation that has a more intense, disciplined commitment to enabling the best of the human spirit and to a nation that values the role of childhood in that quest. Conceptual leadership focuses on improving all early care and education in service to a more just and equitable society.

References

Bennis, W.G., & B. Nanus. 1985. *Leaders: Strategies for taking charge.* New York: Harper & Row.

Gray, B. 1989. *Collaborating: Finding common ground for multiparty problems.* San Francisco: Jossey-Bass.

Koestenbaum, P. 1991. *Leadership: The inner side of greatness.* San Francisco: Jossey-Bass.

Lynch, R. 1993. *Lead! How public and non-profit managers can bring out the best in themselves and their organizations.* San Francisco: Jossey-Bass.

Nanus, B. 1992. *Visionary leadership.* San Francisco: Jossey-Bass.

National Association for the Education of Young Children. [1984] 1991. *Accreditation criteria and procedures of the National Academy of Early Childhood Programs.* Rev. ed. Washington, DC: Author.

Rodd, J. 1994. *Leadership in early childhood: The pathway to professionalism.* New York: Teachers College Press.

Senge, P.M. 1990. *The fifth discipline: The art and practice of the learning organization.* New York: Doubleday.

Terry, R.W. 1993. *Authentic leadership: Courage in action.* San Francisco: Jossey-Bass.

World Organization for Early Childhood Education. 1979. *Listen! The children speak.* Washington, DC: Author.

Zigler, E. 1979. Head Start: Not a program but an evolving concept. In *Project Head Start: A legacy of the War on Poverty*, eds. E. Zigler & J. Valentine. New York: Free Press.

Commentary

by Valora Washington

Kagan and Neuman give voice to the phenomena that most of us simultaneously witness and overlook in the field of early care and education —conceptual leadership. Through the authors' careful articulation, the reader immediately recognizes conceptual leadership as the breakthrough wisdom behind the "ah-has!" of our contemporary professional history. Exemplars among our shared treasures include Project Head Start, as well as the growth of resource-and-referral agencies, center accreditation, and professional recognition. Signifying more than the cumulative effects of programs or financial resources, these exemplars are celebrated by Kagan and Newman as manifestations of conceptual leadership—the long-term vision that we create by thinking together and "visioning" possibilities for our field within the context of a just society. This vision must be broader than, yet inclusive of, any particular program, service, task, or interest.

Far from being an abstraction, this essay implies that the roots of conceptual leadership lie in the utility of ideas.

> Transformation of the social order often begins with acts of imagination that elevate a startling dream of change above the intimidating presence of things as they are. Yet if such dreams are passionate and clear, and if they can call a great many people into their service, they may ultimately give shape to the future. (W.K. Kellogg Foundation 1996, 3)

In this way, the future vibrancy of our profession depends on the igniting of bold ideas, passionately conveyed. Conceptual leadership, then, targets the *what* and *how* that must transcend and unite our field. It calls us to action.

Yet multiple factors impede conceptual leadership. Kagan and Neuman list five impediments, of which I wish to emphasize two: professional risk and fiscal priorities. Transformative dreams defy traditional wisdom and may invite contempt or professional rivalries, even if they ask for nothing more than the granting of basic human rights or for other contributions to the common good. Today's exemplars, for example, often were yesterday's controversies. Project Head Start was not uniformly welcomed, especially in some southern towns (Washington & Oyemade 1989). And, for various reasons, not all of us embraced the Worthy Wage approach to action, which is now gaining a place in the mainstream of our field. Individual leaders and groups of people who initiate the innovations that later become acclaimed exemplars sometimes pay a price in doing so.

The social cost of impeding conceptual leadership can be high. Kagan and Neuman state that in times of crisis, conceptual leadership is most urgently needed but is often neglected in preference for direct services designed to curtail the disaster. Current analysis strengthens the authors' argument for conceptual leadership by revealing that our nation is inclined to invest neither in direct services nor in the long-term planning and quality enhancements that conceptual leadership implies. Consequently, as the risks and needs multiply, apparent opportunities to achieve conceptual leadership become even more scarce.

In this reality, Kagan and Neuman correctly assert that conceptual leadership does not only regard early care and education as a target for change but also considers this reform within the broader context of social change and change in other such systems as education, health care, community development, and welfare. What are we talking about here? In my view, we are talking about the quality of children's lives and the extent to which our society ensures that basic services will be universally available to children. The focus of conceptual leadership, then, must be the children and families we serve. Our domains of work are not the reason for change but rather are the tools through which we seek to enhance, promote, and ensure the development of children. Our professional tools are valued only to the extent that the reasons for change are valued. Conceptual leadership cannot focus wholly on the domains of our work without addressing the fundamental values and attitudes that surround childhood in our society.

In effect, therefore, because conceptual leadership must be willing to challenge conventional assumptions and approaches to childhood, it supports transformational change in the way society thinks about children. Without this fundamental redirection of our thought processes, all of our efforts to improve the old paradigm are bound to be met with limited success. Clearly, we cannot abandon developmental or incremental change—those activities in which we engage as we attempt to improve our skills or implement better practices. Further, in the context of the current paradigm, planned action or transitional change also leads us to important advances. However, I imagine that efforts to create a new destiny for our field will require fundamental changes that affect the values, structures, and processes of our field and in society as a whole. Stated abruptly, we must acknowledge that some of the core principles of our profession are out of alignment with current reality in the public domain about what children need and must have. Achieving alignment will require ongoing and consistent intervention that includes political action, professional enhancements, and community mobilization. This type of change is often proceeded by frustration, confusion, anger, doubt, and pain (Anderson 1985; W.K. Kellogg Foundation 1996).

I wish Kagan and Neuman had emphasized the need to build a constituency in effective conceptual leadership. A primary question that I have about the essay is its dominant focus on learnings that we gather from among ourselves or through collaborations with other professionals. Although our field has relatively strong ties and historical traditions of being close to the "customer," "parent involvement" is too often is a passive substitute for meaningful engagement. Conceptual leadership for the field of early care and education will continue to emerge from within our profession. But the future, I believe, suggests a stronger role for consumers, especially parents, in conceptual leadership. Comprehensive, fundamental change in early care and education will occur through community processes and the aspirations of families themselves.

My experience with an initiative called Families for Kids illustrates, powerfully, that community planning has the capacity to lead to profound conceptual shifts not even imagined by professionals (in this case, social workers and attorneys) acting on their own. Families for Kids emerged from a planning process in 19 communities that invited participants from all walks of life to imagine—from the child's point of view—preferred child welfare system that could provide a nurturing, permanent home to all children in foster care who would not be returning to their families of origin. This active, participatory dreaming ultimately led to five outcomes that constitute a vision of what is desired for kids, and it shaped action plans that are now directing adoption reform in many areas of the country. Visioning activities also generated an unprecedented level of community involvement in determining the direction of system reform. In doing so, they avoided the divisive political style of the times and strengthened civic skills crucial to our democratic process. Child welfare professionals played a vital role in the leadership process, but their roles were guided and influenced by what consumers (families and foster children) want. This broad engagement was crucial in helping transcend the mind-set imposed by constantly experiencing the system as it is; it freed all of us to imagine the system as it could and should be. In such ways, families and communities are not "target recipients" for our visions but fellow dreamers and key stakeholders who work with us on common goals (W.K. Kellogg Foundation 1995, 1996).

Finally, I want to emphasize that conceptual leadership does not necessarily imply a radical departure from all the past ways of knowing, doing, or delivering services. In some cases, conceptual leadership may reject the modes of the past (for example, in moving from housing children in orphanages to placing them in permanent families). Sometimes, however, conceptual leadership may invent a novel way of organizing or communicating existing information and thinking or create a feasible means of doing what we already know works. Creative or intensive applications of existing knowledge may indeed be the breakthrough needed by a given community (see Washington, Johnson, & McCracken 1995). For example, the five outcomes that are the core vision of the Families for Kids strategy do not necessarily articulate previously unknown ideas; rather, the initiative synthesized and captured the ideas in a comprehensive, comprehensible, measurable, and achievable fashion.

Evidence of the strength of conceptual leadership abounds in our field, as Kagan and Neuman point out. The benefits are obvious. However, as our conceptual strength emerges, we must expect and be open to criticism and change. Our success in thinking together on critical issues may in itself attract the attention of potential detractors. Success will further test our willingness to share power with consumers and other community members or business leaders—even when, in our view, they don't get the message quite right. These requirements are quite challenging under the best of circumstances, but they are signs of the metamorphosis of caterpillar to butterfly.

Our heritage as a field has been the continual development of early childhood leaders who have been passionate, active dreamers with our eyes on the best interests of children. There is a strong, compelling need to marshal the best of what we have been to create a clear vision of what we can be.

References

Anderson, L.A. 1985. *Development, transition or transformation: The question of change in organizations.* Berkeley, CA: Being First.

Washington, V., & U.J. Oyemade. 1989. *Project Head Start.* New York: Garland.

Washington, V., V. Johnson, & J.B. McCracken. 1995. *Grassroots success! Preparing schools and families for each other.* Washington, DC: NAEYC.

W.K. Kellogg Foundation. 1995. *Families for kids who wait: Promising directions in community-based adoption reform.* Battle Creek, MI: Author.

W.K. Kellogg Foundation. 1996. *Families for kids: Building the dream.* Battle Creek, MI: Author.

Leadership Challenges

SECTION 3

Chapter 8

Race, Class, and Education

Evelyn K. Moore

My career in the early childhood education field began more than 30 years ago, when I applied for a teaching position in the Perry Preschool program. I was one of four teachers hired by David Weikart, director of the preschool, for an experimental project for disadvantaged 3- and 4-year-old children in a predominantly Black, low-income neighborhood in Ypsilanti, Michigan.

The Perry Preschool provided my first professional leadership opportunity, an experience common to many African American early childhood education leaders: being appointed head teacher. It was in this position that I honed my skills in practice, learning to utilize in the classroom the early childhood theories that had been known to me only in an academic sense. For example, I was able to translate Piaget's theories into creative curriculum ideas for children.

Being well-grounded in theory and practical applications has stood me in good stead as I joined the leadership ranks. I continually urge my younger colleagues to take advantage of opportunities to gain frontline experience in putting theory into practice. However, in addition to a grounding in theory and practice, mentors are also vital to advancement within this field.

The importance of mentors cannot be overemphasized. It was at the urging of David Weikart that I went to the University of Michigan's graduate program in early childhood education. There I later had the opportunity to be mentored by another great man, Wilbur Cohen, who was secretary of the Department of Health, Education and Welfare under President Johnson. At that time, only very few people of color were afforded opportunities such as these.

Thirty years later, access to the early childhood leadership ladder still remains blocked for too many talented individuals. For this reason, the National Black Child Development Institute (NBCDI) has focused, over the past several years, on the issue of leadership in the early education field.

NBCDI has been involved for the last 25 years in the struggle for quality early care and education. One of the structures NBCDI has developed is an annual Early Childhood Leadership Institute. Among the most critical issues identified by early childhood professionals at the Institute has been the paucity of African Americans in leadership positions in the field. Many participants emphasize the need for a strategy to support the advancement of African Americans in the field to benefit not only Black children but also children of all races.

Responding to this concern, NBCDI requested and received a grant in 1993 from the Carnegie Corporation of New York to begin to fill the data void and to develop concrete recommendations to support the advancement of African Americans into leadership positions. The results of the study were published in a report, *Paths to African American Leadership Positions in Early Childhood Education: Constraints and Opportunities.*

After discussions with a number of colleagues, I took the lead in determining how leadership would be defined for the purposes of the Paths study: faculty members of major colleges or universities; researchers; foundation officers; members of advisory boards, commissions, or panels; directors of child care centers or resource-and-referral agencies; directors of licensing agencies; presenters at major conferences; and individuals who have published articles on early childhood education.

We chose to use this traditional definition of leadership roles because we saw a vital need to bring minority representation into these positions. We do not wish to diminish the value of other types of leadership; we recognize that there are additional forms of early childhood leadership in the classroom, communities, and other arenas. However, NBCDI finds that defining leadership in terms of the roles specified in the Paths research provides a clear and concise focus for our efforts to open doors for a more diverse group of early childhood professionals; it is these roles in which African Americans and other people of color have been particularly underrepresented.

Much of this chapter is based on the results of the Paths study as well as more than two decades of NBCDI's institutional involvement in the field. While NBCDI's work on the issue of early childhood education leadership has specifically addressed the concerns of African Americans, this chapter broadens the focus to include leaders from other racial and ethnic groups. Where available, statistical information on Hispanics, Asian Americans, Native Americans, and other groups is provided.

Race, class, and education play a significant yet often ignored role in the development of early childhood education leaders. These variables help to determine whether potential leaders are recruited or overlooked, nurtured or discouraged, selected or rejected as they seek to advance to leadership positions.

The concepts of race, class, and education are intertwined within our society and cannot be examined independent of one another. Therefore, a contextual approach has been taken in the analysis presented in this chapter.

The importance of diverse leadership

Diversity among leadership throughout the education arena is essential to ensuring educational equity for all children. However, diverse leadership in early childhood education may be particularly significant in reversing the current low levels of educational achievement for American children from ethnic minorities because this is where children first enter the system.

The inclusion and advancement of diverse professionals in early childhood education is important because these professionals are in a unique position to build bridges between the early education community and America's ethnic communities. Early care and education leaders who are also members of the communities being served are uniquely positioned to identify, develop, and assess practical approaches to ensuring that parents are able to effectively participate in the education of their children. For example, through its programs, NBCDI has found that African American parents are eager to become more involved in the education of their children—provided they have the necessary support from individuals and agencies that reflect and respect their culture. Furthermore, the presence of diverse leaders in the profession encourages parents to see early childhood programs as extensions of their community rather than as detached institutions.

It is also essential that aspiring early childhood educators of all races see African Americans and other minorities in leadership positions in the field. Individuals of all ages are often influenced by the presence of role models in their field of interest. If more minority-group members were in leadership positions, youth and individuals who are already studying early childhood education or working as aides or assistants in programs might be encouraged to set higher career goals. In addition, increased personal interactions among students and educators of all races would enable them to break down stereotypes and develop mutual respect.

Furthermore, diversity in early childhood education leadership allows varying perspectives to be heard and considered when policy decisions are made. For example, in the development of curriculum, it is important for different perspectives to be heard and integrated in the curriculum. Diversity in leadership is necessary to sensitize administrators and teachers alike to the particular concerns, values, and learning styles of a broader cross-section of American children and families. The development of more diverse leadership may help improve the understanding of children from a variety of backgrounds.

The challenges facing this nation's educational system demand a sophisticated, informed, and diverse educational leadership that actively seeks to include all individuals who can contribute to the field. The early care and education community must begin the process of embracing more fully the entire talent pool to improve the quality of education received by America's young children.

Factors affecting diversity

During a six-month period in 1993, NBCDI assessed the status of African American leadership in early childhood education, explored the reasons for underrepresentation, and identified strategies to increase African American participation as leaders in the field. Three sources of information were used for the Paths to African American Leadership study. First, NBCDI completed a thorough review of existing literature on African Americans in the field. Second, the Institute analyzed the limited survey data that exist. Third, NBCDI interviewed 25 African American early childhood leaders representing all four regions of the country. The 22 women and 3 men included heads of national organizations, associate and assistant professors, college administrators, state specialists, foundation executives, program administrators, and others. Ten had attended historically Black colleges, and 23 had completed at least a master's degree.

The information obtained from existing data and from NBCDI's original study presented an interesting overview of the field but also raised many questions. Because the field of early education encompasses a large number of individuals working in many occupations, the total number of people in the field is difficult to estimate. In addition to working in child care programs, persons with expertise in early childhood education also work in federal and state governments, on the staff of resource-and-referral agencies, and as directors of licensing agencies and organizations. They staff national children's organizations and associations. They are expert advisors to national associations whose mandates extend beyond children's concerns. They work as faculty and research staff in universities and nonprofit research institutes, as program officers in foundations, and as directors of social service agencies and organizations.

However, the data on early childhood professionals do not adequately describe this wide range of occupations. While there is considerable information on staff in early childhood programs—especially those in child care centers—there are no representative data on leaders. Nevertheless, because a substantial proportion of leaders in the field have spent some time as early childhood educators, data on the staff of early childhood education programs shed light on the characteristics of the pool of potential leaders, as well as their mode of entry and progression into leadership positions.

Pool of potential leaders

According to the Bureau of Labor Statistics (1995), in 1994 there were approximately 1.2 million child care workers, including 325,000 prekindergarten and kindergarten teachers, 416,000 early childhood teacher assistants, and 428,000 family child care providers. Statistics for 1990 indicate that approximately 18% of workers in center or preschool programs were African American, and 10% of regulated family day care providers were Black (Kisker et al. 1991). In 1993 one-third of all early childhood teaching staff were women of color (National Center for the Early Childhood Work Force). At the entry level, then, there are many American and other minority staff providing early care and education services comprising a large pool from which leaders could emerge.

However, while diversity exists at the lower levels of the field (including aides, teacher's assistants, and even teachers), it does not at the higher levels (college faculty, researchers, advisory board members, and center directors). Membership lists of several leading early education organizations reveal very little racial diversity. For example, in 1993, fewer than

3% of the 4,800 members of the Society for Research in Child Development were African American (telephone interview with Barbara Kahn, executive director of SRCD, 27 September 1993). In 1992–93, only 6% of the 50 regular members of the National Association of Early Childhood Specialists in State Departments of Education were African American (telephone interview with Cecelia Mobley, treasurer of NAECS/SDE, 21 September 1993). In 1993, fewer than 5% of the more than 400 local, state, and regional Affiliate leaders of the National Association for the Education of Young Children were African American (telephone interview with Marilyn Smith, executive director of NAEYC, 21 September 1993).

The NBCDI Paths study was not designed to examine the experiences of Hispanic, Asian American, or Native American early childhood educators, but the report recommended that organizations representing various groups collaborate with a research entity to collect additional data on leaders of all races in early childhood education. Even without systematic data, we suspect that the experiences of other minority groups—particularly Hispanics and Native Americans—are similar to those of African Americans in many respects. This hypothesis is based on the similarities among these groups in socioeconomic status. As data on other groups accumulate, the hypothesis can be tested. Several factors that appear to affect, positively or negatively, the movement of African Americans into leadership positions in early childhood education emerged in the Paths study and other data. They are summarized in the next four sections.

Basic qualifications

Taken as a group, African Americans in early care and education lack the level and quality of academic preparation received by their White peers (Task Force on Teaching as a Profession 1986). The National Child Care Staffing Study (Whitebook, Howes, & Phillips 1989) of day care center staff found that only 14% of Black teachers had at least a bachelor's degree, compared to 30% of White teachers. Also, 16% of the Black teaching staff surveyed received their education in vocational school, compared to only 4% of Whites. The educational backgrounds of Hispanics, Asian/Pacific Islanders, and Native Americans more closely paralleled that of Whites, with only 6% receiving their training in vocational school.

Between 1973 and 1993, college enrollment rates for Hispanics remained statistically unchanged but increased for both White and Black high school graduates. However, Blacks did not improve their enrollment rates relative to Whites. In 1993, 42% of White high school graduates enrolled in college, compared to 33% of Black high school graduates (Census Bureau 1994).

The lower college enrollment rates among African Americans and Hispanics may be due to a lack of financial resources to attend college. Over the past 20 years, the federal government has decreased funds for grants-in-aid and provided student aid mostly through loans (Jaynes & Williams 1989). For many minority students and families, borrowing is not a viable option, and other resources are not available within the family to support young people in getting a college education. Many of the leaders interviewed by NBCDI during the Paths study were married when they pursued their education and were able to rely on the financial support of their spouses to continue school, but few aspiring college students are so fortunate.

Low wages in the field are a further financial disincentive for anyone deciding whether to enter the field. Those who might be drawn to early care and education generally know about the low earnings in the field, compared to wages for workers in other occupations with lower than average educational levels, such as typists and sales workers in retail establishments. According to the National Center for the Early Childhood Work Force, the average hourly wage for early childhood education teachers in 1993 was $6.70, making the annual income for a 35-hour-per-week, 50-week work year only $11,725.

Wages and benefits are equally low for Blacks and Whites when education and length of time in the field are held constant. However, because a higher proportion of minorities are single mothers supporting their own children and contributing to the support of other family members, low benefits and salaries may keep a greater percentage of minority workers from pursuing careers in the field.

Job experience and mobility

On-the-job experience is another variable that may affect the rise to leadership in early childhood education. However, NBCDI's original analysis of data from the National Child Care Staffing Study (Whitebook, Howes, & Phillips 1989) does *not* support the hypothesis that African Americans have less experience in the field than Whites. To the contrary, Black teachers, assistant teachers, and aides participating in that study had more experience than their White counterparts. Among African Americans, approximately 80% of teachers, 60% of assistant teachers, and 50% of aides had been in the field for at least three years. Among Whites, this was true for about 64% of teachers, 40% of assistant teachers, and 29% of aides. (The Paths study did not analyze data for other racial groups.)

It appears that African Americans have more experience in these positions because lower educational levels prevent them from advancing further. When upward job mobility was compared by race among those with similar educational levels, NBCDI found that African Americans experienced substantial mobility at lower levels in the field, such as moving from aide to assistant teacher. However, a college degree was critical for advancement from teacher to teacher/director. In fact, 18% of African Americans who started as teachers and had obtained at least a bachelor's degree advanced into a teacher/director position. This rate is higher than that (2%) for Whites. At the level of teacher/director, there was no difference between African Americans and Whites in educational attainment or in years of experience. However, the *number* of African Americans in these positions was small.

Leadership experiences

NBCDI interviewed 25 African American leaders, and virtually all of them acknowledged the important role education played in helping them attain leadership positions. Ten percent stated that for them as African Americans, a postgraduate degree was important for proving their qualifications. About 65% credited their graduate school educational experience with at least indirectly giving them the chance to assume leadership positions. However, about half felt that the courses, field experiences, and activities required to obtain the degree were not particularly beneficial as practical preparation for leadership in the field.

Mentors played a significant role in helping African Americans gain access to the leadership ladder. The leaders interviewed by NBCDI felt that having someone to help them learn how to work within the system was important. Eighty-four percent of respondents had at least one mentor when they entered the field. Three-quarters of respondents were mentored by professors or supervisors. African Americans and Whites both served as effective mentors to respondents, once reciprocity and trust were established.

More than half of the leaders NBCDI interviewed stated that a mentor gave them support and encouragement, which helped build self-confidence. Mentors also exposed respondents to opportunities that led to leadership positions. A few respondents published articles with assistance from mentors, and some respondents were nominated for boards or selected for jobs based on recommendations from their mentors. Such activities helped respondents obtain the necessary exposure to be considered for leadership positions.

Mentors were also helpful in pointing future African American leaders toward membership in professional organizations; 20% of respondents became involved in professional organizations at the insistence of their mentors. At the time of the interviews, almost 70% of respondents had been involved in professional organizations for at least 15 years, and every respondent participated in at least two professional organizations. More than 60% of the respondents had gained access to professional networks through involvement in these organizations. These experiences led to leadership positions and national recognition.

But access to key informal networks beyond those provided through professional organizations is also important for attaining leadership in the field. Nine out of 10 of the leaders NBCDI interviewed felt that several such networks existed but that membership on the highest levels was predominantly White. Half of all respondents felt that their access to key informal networks was not limited but the access of most other African Americans was. And the majority of respondents felt that they were not really included in the informal groups but remained on the periphery. NBCDI's observations indicate that the same perceptions probably exist for leaders from other minority groups. This raises questions about racism.

Racism in the field

According to the African American leaders interviewed, racism remains a problem in the field, beginning at least as early as the college years. Support received on campus from faculty and administrators was perceived as different for Blacks and Whites. Although almost 70% of respondents felt that their school administrators and faculty were supportive and helpful while they were in school, 60% felt that Blacks did not receive the same amount and type of support on campus as Whites. These respondents stated that White faculty members did not know how to support African Americans.

Respondents who attended predominantly White undergraduate colleges believed that such environments were generally less supportive and less encouraging for African Americans than historically Black colleges. Respondents felt that they had to do a lot more to get the attention and recognition they deserved. Such comments were less frequent with respect to experiences at predominantly White graduate schools.

More than 90% of respondents reported that they encountered racism in the field; 64% felt they were sometimes treated as token leaders. Few respondents noted instances of blatant racism but mentioned the prevalence of more subtle forms of racism. For example, 15% of respondents stated that their comments were often ignored at meetings, and that African Americans were rarely selected to speak at conferences of national organizations. Others mentioned that only a few minority-group members are asked to be involved in national activities and events.

Respondents noted that the racism they experience is not unique to the early childhood education profession but that until racism is eradicated from the fabric of American society, it will continue to exist in this field.

Making diversity a reality

The effort to lay the groundwork for more diverse leadership must start with increased educational opportunities for the entry- and mid-level educators already in the pipeline. The Human Services Amendments of 1994 to the Head Start Act present opportunities for professionals to ascend the career ladder in one area where there appears to be real job-growth potential, but community-based child care programs must also receive funds for training programs that enable staff to advance.

Institutions of higher education, professional associations, and advocacy organizations must work together to better coordinate existing efforts to support the advancement of minority professionals and to develop new strategies for diversifying the field at the leadership level. NBCDI envisions a cooperative effort that would include early childhood education institutions such as Wheelock College, Erikson Institute, Pacific Oaks College, and Bank Street College; institutions that have strong leadership development programs, such as Yale University; historically Black colleges and state universities, such as Bennett College, Clark Atlanta University, and Howard University; and nonprofit organizations serving diverse populations, such as NBCDI and La Raza. Critical to the success of this effort would be initiatives to identify streams of funding to underwrite the cost of recruitment and training programs for marginalized groups.

The consortium could assist in recruiting ethnically diverse educators to prepare for leadership in the early childhood field, tapping the Head Start and child care communities. It should be made clear to early childhood educators that although the field is currently low paying, this may very well change as our economy becomes increasingly service driven. Building an ethnically representative corps of individuals at various levels will ensure that when the field blossoms, minority communities will be well represented in all positions.

Broad-based fellowship programs could also be established to help individuals already in the field gain exposure to and experience in the policy arena. Nonprofit organizations, foundations, governmental entities, and other institutions would provide ideal settings. They also could also facilitate the development of mentor/proteégé relationships and develop a process to expedite the hiring and promotion of professionals in the field who are ready to assume leadership roles.

In addition to organizational efforts to address the lack of diversity, efforts on the part of individuals are also needed. If the field is to remain viable as the demographics of this country change, the boundaries of the early childhood "inner circle" need to be extended to the "outer rim." This requires farsightedness and a commitment to fairness, inclusion, and mutual respect. A case in point: We seek to help parents learn methods of discipline other than physical punishment, but we do so within a relationship of respect for them and their cultural practices. A number of cultural differences may have to be addressed in sensitive, new ways if early childhood leadership is to become more inclusive.

Initiatives undertaken by individuals would be facilitated by internships and apprenticeship programs as well as by same-race and cross-race mentoring. It is essential that these programs be institutionalized and made systemic. Head Start has already shown leadership in this regard, with the authorization of a fellowship program to provide leadership development opportunities for Head Start staff and others in the early childhood field.

Finally, if diversity is central to the development of the profession, it is appropriate that a national monitoring system be established to ensure that organizations undertake efforts to include minorities at the higher levels of the early childhood education field. An immediate step would be to conduct additional studies—similar to NBCDI's Paths to Leadership study—to collect data on individuals of all races in the field. African American, Hispanic, Asian American, and Native American nonprofit organizations should collaborate with a research entity such as the Institute for Survey Research at the University of Michigan to address the lack of data. Future research efforts should include an investigation of the role of actual and perceived racism in discouraging ambition and otherwise preventing advancement among early childhood personnel of some racial and ethnic backgrounds.

A longer-term strategy would be to establish measurable goals for the field and conduct outcome-based evaluations on a regular basis. The primary evaluation criterion should be actual increases in minority leadership, not just how many individuals were invited to participate in training programs or conferences. The development of a feasible *permanent* system for ongoing data collection would ensure that our plans for achieving diversity do not sit on the shelf collecting dust.

Undertaking efforts to ensure diversity, inclusiveness, and fairness are particularly important at this point in American history. From the Oval Office to board rooms across the country, there is recognition that the future success of our nation will have a great deal to do with how we manage diversity. There is no area where this is more true than with the education of our youngest Americans. The character of the institutions that serve children may very well be reflected in young people's attitudes and actions for decades to come.

References

Bureau of Labor Statistics. 1995. *Employment and earnings* 42 (January). Washington, DC: U.S. Department of Labor.

Census Bureau. 1994. *High school graduation and access to college.* Cendata Census Bureau Online Service.

Jaynes, G.D., & R.M. Williams Jr., eds. 1989. *A common destiny: Blacks and American society.* Washington, DC: National Academy Press.

Kisker, E.E., S.L. Hofferth, D.A. Phillips, & E. Farquhar. 1991. *A profile of child care settings: Early education and care in 1990.* Washington, DC: U.S. Government Printing Office.

National Black Child Development Institute. 1993. *Paths to African American leadership positions in early childhood education: Constraints and opportunities.* Washington, DC: Author.

National Center for the Early Childhood Work Force. 1993. *The National Child Care Staffing Study revisited.* Washington, DC: Author.

Task Force on Teaching as a Profession. 1986. *A nation prepared: Teachers for the 21st century.* New York: Carnegie Corporation of New York.

Whitebook, M., C. Howes, & D. Phillips. 1989. *The National Child Care Staffing Study.* Oakland, CA: Child Care Employee Project.

Commentary

by Josué Cruz Jr.

The notion of looking at leadership from the perspective of race, class, and education is certainly worthy of analysis and an essential step if we are to be inclusive of everyone in the profession. Evelyn Moore makes a very strong case for the need to factor in those variables, and she provides some very useful recommendations for making diversity in leadership a reality.

I would like to build on the definition of leadership used in the research Moore reports, adding the dimensions of language and culture and noting that the act and status of leadership are manifested in many different ways. Leadership is more than being in the limelight and having an impressive title; it is also giving direction to and influencing practice and scholarship via our actions and belief system and being willing to share power.

As one who has been in the field for more than 20 years, I have observed many of the traditional practices that have prevented Latinos from assuming positions of leadership in early childhood education. For example, many Latinos speak both English and Spanish, and with Spanish come cultural nuances that do not always appear to fit in or be representative of mainstream culture. This is further complicated by the fact that within the collective group of Latinos are several distinct cultural and linguistic subgroups.

Given projected demographics—substantial growth of the Latino population relative to other groups over the next two decades—sheer numbers will make Latinos key players in U.S. society and a force with which to contend in the field of early care and education (de la Garza, Fraga, & Pachon 1988). Our profession has a long way to go before it reaches equity, even though it has been more sensitive and has shown greater willingness to be inclusive than most others fields have. It is important to recognize vestiges within our field that prevent Latinos and other minorities from being absorbed and that thwart development of a workable plan of action to do so.

Past practices

Over the years, as I became more involved in the profession, I noted with great interest the few Latinos who were in positions of leadership or at least in perceived leadership roles—head teachers, directors, coordinators, curriculum specialists, trainers, college faculty, researchers, and others. I also became aware of the numerous attempts to recruit Latinos through a variety of training programs that seemed to reflect the prevailing mind set. In most cases, training initiatives designed to identify talent and prepare individuals to assume leadership positions promoted what

I often refer to as the "Fatal Three *Rs* of Latino Leadership Training":

1. Repair: This first step in the training process was based on the belief that most Latinos had an English language problem (accent and/or limited fluency) that needed to be repaired. Failure to show mastery of the language or to overcome an accent was reason enough to deny an individual the opportunity to be considered a viable candidate for a leadership position.

2. Retrain: Having reached this level, candidates for leadership positions were expected to adapt to and master certain skills and behaviors that were not always part of their repertoire or base of experience—for example, marketing, communications, fundraising, delegation of responsibility, staff supervision, business protocol, and parliamentary procedure. Being able to demonstrate the use of those behaviors was an indicator that someone had leadership potential.

3. Recast: Finally, once the language problem was overcome and certain behaviors were successfully mastered, the Latino was expected to talk like, behave like, and look like a different person, molded in the image of those in leadership positions.

This one-size-fits-all approach to leadership training clearly did not allow for diversity to be a part of the overall equation for inclusion. The view that something was wrong and needed fixing was a very defeating and undermining orientation to truly opening the doors to diverse leadership in the profession. Those Latinos who were successful in meeting the demands of the three *Rs* usually were the ones who could most easily adapt to being bicultural and bilingual or those who opted to leave behind their Spanish and certain cultural differences—not necessarily the best leaders or the most representative of the larger Latino community.

Upon entering the ranks of leadership, many Latinos were confronted with yet another set of challenges. Many experienced personal frustration because the existing system did not allow for differences and was severely entrenched in tradition, apathy because of their inability to make a difference and to progress in their careers, and crisis that led to internal turmoil and, in some cases, departure from the field (Gilliland 1992). All of these were symptoms of a broken-down system of leadership and training that was in need of a major overhaul. The continued failure to assure Latinos a place in the leadership structure was not so much a lack of worthy intentions but rather a characteristic of a system that did not make room for diversity (James 1995). It is one thing to advocate for diversity in leadership and quite another to support it when it means a shift in power and a new consensus and infrastructure (Shaw 1989).

More recently, as we have become more enlightened, we have made diversity a cornerstone of our profession. This development, still in the process of evolving, is of enormous importance, but we should not allow ourselves to feel complacent when much remains to be done.

Promising practice and challenges

The goal of bringing diversity to leadership is one that must be shared by all the stakeholders in the profession (American Council on Education 1988). Professional organizations, colleges and universities, government, foundations, and voluntary organizations, as well as members of those groups that have been insufficiently included in the past, must be an integral part of the solution. As a profession, we must be willing to reconsider the definition of leadership in relation to Latinos. For example, here are three fundamental ideas that must be given careful attention if we seek true diversity, not token diversity, in leadership:

• lack of English language mastery and speaking with an accent are not valid indicators of leadership potential,

• personal and professional affiliations will differ from the mainstream, and

• a person does not have to abandon cultural identity and practices to succeed as a leader.

This is not to deny that English professional affiliations and culture are important. The point is that leadership is much more complex and should not be restricted to a mere two or three characteristics that often exclude Latinos and other minorities. Moreover, relying exclusively on mentoring, role modeling, and community relations—important though these strategies are—will not necessarily result in the improved representation of Latinos in the early childhood education field (Schneider 1991; Drummond 1995). We also should be looking for those attributes that will give a common voice and a firm place to the profession in the greater society (Shaw 1989). In this vein, the field is in great need of leaders who have a vision for the improvement of the quality of life for children, are willing to acknowledge their roles as leaders in the profession as well as in their communities, desire to work in collaborative relationships, have a passionate commitment to all children and their families, and can balance data-based knowledge and reason with intuition.

If Latinos and other minorities are going to take their rightful place in the profession as leaders, we as stakeholders must be willing to make a firm and binding commitment to include them in our staffs and governing boards. Too often, members of minorities become second-tier-level associates and are excluded from significant and systematic input in programs and projects under consideration for funding. Latinos and other minorities must be assured of involvement in round-table seminars and similar by-invitation-only professional dialogues. These exclusive blue-ribbon type of gatherings often serve as agenda-setting forums that directly influence funding and policy initiatives by public entities and philanthropic organizations. We also must be willing to identify and implement policies and practices that will promote Latinos and others within the organizational structure. This means that we must confront institutional and attitudinal barriers that prevent Latinos and other minority-group members from being part of the leadership team (Murray 1993). Finally, there should be a commitment to publish and promote the works of minority scholars and experts and to establish professional linkages with organizations that represent minorities.

Conclusion

There is the story of the royal astronomer who looked at the stars and told the kings and queens what the future held in store for them (James 1995). Eventually, as the astronomer got older, his powers diminished and he saw his life coming to an end. Not being able to accept that the world could continue to exist without him, he predicted the end of the world. The same analogy can be applied to leadership and diversity. A look at the demographics can tell us much about what is in store for us as leaders in early education. Down the road is a very different population and with that will come a new set of challenges. We can decide to do something about it or, like the royal astronomer, deny the obvious and proceed with business as usual.

Political moves such as the English-only movement, efforts to deny a public school education to children of illegal immigrants, block grants and cutbacks on funding for bilingual programs, and welfare reform are clearly affecting diversity in leadership. The profession is in need of "transformational leaders" who will move us to a new level of understanding, "renewers" who will reenergize us and help us confront the challenge of diversity, and "servant leaders" who will redefine our commitment to stewardship (Shaw 1989). Through this new breed of leaders, the community of early childhood professionals will bring a sense of mission and direction to what it is that we do.

More and more, leadership in the profession is becoming a matter of equity and quality in leadership (Marshall 1989). Latinos must be part of that overall equation. To be ready mañana, diversity in leadership should not be *tolerated;* it should be *embraced.*

References

American Council on Education. 1988. *One third of a nation: A report on the Commission on Minority Representation in Education and American Life.* ERIC, ED 297057.

de la Garza, R.O., L.R. Fraga, & H. Pachon. 1988. Latinos and state government: Toward a shared agenda. *Journal of State Government* 61 (2): 77–80.

Drummond, M.E. 1995. Minorities in higher education leadership. *Black Issues in Higher Education* 12 (23 March): 43–47.

Gilliland, R. 1992. Leadership, diversity, and Columbus: A manifesto for social change. *Community, Technical, and Junior College Journal* 62 (5): 18–22.

James, J. 1995. Negotiating the Grand Canyon of change. *School Administrator* 52 (January): 22–29.

Marshall, C. 1989. *More than black face and skirts: New leadership to confront the major dilemmas in education.* ERIC, ED 318089.

Murray, G.J. 1993. *Minorities in educational administration: Issues and recommendations.* ERIC, ED 361912.

Schneider, A.M. 1991. *Mentoring women and minorities into positions of educational leadership: Gender differences and implications for mentoring.* ERIC, ED 344843.

Shaw, R.G. 1989. *Leadership for a new century.* ERIC, ED 305970.

Chapter 9

Who's Missing at the Table? Leadership Opportunities and Barriers for Teachers and Providers

Marcy Whitebook

I understand beauty and leadership in similar ways. Both come in many forms, yet in any given culture, we can easily identify the form of beauty or leadership that is most highly valued and acknowledged. My understanding of beauty came to me more than a quarter-century ago, as a college senior in the late sixties, participating in my first women's consciousness-raising group. Ten of us—young, healthy, and lovely in a variety of ways—told our life stories, invariably sharing the familiar pain we all felt about our shapes, features, and coloring. Slowly we came to realize that each of us judged our own appearance in relation to our internalized view of the cultural norm of beauty. (As a woman with dark curly hair, I compared myself most unfavorably to blond Julie Christie, who was then in vogue.) We were failing to appreciate, enjoy, or value our own considerable gifts. That shared understanding released enormous amounts of positive energy, allowing us to acknowledge and value our beauty and, most important, to relax the hold of self-defeating energy.

I would suggest that the early childhood community is likewise caught in the grips of culturally sanctioned notions of leadership and, as a consequence, fails to recognize the full spectrum of leaders among us. In so doing, we stifle important, creative energy in our field, restricting our understanding of who leaders are and preventing the valuable contributions and perspectives of many. Specifically, acknowledged leadership in our field tends to mirror the larger society values that demean caregiving work performed by women and involving children. As a result, the acknowledged leaders in our field typically do not work directly with children, and the leadership qualities of those that do each day are routinely overlooked.

I raise these issues not to invalidate our current leadership but rather to argue for creating a more diverse and representative acknowledged leadership in the early childhood field (I know that my own status in the early childhood field is in many ways directly proportional to my distance from the actual work of caring for children. And yet, I believe, the degree to which I am effective as a leader is directly linked to my own experience working in the classroom and my connection to those who currently are teachers and providers.) Expanded understanding and opportunity for leadership for teachers and providers empower all of us who want to improve the image of child care work. Upgrading societal understanding of the skill and importance of early care and education work is essential to garnering the resources that will lead to greater financial reward for teachers/providers and, ultimately, better services for children and families. If our field does not value the contributions of teachers and providers, it is highly unlikely that the rest of society will.

We cannot fail to remember the crisis in our field. Both the quality of early care and education services and jobs are declining at an alarming rate (Whitebook, Howes, & Phillips 1990). Our current strategies to improve programs for children and jobs for their caregivers are unequal to the daunting obstacles we face. We need new ways of looking at the problems that characterize our early care and education system. The greater inclusion of teachers and providers will expand our leadership not only in numbers but in the breadth of potential ideas.[1]

Characteristics of the acknowledged early care and education leadership

Who currently constitutes the identified leadership in our field? Although only limited studies of early childhood education organizations have been conducted, I have some strong hunches about what more extensive examinations would reveal. My impressions, drawn from more than a quarter of a century working in early care and education and from discussions with teachers and providers, suggest the following characteristics.

The acknowledged leaders of the early care and education field *are not* typically practitioners who spend their days working with children. They may or may not have done so in their past. Frequently, if these leaders worked with children, it was long ago and under dramatically different circumstances. This characteristic of our leadership distinguishes us from other professions, such as medicine or law, in which practitioners rise to positions of status and power. Nurses and K–12 teachers sometimes assume more visible leadership roles, often because their professional organizations explicitly represent their interests and promote them as field leaders. In contrast, the largest professional association in our field, the National Association for the Education of Young Children (NAEYC), as well as most of the other national organizations, seldom even includes teachers and providers in its slate of candidates for the Governing Board.

Acknowledged leaders in our field typically hold advanced degrees beyond the bachelor's. This is somewhat predictable because our field is highly educated. More than half of center-based teaching staff and regulated family child care providers have some college background. Among center-based teachers approximately one third have earned a bachelor's degree or higher (Whitebook, Howes, & Phillips 1990; Cost, Quality, & Child Outcomes Study Team 1995). But because of the low pay and lack of recognition for working with young children, many with advanced degrees in the field leave the classroom or home—even if they would like to continue. The net result is a leadership cadre with few teachers and providers and the impression that leadership positions are open only to those who hold higher degrees.

A high proportion of our leaders are associated with a university or other institution of higher learning. Many others work in a government department or resource-and-referral agency. Few come from the family child care homes and the relatively small, community-based programs, both for-profit and nonprofit, that characterize our field. Center directors who are identified leaders often hold management positions within a larger system or chain, rather than working closely with a particular group of staff and children. Because of their educational backgrounds and jobs, most of the acknowledged leaders in our field earn incomes that are several times greater than even our most highly educated and tenured teachers and providers. As a function of their jobs and income, our identified leaders have greater freedom to travel, attend meetings and conferences, and write about their experiences in the field. The acknowledged leadership also includes a greater proportion of males and Caucasians than constitutes the larger early childhood workforce (National Black Child Development Institute 1993).

Barriers to teachers and providers assuming greater leadership roles

As the analogy about beauty suggests, there is a distinction between acknowledged, or recognized, leadership and actual leadership. In discussing the absence of teachers and providers in acknowledged leadership roles in the field, I do not mean to suggest that teachers and providers fail to show leadership qualities. Rather, their leadership often goes unrecognized by those outside the classroom or home. And teachers and providers too rarely occupy positions of power and visibility in which they could act as spokespeople for decisions and policies that influence the distribution of resources in organizations and programs. A number of intertwining factors discussed below contribute to the dearth of acknowledged leadership among teachers and providers.

Failure to recognize and value teacher and provider leadership skills

As anyone who has ever worked with a group of children knows, effectiveness requires well-honed leadership skills. One has to guide, both directly and indirectly, the interactions and movements of many young children (and adults) through space and time. Facilitating the transition of a group of children, for example, from high-energy outdoor play to more low-key circle time, and then on to a snack, strikes terror in the hearts of many novice caregivers. The leadership skills required often do not resemble the more traditional notion of a leader as someone who commands authority and respect and directs others. Leadership skills in an early childhood environment require a more subtle and participatory style that is barely visible to the untrained eye. While co-workers know who has these skills, because they are invisible in the greater society, which views child care work as the natural proclivity of women, they are often difficult to acknowledge in oneself and in colleagues.

Even less obvious to people are the many adult skills required of teachers and providers as they interact with coworkers, parents, grandparents, foster parents, volunteers, trainees, and other professionals. Effective teachers of young children are also supervisors and teachers, and therefore leaders of adults. The style of leadership utilized by effective early childhood teachers and providers with their peers does not call attention to itself, but it nevertheless requires careful honing and practice.

The leadership skills that teachers and providers develop while working with children and families can be applied relatively easily outside the classroom or home, if there is adequate support and recognition. Teachers and providers can translate what they know about working with children and adults to other situations. But all too often, when they participate in settings outside the center or home, their skills and experience are not recognized or valued, and they are, perhaps unwittingly, excluded from information or processes, which in turn limits their participation. For example, in public policy discussions, child care teachers and providers lack access to the most recent information on proposed legislation and thus remain silent in discussions. Most do not receive newsletters or other bulletins that provide policy updates. But teachers and providers have valuable insights about the implications of policy changes for children and families—implications that often are unrecognized even by those more aware of the nuances of a particular bill. Teacher and provider voices are often muffled by those of us who volunteer our opinions, often repeatedly, and we fail to consider whether our group process encourages or ensures everyone an opportunity to share their perspectives. When our early care and education meetings assume certain types of knowledge, neither recognizing the range of information and perspective that people bring to the table nor people's comfort level in the particular venue, those with the least sanctioned skills and experience are often hushed.

The lack of support for teacher and provider leadership roles is related to another contradictory phenomenon in the early childhood field. Although we identify ourselves as educators, we often restrict what we know about how humans learn to our work with children and pay relatively little attention to adult learning and growth (Jones 1986). Most of our conferences and meetings and much of the writing in our field mirror more traditional forms of pedagogy and communication that are less accessible or inviting to many teachers and providers. Our restricted teaching and leadership styles also fail to reflect or encourage the cultural and linguistic richness that is so evident in the early childhood workforce.

Insufficient compensation and its consequences

Inadequate pay fuels high rates of job turnover among early care and education workers, forcing many of our most experienced and skillful practitioners to seek jobs outside the classroom or home, and even the field (Whitebook, Howes, & Phillips 1990; Whitebook, Phillips, & Howes 1993; Cost, Quality, & Child Outcomes Study Team 1995). Among those who stay, many work second jobs to earn sufficient income to support themselves and their families or, in the case of family child care providers, work exceedingly long hours that make participating in leadership activities difficult or impossible.

The lack of sufficient resources in early childhood settings, combined with practitioners' meager earnings, results in limited access to professional development, participation in advocacy, or other experiences for many teachers and providers. Many leadership activities, such as conferences and meetings, are held during the work week. Teachers and providers usually can attend only if they can be paid for their time and a substitute caregiver can be arranged, but the limited resources in the field make this difficult and all too rare. Payment for travel to meetings, accommodations, and meeting/conference fees are beyond the financial reach of most practitioners.

Insufficient organizational representation for teachers and providers

Relatively few child care teachers and providers maintain organizational ties; only 14% of center staff teachers belong to any professional or occupational group (Whitebook, Howes, & Phillips 1990). Even fewer center staff (4%) belong to a union, although this percentage varies by the sector of the industry (Morin 1991). (Nearly 25% of Head Start workers are represented by unions, and even greater proportions of public school child care teachers work under a collective bargaining agreement, but virtually no workers in for-profit centers have union recognition.) Most family child care providers do not belong to organizations, and many have limited or no contact with other providers (Galinsky et al. 1994). Regulated family child care providers and those who participate in the Child Care Food Program are more likely to be involved in family child care associations (Galinsky et al. 1994). But the majority of child care workers do not participate in organizations that enable them to build sanctioned leadership skills or to assume acknowledged leadership roles among their colleagues.

Most organizational options for teachers and providers also include members from a wide variety of early childhood roles. Typically, teachers and providers are only one of several occupational groups within these organizations, and they must struggle to make their voices heard among a competing chorus of other interests. Within their union locals, child care employees often constitute a small minority of the membership, which may comprise service workers or teachers of older children. The same dynamic operates for teachers and providers within NAEYC.

By far the largest organization in the early childhood field, NAEYC has experienced growth paralleling that of the industry as a whole in the last two decades. From modest beginnings in the 1920s as the National Association of Nursery Educators, which represented nursery school teachers and university-based child development professors, NAEYC now numbers 96,000 members, organized in several hundred regional Affiliates. From 1975 to 1990 alone, NAEYC's membership grew four times larger. Only a handful of teachers or providers have been elected to the Governing Board in recent years. Similarly, while the organization's peer-reviewed journal *Young Children* publishes articles for frontline practitioners and includes practitioner-written articles, in fact, few of the articles are written by teachers not associated with an institution of higher learning.[2]

Promoting teacher and provider leadership roles

Articulating and validating the skills involved in child care work, building a career development ladder that supports better compensation and rewards training, and consciously creating organizational roles for teachers and providers are all necessary steps toward building a more diverse leadership in the field. (These efforts will help diversify the leadership not only by job role but also by ethnicity, as teachers and providers are disproportionately women of color.) In recent years, targeted efforts have been made to acknowledge and build leadership roles for teachers and providers. Profiled below are the Worthy Wage Campaign and early childhood mentoring programs.

The Worthy Wage Campaign, initiated in 1991 by members of the Child Care Employee Caucus within NAEYC, is coordinated by the National Center for the Early Childhood Work Force, formerly the Child Care Employee Project. The campaign is a nationwide grassroots effort to empower child care teachers and providers to mobilize to reverse the early care and education staffing crisis. It now consists of more than 200 member groups in 39 states, plus the District of Columbia and Canada. The campaign is organized around the following three principles:

1. creating a unified voice for the concerns of the early care and education workforce—which overwhelm-

ingly comprises teachers and providers—at the national, state, and local levels;

2. fostering respect for those who work with young children by improving their wages, benefits, working conditions, and training opportunities; and

3. promoting the accessibility and affordability of high-quality early care and education options that meet the diverse needs of children and families. (*Child Care Employee News* 1992)

The campaign recognizes the importance of local efforts by child care teachers and providers in bringing the staffing crisis to awareness in their communities yet acknowledges that this voice remains weak or absent in most communities. As the campaign evolved over the last several years, local membership groups have developed and many teacher/provider leaders have emerged. As one Seattle-based teacher explains, "The Worthy Wage movement is the nest where in the last three years I have grown tremendously as a leader and a believer in myself and my work with kids" (B. Wiley, personal communication, June 1994). Local campaigns engage in a variety of activities to build the confidence and skills of teachers and providers as spokespeople for the profession in their communities.

Recently, the National Center for the Early Childhood Work Force, responding to requests by local campaigns for assistance, created the Leadership Empowerment Action Project (LEAP), a curriculum and training process for child care teachers and providers. The training is geared to people at a variety of levels of experience in leadership, organizing, community action, and advocacy—newcomers meeting with other teachers and providers for the first time, budding leaders who have some experience but want to strengthen their skills, and experienced leaders who need help in nurturing new leadership and replenishing themselves. The curriculum is designed around the three critical stages of empowerment: coming to awareness, engaging in inquiry and analysis, and taking action. The training helps teachers and providers articulate their own stories, interpret these experiences in the larger context of history and community, and use that knowledge to identify appropriate steps toward change.[3]

Early childhood mentoring programs, another significant development in recent years, promote teachers and providers as leaders in the field. Though the programs vary in structure, often because of state and local regulations and sources and amounts of funding, most of the several dozen now in operation across the country are committed to four common goals:

1. retaining experienced and skilled teachers and providers in early childhood classrooms and homes by providing them with financial incentives and recognition of their skills;

2. offering learning opportunities for skilled teachers and providers, particularly in the areas of peer coaching, reflection, leadership, adult development, antibias work, and advocacy;

3. providing learning opportunities for novice caregivers (protégés) with their more experienced teacher/provider colleagues to further their joint professional development; and

4. improving the overall quality of early care and education programs in the community. (Whitebook, Hnatiuk, & Bellm 1994)

Mentoring programs build leadership by acknowledging the skills teachers and providers already have and by helping them to extend their abilities. In so doing, mentoring programs help stem the turnover that is so destructive to our field and enable new teachers and providers to see that they can be recognized for their work with children *and* adults. Mentors speak eloquently about the process.

> I've been a family child care provider for 20 years. By becoming a mentor and responding to people's questions, I am realizing how much I know. (Whitebook, Hnatiuk, & Bellm 1994, 15)

> Becoming a mentor is another step in learning from each other. There is so little respect for this field that we don't recognize what we know or have to offer. The mentor program has changed that—there is a new sense of professionalism and respect. . . . It's different because teacher and providers are talking instead of being talked about. (p. 17)

> The program encouraged me to find the strength inside of me. It gave me a voice. We need change, and it can't happen unless we are heard. (p. 12)

> Her work with children almost seemed magical; she had such an easy way of guiding and nurturing. Since she has become a mentor . . . she uses the same skills with student teachers, gracefully helping them to question and adapt what they do. (L. Gardinier, personal communication 1995)

Almost all of the mentoring programs create time and offer support that enable providers and teachers to become involved. Most include some financial reward for the mentor through a stipend or raise in salary. The programs recognize that good teachers are good advocates and help mentors work on a wide range of skills. Several programs include set aside time for mentors to engage in the larger community as advocates and spokespeople.[4]

Beyond these more formal projects, a number of programs and organizations support and promote teachers and providers by pursuing a combination of strategies. Underlying each of these strategies is recognition of the importance of bringing child care teachers and providers to the tables where decisions are made, and, equally important, the necessity of creating appropriate resources that permit those who work directly with children to take advantage of these opportunities. The strategies include

• more convenient scheduling, coverage, release time, and financial assistance. Meetings, conferences, and advocacy events can be planned to accommodate teachers' and providers' schedules. Paid leave time can also increase participation in these activities by practitioners. Paid, reliable substitute coverage reduces the conflict that workers feel in leaving the children in their classroom or home program to pursue professional development activities. Groups wanting to involve teachers and providers should consider providing financial assistance for child care, transportation, program fees, and accommodations which otherwise limit access to activities outside the home or classroom.

• acknowledgment of the full range of teacher and provider skills. Teachers' and providers' efforts to build skills related to their work with adults, as well as their work with children, require support. Inservice or community training for teachers and providers can focus on adult relationships within early care and education settings and related issues of adult learning, diversity, and leadership styles. Teachers and providers recommit to the field through engagement in learning processes that validate the full range of their job duties and contributions. Redefining leadership, for example, to include teamwork or sensitive support for a child with special needs serves as important professional recognition.

• support for advocacy as a vital part of professional development. The definition of career development for teachers and providers can be expanded to include advocacy activities and participation in community forums as representatives of the early care and education field (Whitebook 1994). To facilitate teacher and provider participation, paid leave and substitutes or other coverage are essential. For example, when centers are asked to send a representative to a community meeting, they may select and support a teacher to attend. United Front Child Development Program in New Bedford, Massachusetts, offers teachers not only annual paid professional-development leave but also three days of paid advocacy leave so that they may participate in community rallies or other events to improve early childhood services. Workers at the United Front Child Development Program are unionized, so they also have the option to take union leave from their jobs, without loss of seniority and with a guarantee of employment. During the leave they may work for their union and be trained in local organizing and other aspects of teacher representation.

Teachers and providers should be encouraged to participate in other advocacy efforts that encourage their leadership (e.g., the Worthy Wage Campaign, mentoring programs, the leadership and diversity projects coordinated by NAEYC Affiliates, or the new Head Start Leadership Fellowship). Centers and organizations can provide supports to enable teachers and providers to participate. For example, Step One School in Berkeley, California, provides release time to teachers working on community education efforts for Worthy Wage Day. Some NAEYC Affiliates and family child care organizations provide scholarships or stipends to enable their members to take advantage of career development opportunities in the community.

• restructure leadership bodies of early care and education organizations, including centers. Teacher and provider representation in leadership positions must be proactively sought if it is to be assured. For the teachers and providers who constitute one third of the National Center for the Early Childhood Work Force board, the organization covers all travel and leave costs, for example. For other organizations with limited contact with teachers and providers, such policies require active outreach and recruitment. Because of the lack of value placed on their work and the lack of recognition for their leadership, teachers and providers may not see themselves as capable of participating. At the center level, encouragement and support may mean reserving slots for teachers on governing committees and providing compensation for additional hours beyond the scheduled workday.

• attention to diversity. As leadership positions in the field open up to those people who work directly with children, we must ensure that these opportunities reach teachers and providers from the full spectrum of ethnic, cultural, and linguistic backgrounds. This may require programs and organizations to examine their approach to diversity and their assumptions about leadership and learning and to develop multilingual training and other resource materials and/or provide translation services. (See Moore, chapter 8.)

Conclusion

Those of us who participated in women's consciousness-raising groups years ago have not escaped the influence of cultural norms of beauty. But as we now come to terms with our middle-age faces and bodies, we have an understanding that helps us navigate the years with more self-acceptance and appreciation for ourselves and other women. And I think we contribute in some indirect ways to a broader understanding of the range of physical attractiveness.

My hope is that the early childhood field will begin to recognize and challenge the cultural standards of leadership that silence many of our most creative and dedicated colleagues. We can challenge the internalized low value placed on child care work in the greater society that is reflected in the limited presence of teachers and providers as our acknowledged leaders and spokespeople. By so doing, we can develop a group of leaders who are willing to question the status quo and to take the necessary risks to make working with young children a career that people can afford to pursue and a career that is respected.

Notes

1. Thanks to members of the Worthy Wage Campaign and the Early Childhood Mentoring Alliance for their assistance in helping me understand leadership issues in the field. Special thanks to Dan Bellm, Alice Burton, Robert French, Laura Gardinier, Patty Hnatiuk, Rosemarie Vardell, and Claudia Wayne for their assistance with this article.

2. A number of teachers and providers within NAEYC want the organization to take a stronger position on compensation. These members tend to be college trained and educated, and many identify strongly as professionals. These teachers and providers view NAEYC as the organization that should represent them on economic issues. In part, many want this because NAEYC does a very good job providing its members with the latest in research and other information relevant to their work with children. It seems to them a logical extension of NAEYC's function as a professional organization. Many also believe, however, that NAEYC's success as an organization is relatively independent of teacher/provider membership. NAEYC ironically has experienced enormous growth during the same period that teachers' and providers' wages and levels of program quality have dropped substantially. Many in the NAEYC leadership would like to see compensation improve, but the issue carries less urgency than it does for teachers and providers struggling to make a living for themselves and their families (Katz 1994; From Our Readers 1995).

3. Training can be arranged through the National Center for the Early Childhood Work Force office (1-800-URWORTHY).

4. For more information about specific programs and the network of individuals and groups involved in mentoring, contact the Early Childhood Mentoring Alliance, coordinated through the National Center for the Early Childhood Work Force.

References

Child Care Employee News. 1992. 11 (Fall): 4.

Cost, Quality, & Child Outcomes Study Team. 1995. *Cost, quality, and child outcomes in child care centers. Public report.* Denver: Economics Department, University of Colorado.

From our readers [Pelo, Morin, Curtis, Draude, & Whitebook letters]. 1995. *Young Children* 50 (2): 3–4, 82.

Galinsky, E., C. Howes, S. Kontos, & M. Shinn. 1994. *The study of children in family child care and relative care: Highlights of findings.* New York: Families and Work Institute.

Jones, E. 1986. *Teaching adults: An active learning approach.* Washington, DC: NAEYC.

Katz, L. 1994. From our president. *Young Children* 49 (6): 2.

Morin, J. 1991. *Taking matters into our own hands: A guide to unionizing in the child care field.* Berkeley, CA: Child Care Employee Project.

National Black Child Development Institute. 1993. *Paths to African American leadership positions in early childhood education: Constraints and opportunities.* Washington, DC: Author.

Whitebook, M. 1994. Advocacy to challenge the status quo. In *The early childhood career lattice: Perspectives on professional development,* eds. J. Johnson & J. McCracken. Washington, DC: NAEYC.

Whitebook, M., P. Hnatiuk, & D. Bellm. 1994. *Mentoring in early care and education: Refining an emerging career path.* Washington, DC: National Center for the Early Childhood Work Force.

Whitebook, M., C. Howes, & D. Phillips. 1990. *The National Child Care Staffing Study: Who cares? Child care teachers and the quality of care in America.* Oakland, CA: Child Care Employee Project.

Whitebook, M., D. Phillips, & C. Howes. 1993. *The National Child Care Staffing Study revisited: Fours years in the life of center-based child care.* Oakland, CA: Child Care Employee Project.

Commentary

by Alice Walker Duff

The famous John F. Kennedy quotation "Ask not what your country can do for you—ask what you can do for your country" always reminds me that the key to success is finding the right questions to ask. In her chapter, Marcy Whitebook asks, "Who's Missing at the Table?" In this commentary I attempt to amplify the Whitebook chapter by asking different questions about leadership in early care and education. The questions are tools to help clarify current understanding of leadership in our field and to better appreciate the Whitebook chapter. The goal is for all of us to envision possibilities that, when realized, will substantially improve our field.

Improving the field is the point of the Whitebook chapter. After asking the title question, Whitebook explains why she thinks early care and education teachers and providers are not acknowledged leaders or spokespersons in their own field. Describing successful programs that challenge current cultural standards of leadership, she suggests how teacher/provider leaders can develop. However, the fundamental question—Why does it matter?—is not asked and is only partially answered in the text. That omission is intriguing. Only when we understand the importance and value of inclusion are we motivated to achieve it.

The Whitebook chapter generates a myriad of questions for each of us in the field. From my perspective the most important one is, Are we telling the truth? It is closely followed by others: Do we mean what we say? Are we taking responsibility for our beliefs and actions? Are we holding others accountable for their beliefs and actions? Are we doing what we can for ourselves and not hiding or waiting for someone else to do it for us? Are we seeking positive outcomes for everyone? Do we want success more than we fear failure? Are we people—not saints, victims, or martyrs? Until we can answer these questions in the affirmative for ourselves and the field in general, teachers and providers will continue to be devalued, unfairly compensated, and absent from the policy table. In addition, the majority of the care we provide will be mediocre. Quality, affordability, and accessibility will continue to elude the vast majority of us. Why? Because complex questions get inadequate answers when meaningful participation from significant segments of relevant populations is missing. Inclusion makes us stronger and more effective.

We are not telling the truth about leadership in our own field, and I believe it is debilitating us. I attempt in this commentary to tell the truth as I see it. The purpose is not to assess blame, or ignite guilt, but to encourage a rigorous, honest look at leadership in our field for the purpose of its well-being. This well-socialized provider has been reluctant to speak difficult truths in public, but serious times require risks. From this beholder's eye, leadership in our field is in serious condition. We are faced with unprecedented challenges without confidence in how to resolve them. Never before have so many families and children needed our services. Not since the Great Depression has the perceived relationship of need to identified resources been so out of balance. As I see the unspoken, but broadly accepted, truth, we in the field are self-interested, territorial, competitive, defensive, and scared. We do not seem to accept that we are human.

The problem is not that we have these human traits. The problem is, we do not know how to effectively handle them. In self-defense we deny them. Too frequently we are dishonest about our motives and beliefs. Our beliefs seem to scare us. Having talked to, worked with, and observed legions of people in this field, I think we fear that the best and the brightest are not in this field. We fear challenges to our assumptions. We fear our fundamental societal problems are not "fixable." We fear that if we win, someone else must lose. We fear that we don't have the answers to our most difficult questions. And we are afraid that we do not have the power, or are not able, to effectuate the answers we do have. We are afraid of the truth because we think it is too difficult or too ugly. Do these fears sound familiar to you? What is your list of unspoken truths?

Whatever the truth is, we are not saying it where and when it matters. We even question if it matters. We need the courage to speak the truth to people who have recognized power. First, and most important, we must gather the courage to let down our well-developed defenses and speak the truth to ourselves.

It may be hard to understand or appreciate why it is important to speak difficult truths in public. It may seem that all it does is expose dangerous weaknesses and thus make us more vulnerable. In fact it does. However, it does something else that is less obvious but more powerful. The truth unleashes incredible positive energy. Whitebook and her friends experienced the release of positive energy when the truth of their beauty was recognized and spoken. Speaking hidden truth also allows attention to be focused on fundamentals. An incredible amount of individual and organizational energy is used trying to keep secrets, maintain illusions, and avoid reality. Thus, in addition to finding new energy, truth eliminates huge time wasters. It actually enables accomplishment of goals and exchange of ideas. What about those exposed weaknesses? Will they be our demise?

If they are exposed and left unattended, probably so. But, if they are exposed and attended to, they increase our strength exponentially and increase our power.

In our imposed or selected roles of victim, saint, or martyr, we deny that we are powerful individuals. That denial keeps us trapped in the status quo and keeps us from being leaders. How do we change the status quo? It is a skill that can be taught and must be taught to a wide spectrum of people, especially teachers and providers. It starts with at least one person confronting a consequential question of value and will. While the answer lies within each individual, the solution requires both individual and collective action, conducted both locally and nationally. While articulating and assigning priorities is important, matching time, talent, and financial resources to priorities is essential. Setting goals and time lines, monitoring progress, seeking feedback, revising plans, and working daily is how change occurs. Knowing this, why have we not significantly improved the compensation of early care educators? Tell yourself the truth—about yourself and those you know.

Reading Whitebook's thought-provoking chapter, I ask myself, Am I part of the problem or the solution? What have I done to create, promote, allow, or accept the conditions she describes? I hope this commentary prompts you to ask yourself the same questions. The answer for me is that leadership for direct-service providers has not been a priority. I have not taken responsibility for changing the status quo for teachers and providers, and I have missed opportunities to raise issues of inclusion and compensation.

The next time you attend a gathering focused on any level of policy, ask yourself the following questions: What is the purpose of this meeting? Who are the stakeholders? How are their experiences and concerns included in this meeting? Do we have sufficient inclusion? What would be a better way—in terms of outcomes and resources—to be inclusive? What can be done to make meaningful inclusion possible? What can I do about it? Do not be afraid to ask these questions in the context of race and gender. Solutions may seem impossible, but when time frames are expanded, the seemingly impossible becomes possible.

What is the truth that keeps teachers and providers, African Americans, Latinos, and other people of color away from the table where decisions are made? As Whitebook pointed out, we in early care and education tend to mirror the larger society. We do not understand the value and need for diversity. We hold values that demean caregiving work performed by women involving children. Likewise, we mirror the values that demean people of color, especially men of color. As Whitebook observes, our values result in excluding people who work with children and people of color as our acknowledged leaders. If inclusion is not convenient, we do not extend opportunities to use

and develop leadership skills. My experience matches her hunches about the leadership in our field.

Not only is our view of leadership mired in dysfunctional values, but it is also limited by narrow frames of reference. As Kagan and Bowman point out in chapter 1, attention to early childhood leadership issues has been sparse, despite the acknowledged importance of the subject. We still act as though leadership comes naturally.

In addition to Whitebook's illustrations, here are some specific suggestions to improve our leadership abilities. We need to spend money on leadership development. Personal, agency, corporate, association, and governmental budgets must reflect this priority. When parents become true partners with caregivers, greater personal and political will develops to support the field. We must recognize, celebrate, and reward—both financially and psychically—leadership.[1] Early care and education professionals need to seriously consider politics for themselves.[2] As we use mass media and technology to support our field, we can develop our leadership skills and improve the status of the field. Responding to talk radio shows, writing letters to the editor, and communicating on the Internet through home pages and chat rooms are powerful development activities and ways to raise the public consciousness.

I expect that a common reaction to the Whitebook chapter is, It can't be done, because we can't conceive of how to do it now. We do not have highly developed skills in management or systems change or inclusion. But there are ways to have meaningful inclusion at policy tables and ways to develop early care and education leadership and improve our field. We will find them and implement them if we speak the truth not only to power brokers but also to ourselves. We need to heed the wisdom of Nelson Mandela, prime minister of South Africa, who points out that our worst fear is not that we are inadequate. He insists that our deepest fear is that we are powerful beyond measure. If we don't tap into that power now, teachers and providers will continue to be undercompensated, undervalued, and exhausted—and they will be unavailable for our children, families, economy, and future.

Notes

1. The National Black Child Development Institute, for example, recognizes leadership with the annual bestowing of the Sarah Harbin Award. Think about the consequences of every organization doing so and publicizing it in the media. I look forward to the day when the Sarah Harbin is as famous and sought after as the Oscar.
2. Maxine Waters from South Central Los Angeles is an examplar. Grounded in her Head Start experience, she has been a leader for early care and education in both the California State Assembly and the U.S. House of Representatives.

Chapter 10

Reflections on Early Childhood Leadership Development: Finding Your Own Path

Anne Mitchell

So, you want to become an early childhood leader? If a primary school principalship is what you have in mind, the path is relatively clear, wide, and well marked. Unfortunately, if any other leadership position in the early childhood field is your goal, the paths are neither clear nor obvious. In most cases there are few guidelines, no required certifications, and very limited access to educational preparation. You have to create your own path.

Various routes to leadership

Public schools

The route to becoming a principal, although not always straightforward, is fairly well established. First, one goes to college to become an early childhood educator qualified to teach in a public school. Then, usually after teaching for a couple of years, he or she enrolls in a graduate program in educational administration (sometimes also called educational leadership) at the local college or university and completes the state requirements to be certified as a school administrator. The theoretical knowledge gained from the courses and the practical knowledge from administrative internships will prepare the individual to be a good principal. Making the connection with at least one mentor, through course work or internship, supports the early childhood educator's learning and helps launch a leadership career. Through a combination of experience, education, and mentoring, a principalship is often secured, preferably in the desired school district.

Child care

How does one prepare to become the director of an early childhood program? Experience as a teacher helps. Education in such areas as program administration, staff supervision, financial management and legal issues also helps. But there are only a handful of college-level programs specifically designed to prepare early childhood administrative leaders. Even fewer continuing education opportunities exist for early childhood leaders.

Experience suggests that many people who are early childhood directors rose to their positions from the teaching ranks and learned what they needed to know about administration on the job, under pressure, at the point when they needed to learn it to survive. A few directors move into center directorships from positions running successful family child care operations, which means that they had some experience running a small business as well as teaching. More than 80% of child care directors were classroom teachers prior to becoming administrators, and the majority had no prior training in early childhood administration (Norton & Abramowitz 1981; Bloom 1989, 1992). For some directors, state licensing regulations are their training manual. If the regulations say a center has to have an admission form, a health policy, or a personnel manual, then the director must create one. If directors need help, they can ask the regulatory agency for guidance.

Some directors do prepare for their leadership roles by working as assistant directors under the nurturing guidance of a mentoring director in a large center. There are other ways to learn from predecessors—

especially by not repeating their mistakes. For instance, as the new director of a midsize, nonprofit child care center, I learned a great deal about the technicalities of labor relations when I had to represent the center before the National Labor Relations Board in a seven-year-old case that involved an alleged illegal firing.

Head Start

There are somewhat better-marked trails for Head Start directors to follow. Like child care directors, most Head Start directors come up through the ranks, first teaching, then often becoming component coordinators before assuming directorships. Head Start is a distinctive program that takes a while to understand, so experience helps significantly. Directors who come from outside Head Start usually have extensive experience in working with low-income populations and/or in early childhood administration in another type of program.

On-the-job learning and previous experience as a teacher are common elements between Head Start and child care, but the similarity ends there. Head Start administrators have access to training and technical assistance; the regional Head Start offices, the regional technical assistance support centers, and the national Head Start Bureau all offer support to directors. Tailored administrative consultation, as well as new director workshops and week-long regional training sessions for directors and component coordinators, are offered. Within many regions, there is an informal mentoring system; more experienced directors help newer directors, giving them information and support. The Head Start Directors' Associations (national, regional, and state) offer formal and informal peer support as well as some specific training, mainly at conferences. Advanced training is available free of charge to Head Start directors on a competitive application basis through the Head Start Management Fellows program at the University of California at Los Angeles.

Other kinds of leadership

What about other kinds of leadership? There are obviously many administrative roles in the early childhood field: directing a child care center, heading a child care resource-and-referral agency, managing a Head Start program, administering a family child care home or network. But there are many other ways to lead. A teacher who speaks out effectively about child care working conditions is a leader. A college professor of child development who inspires students to become early childhood educators is a leader. Advocates and lobbyists, vocal parents, and creative state-level administrators of public child care agencies are also leaders.

Essentially, no one way prepares someone to become an early childhood administrative leader; it more or less just happens. Interest and experience land an individual the job, and he or she rises to the occasion. Mentoring may play a role, and education helps—if appropriate administration courses are available. But learning through on-the-job experience—from both mistakes and successes—is the primary method of preparation.

Clearly, fragmentation of the field and lack of access to preparation and continuing education in early childhood administration are problems for anyone who wants to be anything other than an elementary principal. But more fundamental issues must be considered: What exactly is early childhood leadership? How do people develop into early childhood leaders? Can there be a "training" system for leadership? What would an early childhood leadership development system look like?

What is early childhood leadership?

Leadership plays critical roles in both creating and maintaining good early childhood programs and in advancing public policy to create the conditions to nurture good programs.

Leadership affects programs and children

Considerable research evidence shows the efficacy of high-quality early childhood programs for children's later school and life success (e.g., Consortium for Longitudinal Studies 1983; Whitebook, Howes, & Phillips 1989). Such research points to specific elements that produce good child outcomes: Teacher-child interactions are influenced by teachers' educational backgrounds (their ability to create appropriate learning environments), the conditions of their work (compensation, turnover), and the structural elements of the child's environment (ratio, group size, materials, and equipment). Oddly, leadership is not discussed much in this literature, leaving an impression that these conditions can magically appear without it. (The exceptions are two studies that relate director experience to center quality [Phillips, Scarr, & McCartney 1987] and director experience to children's outcomes [Kontos & Fiene 1987].)

Anyone who has ever worked in or enrolled a child in a good program knows that leadership is critical—the administration makes the decisions that create the conditions for good child outcomes. Recently, evidence of the influence of leadership at the program level has emerged. The Cost, Quality, and Child Outcomes Study (1995) provides clear evidence that administrator experience, level of education, and degree of involvement with program planning all have positive program and child outcome effects.

Defining leadership

To discuss leadership development requires a working definition of leadership itself. One distinction is between leadership *roles* and leadership *behavior.* Clearly, people who fill leadership roles (administrative and management positions), such as child care center director, Head Start director, director of the local child care resource-and-referral agency, or president of the local early childhood association (AEYC), need to have a set of skills and competencies to fill the role effectively.

On the other hand, people who want to change (improve) circumstances for children and families—for example, parents, community leaders, early childhood teachers, or university professors—can act as leaders regardless of role. To be effective, they need to develop a set of skills and competencies similar but not identical to those that people need to fill leadership roles. These two categories of leadership are not mutually exclusive: people who fill leadership roles also demonstrate leadership behavior within their workplace and usually exert leadership beyond their center or organization.

In the older leadership literature, role-related leadership is sometimes described as *transactional* leadership, meaning having the skills and abilities to make an organization function. Newer theories of leadership alter the static quality of this definition to incorporate vision, teamwork, and adaptation. This is collaborative leadership for change, or *transformational* leadership (Culkin n.d.).

There appears to be a good deal of consensus around the skills and competencies required for early childhood leaders—in whatever role.[1] The six generally agreed-upon competencies are

1. the ability to articulate organizational mission, goals, and direction;

2. communication skills (written and verbal);

3. analytic skill (problem solving);

4. interpersonal skills (e.g., motivate and inspire others, get along with others, collaborate, resolve conflict);

5. attitudes/dispositions (e.g., flexibility, openness to change, ability to accommodate divergent viewpoints); and

6. child and family development knowledge.

Four other competencies are necessary for leadership roles that involve the management of people and organizations:

1. fiscal management and planning;

2. creation and development of organizational culture;

3. staff development and supervision; and

4. supervision for creating coherent, well-understood curriculum.

Conceptually, the definition of early childhood leadership encompasses both the ability to create and run excellent programs for young children *and* the ability to be effective and powerful in decisionmaking that affects children and families—being "at the table" and influencing decisions wherever that table may be.

Developing early childhood leaders

When recognized leaders in our field (at the national, state, or community level) are asked how they came to be leaders, they offer a number of revealing answers. Before writing this chapter, I informally interviewed a number of well-known leaders in the field. Many said that a large part of their leadership is grounded in a powerful sense of self-confidence, instilled early on and nurtured by their parents (usually their mothers). The unconditional love and support these individuals experienced in their childhoods prepared them to be leaders in whatever field of endeavor they might have chosen. As one leader said, "It never crossed my mind that I shouldn't be in the leading roles I have had."

Other leaders reported that their leadership ability developed over time through successive positive experiences in a series of roles characterized by increasing responsibility and scope. Years of practice and progressive challenges honed their leadership skills. Other leadership know-how was acquired through peers with whom they had a close relationship—e.g., in directors' support groups. Some leaders credited the cohort of students in their college degree program. These cohesive support systems sometimes continue for years beyond graduation.

Nearly every leader mentioned particular people—role models—who inspired them by showing how leadership is lived, demonstrating leadership by example. These may be people in leadership roles or those who are leaders regardless of their role. Some role models can be observed only from afar, but the more accessible role models are generally described as mentors—people who give developing leaders a chance to learn under their guidance, to practice and develop with personal support. This mentoring takes many forms, ranging from invitations to work on a project or assist in teaching a course to an introduction to other leaders in the field or a referral to a better job.

Connections with role models, peers, and mentors are often made in college courses, institutes, and workshops. But no leader indicated that course content in itself was the spark that ignited their leadership.

The reflections of early childhood leaders on the development of their own leadership suggests three things.

1. Leadership is related to emotional characteristics that have their roots in the early childhood years.

2. Leadership primarily develops through unique personal relationships and experiences.

3. Leadership development involves both knowledge acquisition and opportunities to practice leadership in actual settings.

Is it possible to design a system to ensure these characteristics?

The current training system

Given how leaders describe their own development, a helpful way to discuss the current state of leadership development may be to distinguish intentional or purposeful methods of preparing and continuing to develop leaders from methods in which leadership development is an indirect by-product of activities undertaken for another purpose. Purposeful methods to develop the skills and competencies of early childhood leadership might be called *direct* approaches, such as those offered by a college degree program or a specific leadership institute. Necessary leadership skills and competencies also can be developed via *indirect* pathways, such as through participation in various initiatives that are not designed to train leaders but by their nature build leadership skills—for example, early childhood community planning projects or professional organizations.

Direct approaches to leadership development

Higher education. The most obvious direct route to develop leaders is through college degree programs. There are, predictably, few (except those that are for public school administrators). Child care regulations in most states require that administrators of centers have some early childhood teaching experience or qualifications, but very few require any administrative preparation. None require that directors have any credential. Texas is the only state whose regulations mention a credential for directors. As a result, only a handful of colleges across the country offer a bachelor's and/or master's degree in early childhood leadership.[2] A movement is under way in a number of states (and one national organization) to create a director's credential, which would usually include some amount of college-level course work. When (or if) a credential becomes required, appropriate college-level course work and college degree programs would likely increase, as the higher education system (especially community colleges) designs programs to prepare people for the credential.

Leadership institutes. Another direct method for developing leadership is through institutes or fellows programs (which may or may not offer college credit). The leading examples are the Head Start Management Fellows Program offered through the UCLA School of Management, the North Carolina Early Childhood Leadership Development Fellows Program, National-Louis University's Taking Charge of Change Institutes, and Wheelock College's Advanced Child Care Seminars (which celebrated their 20th anniversary in 1995). These kinds of programs can be exclusive—the UCLA program, for example, is for Head Start directors only—but are usually open to a wider range of early childhood folks and offered at more than one location, such as the Advanced Child Care Seminars that Wheelock holds in Boston and at other sites around the country.

Seminars, institutes, and similar methods that draw participants from diverse sectors of the early childhood field (and from related child/family service-related fields) provide knowledge and new information about a range of topics as well as offer a valuable network for established and emerging leaders from across the country who work in child care centers (including Head Start), resource-and-referral agencies, family child care homes, government, among other settings.

Interprofessional approaches to leadership development are especially important in the early childhood field because the needs of young children and families are multiple and require programs to work cooperatively. Working (and leading) collaboratively is a distinct skill. Some colleges that offer degrees in early childhood leadership (e.g., Wheelock) have developed interdisciplinary approaches in their degree programs. The North Carolina Early Childhood Leadership Development Program offers the only nondegree program designed to develop local collaborative early childhood leaders across systems.

By their nature, seminars and institutes are intense and concentrated. They often lead to significant transformational experiences among participants, including myself. In 1978, as the director of a large child care center in Vermont, I attended the Wheelock Advanced Child Care Seminar on social policy. In many ways, my current work is a direct result of that experience.

Civic organizations' leadership programs. Another direct route to developing some of the necessary early childhood leadership skills is the leadership programs offered by such organizations as the Chamber of Commerce and Kiwanis to their members in a given community or state. According to early childhood leaders who have participated in these programs, integrating early childhood people with the larger business and civic community has double benefits. First, good leadership training is made more available and accessible than through other kinds of programs simply because such organizations are common and widespread. Second, key opinion leaders develop community awareness of early childhood issues, thus building public support for early childhood programs. The only downside is that the child/family content of early childhood leadership is not addressed, although that may not be much of an issue since directors feel confident about their knowledge of child development and developmentally appropriate practices (Bloom 1989).

Indirect approaches to leadership development

Leadership appears to develop from an individually unique set of experiences. These usually include direct approaches to learning skills and acquiring knowledge, but leaders report that learning by example and being offered opportunities to lead through a mentor relationship are key elements. Supportive relationships (mentoring) can develop on the job, in college, or in projects that are designed to bring people together. The following are examples of programs and projects that offer *indirect,* yet significant, opportunities for leadership development.

Mentoring and other approaches. The Mentoring Alliance, cosponsored by the Center for Career Development at Wheelock and the National Center for the Early Childhood Work Force (NCECW), is a network of local mentor teacher projects from around the country. While mentor teaching is primarily seen as a compensation and retention strategy that gains recognition for expert teachers, it also develops leaders. Mentor teachers learn to lead new teachers into the profession and take on more visible roles in their programs and communities. The TEACH (Teacher Education and Compensation Helps) project in North Carolina has similar effects. The Worthy Wage Campaign (also an NCECW project) is a network of local groups working to improve compensation of early childhood workers. NCECW supports the network with training

in public speaking, problem analysis, community organizing, and other areas that develop leadership.

Community planning. Early childhood community planning is also an indirect leadership development strategy. These are typically broad-based efforts that attract a diverse group of community leaders and concerned citizens who can learn leadership by example and through direct experience with each other. The projects that are more focused on early childhood services (rather than broadly on child and family conditions) probably offer better leadership development possibilities. For example, the Child Care Careers Institute in Boston has done an excellent job of finding and elevating early childhood directors and trainers from the Latino, Asian, and African American communities. These individuals, who have become active in overall planning and implementation of various projects of the institute, are now seen as key leaders in the local early childhood community.

Early childhood system building. By the same token, system change projects sponsored by many national organizations in states and communities are based on principles of empowerment, capacity-building approaches that indirectly aim to develop local and state leaders. The Child Care Action Campaign, the Children's Defense Fund, and Wheelock's Career Development Center are prime examples. These efforts usually work through committees, task forces, and work groups composed of diverse representatives who learn from one other and from the national leaders. The effectiveness of either community planning or system building as leadership development depends on whether leadership development is an explicit objective that receives sufficient attention within the larger project's goals.

Implications

If we merge what the early childhood leaders said about their own development with the list of leadership competencies, we begin to define the outcome we are trying to reach with leadership education. From the competency list, we get what potential leaders have to know and be able to do. From the leaders' reflections, we see how these things are best acquired: through mentors, in practice, and in personal relationships.

Assuming we agree on *what* one has to know to be a leader (the content) and *how* she or he acquires the competence (the process), we can ask whether an individual must have it all before becoming a leader. Leadership may be a little like a child walking. When adults say a 12-month-old is walking, they don't mean the child is a completely competent walker, only that she has taken the first recognizable steps. Similarly, leaders become more and more competent with practice in a supportive and encouraging environment. In short, leaders develop.

The direct, purposeful approaches to leadership development are more likely to provide the relevant content knowledge and do so through appropriate processes and experiences. By definition, they are designed to develop leadership, requiring an explicit definition of the content. Such programs may use the processes that work—combining theory and supported practice, learning from experience, and mentoring. Programs of shorter duration, such as institutes, can meet the content criteria and offer opportunities to learn through personal relationship, but they are not usually designed to provide for supervised practice. Longer programs, such as graduate degree programs, have time to include supported fieldwork and mentor opportunities. Of course, any specific direct-approach program of leadership development may nonetheless fail to provide both appropriate content and effective processes. Programs may be didactic in the delivery of course work and internships or they may be content-rich models of appropriate adult learning.

Leadership is about creating vision, communicating, and motivating others—competencies that rest on personal qualities such as emotional strength. To develop these competencies, leadership development approaches must reflect the reality that leadership is both personal and professional. Purposeful approaches that incorporate continuous advisement develop both professional knowledge and skills and the personal strengths to be a competent leader (e.g., Bank Street's graduate programs do this systematically by including advisement as a regular course taken simultaneously with fieldwork over a full year).

Indirect approaches offer opportunities to practice leadership and gain certain skills (e.g., vision setting, moving groups toward a goal, or negotiating political processes). These indirect ways are important because there currently are not enough affordable direct methods. (One volunteers in a community planning process but has to pay to go to graduate school.) However, indirect methods are not systematic enough to be the main approach to leadership development. These could be made more purposeful if project designers thought about leadership development as an explicit goal, along with the other goals articulated for the project.

Today's leadership development opportunities are a very modest foundation on which to create a system of leadership development. Programs may match both the content and process requirements for leadership development, with purposeful approaches more likely to achieve both than indirect ones. But there is no guarantee that any particular program is a good match. Even if every program were excellent today, the major problems of fragmentation and extreme scarcity of programs remain.

Designing an early childhood leadership system

Ideally, the system of leadership education should reflect best practice in both content and process, be easily accessible, be connected to the higher education system, and be available both before and after someone assumes a leadership role. Some leadership training should be built into all early childhood professional development, because we never know who might become a leader or when.

Each state or regional group of states would have an articulated set of excellent early childhood leadership programs. Many programs would be offered in community colleges, leading to advanced degree programs at a four-year college or university. Each state also would have an early childhood leadership fellows program (or institute or ongoing seminars) for continuing education and renewal. National early childhood professional associations would support their developing leaders and offer advanced certificates in leadership. Excellence in leadership would be recognized and rewarded. All early care and education leaders, throughout their careers, would mentor new and emerging leaders as a matter of professional behavior.

Higher education

Because research shows that level of education is related to program quality *and* because higher education is valued in our society, leadership education should be offered by institutions of higher education in credit-bearing sequences that lead to certificates and degrees. When leadership development is offered through community-based organizations or professional associations, it should be directly connected with a college or university so that course credit is available.

Best practice in content and process

Good leadership development programs distinguish between those aspects of leadership that can be taught through a combination of theory and practice, those that are learned through personal relationships (such as mentoring or peer support) and those best learned by doing (on the job or in supported practice).

What can best be learned through on-the-job experience? Experience as a teacher helps a director to know how to work well with staff and to understand what children really need. But teaching experience may not be sufficient preparation for working with families and the community or for putting together a budget. Family support principles and community relations are distinct sets of management skills and knowledge that a leader must learn and practice. Likewise, the skills of financial management and planning (financial projection) have to be first learned and then honed in practice.

While some aspects of leadership (e.g., finances or staff supervision) seem almost generic—or at least very similar across fields of endeavor—leadership is not content free. To be a leader in one's field implies deep knowledge of that field. Someone who is a recognized and respected leader in the travel and tourism industry, for example, could not immediately switch to being an early childhood leader. The individual has to learn the theories, practices, and practical realities of working with children and families. Early childhood leadership rests on knowledge of child and family development. Content knowledge is one key element of early childhood leadership that we know can be taught and learned, and there are many courses at all levels of education.

Most directors know where their knowledge base is sufficient and what they need to learn more about. Directors say they feel most confident about their knowledge of child development and least confident about fiscal matters and organizational development (Bloom 1989).

Relationships

Mentor relationships and peer support are key to leadership development, but neither can be guaranteed in a training system, even one that includes significant amounts of internship. Mentor and peer support relationships very often are based on interpersonal chemistry. One cannot force or even facilitate such relationships. Like love, they just happen. It seems logical, however, that the more opportunities for building personal relationships that are offered (e.g., through internships, fellowships, or intentional mentoring), the more likely that supportive interpersonal relationships will develop.

Personal networks for peer support and mentoring that can offer opportunities for advancement are a critically important part of leadership development and have profound consequences for the whole field. Early care and education's leadership levels lack diversity in part because most personal networks are monochromatic, constrained by individual and societal biases that lead to class and race segregation. If you think otherwise, scan your own Rolodex file to check the diversity of your own network. If personal networks were more integrated, so would be all the professional levels of our field.

Recognition and reward

Recognition for a job well done motivates people to keep on doing well. An effective leadership development system has rewards and recognition for excellence. The Head Start Association (or the Head Start Bureau, or both together) could systematically search for and highlight (even give awards for) innovation and excellence in management in the overall program and for exemplary quality in specific program components (Schultz 1993). An early childhood directors' organization might give annual awards for excellence in management, similar to the 100 Principals of Distinction named by the National Association of Elementary School Principals. *Child Care Information Exchange*'s cover photos of directors and its lead stories about directors and their programs give national recognition to good programs and acknowledge the directors' role in the achievement.

Continuing education

Leadership development is an ongoing process that should be supported with continuing education. Job experience deepens what has been learned and rekindles curiosity. New questions and needs emerge. In my 10-year experience with the Early Childhood Leadership Masters program at Bank Street College, I found that directors seek out leadership education at predictable points in their careers. Directors in the first year on the job are desperate for anything to help them make sense of their new responsibilities—they want the nuts and bolts (e.g., finance and supervision). Directors who have five or so years of experience seek leadership education to extend and deepen their skills in certain areas (e.g., supervision for curriculum development or community relations). Directors with 10 to 15 years of experience are looking for renewal. Often they are ready to move into early childhood positions that have more responsibility or wider scope, and they feel they will benefit from having an advanced degree.

Barriers to a new system

Describing an ideal early childhood leadership development system is easy compared with the effort of getting from here to there. The barriers to achieving the ideal early childhood leadership development system are many—some structural, others attitudinal.

Lack of qualification requirements

In other fields (and for public school leaders), the availability of preparation and continuing development is directly related to the requirements for doing the job. One cannot be a principal without the appropriate credential, which generally includes specified content and set amounts of course work and internship.

By contrast, there are very few qualification requirements for early childhood administrators. The Head Start system has no credentials for directors; no part of the Performance Standards covers administrator qualifications. State regulations governing child care centers sometimes specify that directors should have education, training and/or experience in child development or early education, but 22 states have no preservice requirements whatsoever for directors. Just 10 states mention administrative knowledge in their requirements for directors, and only one (Texas) requires directors to have both business management *and* child development knowledge. Only 16 states require directors to participate in any continuing education. Establishing requirements is a necessary step to increasing the availability of professional development opportunities in early care and education.

Insufficient professional associations

Early childhood professional organizations, especially those with local and state-level affiliates, serve a number of leadership development functions. Associations are often a good way to find peer support. Serving as an association officer is a form of indirect leadership training. Associations make the most of these opportunities if they offer leadership training for their affiliate officers and actively seek to diversify their leadership to match the diversity of the field. But they could do more.

Professional organizations in many other fields, building on the foundation of required qualifications, offer advanced leadership opportunities. The American Nurses Association is one example among many (Mitchell 1994). Even without specific personnel licensing requirements, a professional organization can set the standards. For instance, there is no standard license for health care (hospital) administrators, but their professional organization, the American College of Health Care Executives, offers three progressive levels of credential that are required for continued membership in the organization.

Another barrier to leadership development may be that most early care and education administrators do not have a professional organization of their own, let alone one that offers credentials. Head Start directors and elementary school principals do (the National Head Start Directors Association and the National Association of Elementary School Principals, respectively). Directors of for-profit centers have the National Child Care Association, and directors in a few states have created directors' organizations. But on a national scale, there is no broad early childhood directors' organization. Perhaps USA Child Care could fill the niche. It is clearly organized around child care concerns, and most of its members are early childhood directors. But the organization is young. It will need a few more years and probably some outside funding to develop enough strength as a professional association—and the strategic alliances with other directors' groups—to become a magnet for directors and to offer advanced credentials.

Undervaluing leadership

An obstacle unique to our field is the low regard we have for authority and, by extension, leadership. Early childhood practice is about promoting growth and development—children make choices, families are partners—not about directive teaching or hierarchical relationships. We value equality and sharing and shy away from power and authority. We may value leadership when we mean nationally recognized leaders or scholars, but we devalue program management. We tend to think the real work of the early childhood field is directly interacting with children; managers are not doing the important work. But good program management is a critical kind of leadership.

Too often we equate authority with position—the director has authority. But authority is granted to leaders by followers. Leadership is participatory. We also confuse authoritarian leadership with authoritative leadership. Dictators are authoritarian; leaders we freely choose to follow are authoritative. Leadership is a power-sharing relationship in which everyone involved benefits and grows as a result.[3]

Options for moving ahead

The ultimate goal of a system for developing early childhood leaders is to improve programs for young children and their families. To accomplish this, we need leaders at the program (or direct-service delivery) level, in state (and federal) agencies that fund and regulate child care, in the early childhood units of state departments of education, in state legislatures and Congress, in state and national professional associations, in community organizations such as resource-and-referral agencies and community colleges, and throughout the higher education system. We need well-prepared and supported early care and education leaders in any positions where decisions that affect early childhood program quality are made.

Standards

One way to stimulate leadership development is establishing standards for leaders. Given the overall goal of early childhood leadership, these may best be developed by building on recognized quality-assurance systems such as program accreditation and performance standards.

Head Start Performance Standards cover all aspects of Head Start operations except management. In recognition of the importance of management to program operations, management standards similar to those for the program components could be developed and introduced into the monitoring system. Or management could be addressed as a personnel issue. The Performance Standards are specific about qualification requirements for teachers (the Child Development Associate). Perhaps there should be a CDA for directors—a "CDC" (Competent Director Credential). On the other hand, separate credentials reinforce separation among programs. Is leading a child care center really that different from leading a Head Start program? Probably not. There probably is more difference between a large multisite program and a small single-site program than between Head Start and other child care programs.

Accreditation

Support for leadership development could be built into national early childhood program accreditation. Currently, there are administrative and managerial items in the accreditation criteria, with a suggested range of qualifications for directors. But there is not a specific focus on the role of directors in program improvement. Such criteria could be developed, based on current knowledge and the competencies identified, as director credentials gain hold. Criteria for directors, even a specific credential, could be required, or at least strongly encouraged, in accreditation.

Credentials

The most promising avenue for leadership development is the grassroots movement to create director credentials and the training to go with them.

Leaders and potential leaders themselves are in charge. Early childhood leaders in states as diverse as Georgia, Texas, and Wisconsin recognize that directors' competence is a key to quality and that professional development for directors is scarce, and they are inventing director training and credentialing paths. An informal national caucus has emerged to share information about director credentialing. The philanthropic and business communities have expressed interest in leadership development and begun to support some of these efforts. As this movement gathers strength, we will begin to agree on a definition of early childhood leadership, our experience with methods of leadership education will accumulate, and the stage will be set for making progress toward a system of leadership development.

Eager as we are for rapid progress, we should remember that our field is still very young. Head Start is just entering its 30s. The availability of child care has waxed and waned in response to shifts in federal policy interest over the last 50 years. The general public has recognized child care as an occupational field only in the last decade, as the proportion of working families has increased substantially and the need for child care has become so prevalent. By contrast, public education has been commonplace for more than 100 years.

The presence of leadership development opportunities in a given occupational field seems to be related both to the maturity of the field and to the degree of public support the field enjoys. Society long ago agreed that the public is collectively responsible for educating children and for funding that education. Head Start, though much younger, functions like a public preschool system for very poor children. Society has come to believe sufficiently in the value and efficacy of Head Start to allocate public funds to support it, albeit with some ups and downs over time. Child care has only very recently achieved any degree of recognized public support. The debate surrounding passage of the federal Child Care and Development Block Grant of 1990 was about *how,* not whether, to support child care. But we have a way to go before early childhood is firmly rooted as a public (or semipublic) responsibility.

My prediction is that as public support grows and the early childhood field matures, leadership development opportunities will increase in direct proportion. Let us hope for progress in our lifetimes.

Notes

1. The lists were compiled by drawing on the thinking of Paula Jorde Bloom, Roger Neugebauer, Gwen Morgan, and Carol Brunson Phillips, among others.

2. Degree programs in early childhood leadership at the graduate and/or undergraduate levels are offered at Bank Street College (New York City), Wheelock College (Boston), Pacific Oaks College (Pasadena, California), Erikson Institute (Chicago), National-Louis University (Evanston, Illinois), Nova University (Fort Lauderdale, Florida), Belmont College (Nashville, Tennessee), and Lesley College (Cambridge, Massachusetts).

3. I am grateful to Gwen Morgan for her insight on these ideas.

References

Bloom, P.J. 1989. *The Illinois Directors' Study: A report to the Illinois Department of Children and Family Services.* Evanston, IL: National College of Education.

Bloom, P.J. 1992. The child care director: A critical component of program quality. *Educational Horizons* (Spring): 138–45.

Consortium for Longitudinal Studies. 1983. *As the twig is bent . . . Lasting effects of preschool programs.* Hillsdale, NJ: Earlbaum.

Cost, Quality, & Child Outcomes Study Team. 1995. *Cost, quality, and child outcomes in child care centers.* Denver: Economics Department, University of Colorado at Denver.

Culkin, M. n.d. Literature review about early care and education administrators as leaders/managers. Unpublished manuscript.

Kontos, S., & R. Fiene. 1987. Child care quality, compliance with regulations and children's development: The Pennsylvania Study. In *Quality in child care: What does research tell us?* ed. D. Phillips. Washington, DC: NAEYC.

Mitchell, A.W. 1994. *Preparation and credentialing: Lessons from other occupations for the early care and education field.* New Haven, CT: Quality 2000, Bush Center at Yale University.

Norton, M., & S. Abramowitz. 1981. *Assessing the needs and problems of early childhood administrators/directors.* ERIC, ED 208963.

Phillips, D., S. Scarr, & K. McCartney. 1987. Child care quality and children's social development. *Developmental Psychology* 23: 537–43.

Schultz, T. 1993. *Leadership development: The missing connection in early childhood policy and practice.* Alexandria, VA: National Association of State Boards of Education.

Whitebook, M., C. Howes, & D. Phillips. 1989. *Who cares? Child care teachers and the quality of child care in America: Final report of the National Child Care Staffing Study.* Oakland, CA: Child Care Employee Project.

Commentary

by Roger Neugebauer

Three years after my wife, Bonnie, and I launched *Child Care Information Exchange*, a management magazine for early childhood directors, I penned an article, "Piaget's Theory of Director Development" (September/October 1981), under the pseudonym Fred Piaget. While this article was slapped together in one all-night session with the invaluable aid of a six pack of generic brew, it did seem to touch a responsive chord with my audience. In fact, 15 years later, it is still the most popular of the hundreds of articles I have written about center management—much more popular than articles in which I invested months of in-depth research and thoughtful wordmanship.

For years I assumed that the article was a big hit because it was just so darned clever. However, upon re-reading it recently, I realized its success had more to do with the fact that, in a nonthreatening manner, it talked publicly about the rocky road most directors traverse in honing their own leadership skills.

Anne Mitchell is right on target when she concludes, "Essentially no one way prepares someone to become an early childhood administrative leader; it more or less just happens." The vast majority of directors develop their skills through a patchwork of on-the-job trial and error, midnight calls to fellow directors, community college classes, NAEYC conference presentations, and management articles ripped out of airplane magazines.

Mitchell is also correct in her observation that, although the paths directors follow to develop their skills are infinitely varied, "directors seek out leadership education at predictable points in their careers." The stages of director development I poked fun at in the Fred Piaget article do, in fact, correspond to some common teachable moments in directors' lives.

I will take the liberty of falling back on excerpts from this tongue-in-cheek article to make four observations on the state of the art in early childhood leadership development. Mitchell's analysis of the state of leadership development and her recommendations on where it needs to head are right on target. My observations here, which stem from my experience in working with directors for so many years, are intended to lend emphasis to factors that I have come to see as crucial.

The Pseudomanagerial Stage

Stage I, also known as the Paper Tiger Stage, starts the first day on the job for a new director. . . . At this stage the director is terribly impressed with the trappings of power—with the title of director, with having a desk with pencil holders and in-boxes, with being able to give orders and make important decisions. This infatuation with power goes hand in hand with naive expectations about the effects of this power. Rookie directors are known for having assumptions such as "When I make a decision, the problem is solved" and "Now that I'm in charge, nothing will go wrong." I observed that fledgling directors cannot grasp the concept of "problem permanence." They believe that when they close their office door, the problems of the center go away because they can't see them or hear them anymore.

Mitchell observes that the vast majority of center directors rose to their positions from the ranks of teachers. Most trainers cite this as a shortcoming of the profession—our centers are led by people trained to take care of children, not to lead an organization. I have a different take on this: I believe a center benefits in the long run from being led by someone who understands the problems of caring for children in a group setting from the ground up.

For several years I taught a night course in center administration at a community college. This course was open to students pursuing a two-year degree in early childhood education as well as to current directors who desired to fine-tune their skills. Invariably, the younger students drove me crazy. They approached the course no differently than they did Math 101—they were more concerned about how grades were awarded than about the content of the course. To maintain their interest in discussions of parent relations and staff conflict, I found myself having to be more of an entertainer than a teacher. I cringed at the thought of these paper tiger directors naively assuming control of a center.

On the other hand, the directors in the course were a joy to work with. They were there not merely to earn three credits but to find answers to problems they were experiencing in real life. They were highly motivated to learn and were fully aware of the gaps in their knowledge.

I am not concerned with the lack of preservice training opportunities for directors. I am convinced that what we need is to provide directors with a range of flexible training options that they can dip into periodically to support their on-the-job learning.

The Premanagerial Stage

The new director soon learns that power isn't all it's cracked up to be. In Stage II, often referred to as the Excedrin Headaches #1-99 Stage, reality comes flooding in. A premanagerial director's assumptions about the job reflect her declining sense of confidence and competence: "When I make a decision, the problem gets worse." At the Premanagerial Stage a director has generally assimilated the concept of problem permanence—by now she realizes that, in child care, problems never go away. The Stage II director is also coming to grips with the concept of conservation—she realizes that no matter how she reshapes the budget, there will never be enough money to go around.

One point in Mitchell's analysis that might easily be discounted as a peripheral issue is the value of mentoring and peer support. A director's job can be a very lonely one. In the early stages of his career, when every problem seems insurmountable, a director needs a shoulder to cry on, a seasoned director to turn to for advice, a support group of directors struggling with the same issues and searching together for answers.

One of the tragedies of our profession is the number of young directors with high potential who burn out before they realize their potential. Any successful leadership development effort must create a support network, or build upon an existing network, to provide ongoing nurturance for developing directors.

The Concrete Managerial Stage

The transition from Stage II to Stage III occurs gradually. The director doesn't even recognize she is changing until one morning she realizes she is actually looking forward to going to work. The director at this stage . . . is finally starting to get a handle on the job. She is in control again. However, whereas the Stage I director's feeling of control derived from a sense of power, the Stage III director's derives from a sense of mastery. The director's assumptions about her role now reflect her growing sense of confidence and competence: "Any problem can be solved with sound management decisionmaking."

Mitchell makes the point that "leadership is grounded in a powerful sense of confidence." For most directors who were thrust into that leadership role with little prior training, this sense of confidence is hard-won. It is the result of overcoming a seemingly never-ending series of frustrations, wrong turns, right turns, and little victories.

In fact, I think this key ingredient is not so much confidence as it is hardiness—the ability to persevere in the face of seemingly impossible obstacles. To be truly effective leaders in a center, directors need to be able to weather the daily storms of clogged toilets, angry parents, shrinking resources, and underpaid staff. They need to focus the organization's energy on continually moving forward to achieve its mission.

A leadership development program cannot teach Hardiness 101. But it is important that it not only provide directors with the skills they need to overcome obstacles but also inspire them with real-life testimonials of what effective directors have accomplished. Directors must leave a training program with an appreciation of the difficulties they will face, along with a conviction that they can make a difference.

The Formal Managerial Stage

Stage IV is often referred to as the Philosophical Stage because with its attainment the director is able to take a more philosophical view of her role. The Stage IV director is able to transcend immediate here-and-now problems and concern herself with broader, long-range issues. Her assumptions about her role reflect this broader view: "In decision-making, it is the process not the product that is important" and "If anything can go wrong, it probably will—but then who really cares anyway?"

The point at which directors become truly effective is when they rise beyond being managers to become leaders. The director as manager sees herself as the administrator of financial, personnel, and maintenance functions. The manager keeps the center running. The director as leader sees herself as the guardian of the organization's mission. She sees it as her responsibility to focus everyone's efforts on service excellence, to keep the organization growing and improving, to maintain momentum toward a long-range vision.

Many director development programs aim no higher than developing managers. Courses on budgeting, nutrition, and staff management are essential but do not imbue participants with a commitment to leadership. A leadership development effort that makes a difference must have the goal of developing visionaries and keepers of the faith.

Chapter 11

Personal Dimensions of Leadership

Linda M. Espinosa

When difficult issues arise that are likely to arouse bitter animosities, who among us is willing to take a position and advocate for policies that are unpopular and possibly even risky? What is it in one individual that allows him or her to carve out a position, state it clearly, and not back down when faced with certain opposition, possible ostracism, or even alienation? What personal qualities allow one to envision a better future and inspire others to share this vision? Why do some people surface as lightning rods for the beliefs and hopes of the profession, while others hang back content to follow the crowd or fail to find a consistent audience for their points of view?

This chapter argues that what is needed for leadership to emerge is not necessarily more training, education, or experience but the careful nurturing of certain personal characteristics. In my view, certain personal qualities are essential to the exercise of responsible leadership. There are always thorny dilemmas of policy and practice that require balanced thinking and inspiring leadership. When we think about our great leaders of the past, we may consider what they have in common and wonder who among us is capable of carrying the profession forward. What qualities should we be striving to nurture within ourselves and our colleagues? When all the courses are completed, the budgets balanced, and the skills mastered, it is those deeply personal qualities that grow from within that allow us to lead others.

Definition of leadership

Several years ago at a Western States Leadership Conference, Lilian Katz asked me my definition of leadership. At that time I thought of leadership as a *big* concept, difficult to get your mind around and fully understand, a lot like the notions of love or culture. You recognized it when it was present and you knew when it was missing, but it was hard to explicitly define and almost impossible to deliberately develop. It seemed like any definition was incomplete or shallow. Since that time I have researched and thought about this elusive concept and decided we need to have clarity to ensure that future leadership is not left to chance but systematically nurtured.

For the purposes of this chapter, I am using the term *leadership* to mean the ability to influence, inspire, motivate, or affect the thoughts, feelings, and actions of others. Leaders are those who provoke or nudge or elevate others into thinking, feeling, or behaving in ways they would not otherwise have demonstrated. Leadership is sustained influence over others, shaping the course of events and bending the will of others by word or personal example. Harry Truman defined a leader as "someone who has the ability to get other people to do what they don't want to do and like it" (cited in Gardner 1995a, 8).

For me to be inspired by another person, to want to follow her example, to open myself up to be influenced by her thinking, I must trust in this person's professional and personal integrity. It is not enough for someone to simply hold a position of authority or espouse a provocative idea. To inspire me to change my thinking or behavior in significant ways, a person must also exemplify the qualities I describe in this chapter. Anyone with a compelling point of view can pique my interest for a moment, but to have a sustained effect on me over time, that individual must represent the personal qualities that elevate my thinking and being.

When I think of leadership in our profession, I first think historically of the courageous individuals who challenged conventional wisdom about the nature of childhood and the importance of early experiences.

Rousseau, Froebel, Montessori, Jane Addams, and even Freud and Piaget, for example, took great personal risks in the name of their professional convictions. Their beliefs and their ability to convince others of the importance of their visions forever altered our conceptions of childhood.

While it is more difficult to identify current leaders of the same stature, a cursory scan of the current landscape reveals leaders at every level: those who define and build child care solutions in local communities, those who boldly advance early childhood scholarship, teachers who introduce new models of teaching and learning at their school or center, and our leaders who tirelessly advocate for national policies that support children and families.

What is it that allows some voices to touch and move our hearts and minds while others are never heard? One always needs to consider the context or ecology of individual behavior and its relationship to external social, cultural, institutional, and economic factors, but it is clear that it takes individuals capable of courageous leadership to make progress in any profession.

I would argue that knowledge, experience, and training are necessary but not sufficient requirements for early care and education leaders—and in some cases these are not even necessary. The issues that we confront in today's complex, rapidly changing society—such as how and when to include young children with severe disabilities in regular environments, how to truly embrace diversity even when basic values may be in conflict, how to squeeze out decent teacher salaries and benefits from meager budgets, how to ensure high-quality programs for all children—these are the kinds of dilemmas that will require our best thinking as well as our most competent leadership to forge new understandings and a clear direction for our future.

Moral principles

The integration of one's personal principles and professional voice is what brings strength, passion, and power of persuasion to leadership. The ability to lead others stems from the values, perceptions, norms, and ideas that are based on our set of personal principles. These principles shape our beliefs about how we treat others, what we consider important, how we approach conflict, and ultimately, which direction we choose to take. They help us to see the higher good, empower others, inspire best effort, and remain humble and open-minded. The struggle to understand and live by a set of moral principles is never easy, as evidenced in the lives of great historical leaders such as Abraham Lincoln, Franklin Roosevelt, Mother Theresa, Mahatma Gandhi, and Martin Luther King Jr.

Of course, many leaders and movements not based on moral principles emerge and flourish. In fact, history is replete with examples of misguided and sometimes evil exercises of power. In today's political and social climate, examples of manipulative and deceptive leadership are abundant, yet fortunately they are usually short-lived. This is not to say that one cannot become a powerful leader using fear or coercion, only that enlightened leadership that guides us in a direction of greater humanity and productive progress is centered on personal principles and relationships of trust and integrity. As Hans Selyem points out, "Leaders are leaders only as long as they have the respect and loyalty of their followers" (cited in Covey 1990, 18). This respect and loyalty come from shared values and a belief in the rightness of the leaders' intentions. The willingness to follow is created when leaders are perceived to be honorable, trustworthy, and working toward common goals. Each of us wants to be touched, inspired, and led by a great person who enriches and enhances our personal abilities. I believe that those who become respected leaders over time embody these personal qualities that are born of struggle, self-knowledge, and personal development.

In our field, it is also necessary to behave in ways that are consistent with one's stated positions. For instance, if we promote equity, diversity, and inclusion, our behavior toward others should be accepting and free of prejudice. If we publicly advocate for a position because it is popular or politically expedient, but we haven't worked through our deepest personal beliefs, it is possible to act in opposition to one's true self or conscience. In this case, a personal schism develops that can lead to a lack of integrity. This lack of consistency or integrity weakens one's personal power and ability to lead.

Steven Covey, in *Principle-Centered Leadership* (1990), identifies specific ways that a leader can increase legitimate power with others.

1. Persuasion—sharing reasons and rationale, explaining your position while maintaining a genuine respect for followers' perspectives, telling why as well as what, committing to the communications process until mutually beneficial and satisfying outcomes are reached.

2. Teachableness—operating with the assumption that you do not have all the right answers or insights and valuing different viewpoints, judgments, and experiences followers may have.

3. Acceptance—withholding judgment, giving the benefit of the doubt, requiring no evidence or specific performance as a condition for sustaining high self-worth, being focused on the well-being of others.

4. Kindness—being sensitive, caring, and thoughtful, and remembering the little things (which are really the big things) in relationships.

5. Openness—acquiring accurate information and perspectives about followers, recognizing what they can become while respecting them for what they are now, regardless of what they own, control, or do; giving full consideration to their intentions, desires, values, and goals, rather than focusing exclusively on their behavior or position.

6. Compassionate confrontation—acknowledging error, mistakes, and the need for followers to make "course corrections" in a context of genuine care, concern, and warmth, making it safe for followers to risk.

7. Consistency—ensuring that your leadership style is not a manipulative technique that you bring into play when you don't get your way, are faced with a crisis or challenge, or feel trapped; rather, using a set of values, a personal code, a manifestation of your character to define who you are and who you are becoming.

8. Integrity—honestly matching words and feelings with thoughts and actions, with no desire other than for the good of others, without malice or desire to deceive, take advantage of, manipulate, or control; constantly reviewing your intent as you strive for congruence.

To some, these ideals and the principles they represent may seem like an admirable but unrealistic list of personal virtues—a litany of merit badges. To others they may even seem preachy and simplistic. While there is no empirical evidence that these are necessary characteristics of effective leaders, and despite the fact that lists often become meaningless, the personal traits associated with these characteristics provide a perspective that is worth considering. This view places issues of character and moral principles in the forefront of the leadership discussion. Although many of us would not agree with every one of Covey's recommended practices, I think the central point is valid and applicable to early care and education leadership—namely, that one's stance toward life and one's willingness to develop a personal credo or set of principles ultimately determine one's stature as a leader. Simply having leadership skills is not enough; the voice that carries and connects is the one that has grown from personal conviction and is grounded in integrity.

Can an ordinary person with average abilities become such a notable leader? Mahatma Gandhi thought so.

> I claim to be no more than an average man with less than average ability. . . . I claim to be a practical idealist. Nor can I claim any special merit for what I have been able to achieve with laborious research. I have not the shadow of a doubt that any man or woman can achieve what I have, if he or she would make the same effort and cultivate the same hope and faith. (cited in Gardner 1995b, 38)

At the heart of what Covey and Gandhi and many others have said is what I believe separates the truly great leader from an opportunistic leader: having a moral compass that points the way and allows one to rise above personal limitations. Covey (1990) would call this being principle-centered, Kohlberg (1976) would term it as the seventh stage of moral development, others might simply say it is faith in a higher good, but I like to think of it as the willingness to engage in the daily struggle of confronting one's limitations and investing in character development.

This is true at every level of leadership, from policymakers to classroom teachers. In fact, at the classroom level, teachers are confronted with some of the greatest challenges to their personal principles. When a young child from another culture and background behaves in a way that is contrary to a teacher's values, her reaction and subsequent reflection will reveal her deepest beliefs. For instance, I once worked in a school that was being racially integrated for the first time. When a large group of Spanish-speaking Latino children enrolled, several teachers—who espoused a belief in equity and integrated schools—started to have management problems in their classrooms. At this point, they could have chosen to address the problem in a variety of ways: change their approach to meet the new demands, work more closely with the families to try to understand the children and their culture, work with other teachers to find solutions, or identify the children as the problem and work to remove them from their classrooms. Unfortunately one of the teachers chose the last approach and had several children suspended and ultimately reassigned to another school. While this is an overly simplistic portrayal of the events, it illustrates when teachers are called to leadership and shows that it often takes a deeper sense of our true values and principles to exercise educational leadership.

Vision

Having a personal vision or view or dream of what early childhood education can be has frequently been cited as necessary for effective leadership. For it is this vision of what can be, of how all the small everyday details add up to a coherent whole, that reflects our values, goals, and beliefs. Our behavior toward colleagues, subordinates, and authority figures; how we respond to the needs of others; how we fulfill our daily obligations—all express our inner selves. In my experience a personal vision is just that, personal and unique, developed over time, and often a personal synthesis of multiple points of view. It is not simply an adoption of someone else's vision but a personally constructed vision that embodies one's unique experiences and knowledge. As Mother Theresa says, "There are no great acts of love, only small acts done with great love." It is how we view these small everyday acts and what meaning we attach to them that create the vision we hold for our field. We need to achieve clarity about what it is we want for our children and how this vision can be expressed in practical terms.

Having the vision is one thing, but sharing the vision so that it permeates every aspect of our work again depends on our personal qualities as a leader and skills as a communicator. Harnessing the energy and individual creativity of followers to a dream unleashes the collective power necessary to realize that dream. A leader's ability to clearly communicate her vision goes back to her relationship with others. Open and clear communication is only possible with trust. The skills of effective communication can be learned and used for manipulative purposes, but the ability to lead over time requires a relationship of reciprocal trust and shared purposes.

Howard Gardner, in *Leading Minds* (1995a), portrays a leader as someone who has a compelling story to tell; she is able to forge a group identity and sense of community through her effective storytelling. Gardner explains, "I have argued that a key—perhaps the key—to leadership, as well as to the garnering of a following, is the effective communication of a story" (p. 62). He quotes Charles Cooley: "All leadership takes place through the communication of ideas to the minds of others" (p. 41).

In *Lincoln on Leadership* (1992), Donald Phillips portrays Lincoln as a leader who made his points and communicated his message through the use of parables, yarns, humorous anecdotes, and colorful stories. Storytelling is a means of communicating the substance of who we are and what we stand for. The vision we hold for children, for early childhood programs, and for families can be vividly captured in the stories we choose to remember and repeat. (See Crompton, chapter 6, pp. 50–51.)

Marian Wright Edelman, probably more than any other single individual in this country, has managed to consistently and convincingly envision a world that is safe for children, a world where every child's birthright is to grow up loved and well-cared for. Through her unshakable personal convictions and powerful moral voice, she has inspired, motivated, and renewed countless early childhood professionals, as well as other educators. Elementary and secondary educators come away from one of Marian's brilliant speeches convinced of the need to redouble their efforts on behalf of children. It is as though they needed Marian Wright Edelman to elevate them from the daily discouragements and constant compromises they face, to remember their commitment to children. It is noteworthy that Marian Wright Edelman is not a trained early childhood educator but a lawyer who saw a need in this country and responded by creating an organization (the Children's Defense Fund) devoted to the welfare of children.

Courage

To be able to lead others, one must have a capacity to influence people; to influence people, one must first have a relationship with them. Through our relationships, our daily interactions, our attempts to influence others, we reveal our inner character. True leadership flows from a trusting relationship that is based on mutual best interests. It takes courage to build open relationships that are trusting, honest, and sincere.

Courage is a central characteristic of effective leadership. It is the courage born of self-knowledge and inner security that allows one to have beliefs, convictions, and confidence. Ira Chalfee, in *The Courageous Followers: Standing Up To and For Our Leaders* (1995), identifies five dimensions of courageous "followership" that I believe apply to courageous leadership as well:

• the courage to assume responsibility,

• the courage to serve,

• the courage to challenge,

• the courage to participate in transformation, and

• the courage to leave.

Because the relationship between leaders and followers is a fluid and sometimes interchangeable one, I see courage—and, in particular, these aspects of courage—as essential for both leaders and followers. The courage it takes to lead and the courage it takes to follow, particularly when one is risking reputation, criticism, or even failure, is born of the personal belief in the greater good benefiting us all. Personal growth and self-worth are enhanced when one acts to advance the principles one believes in. Ultimately, we are diminished when we fail to take the lead or, in some cases, fail to follow others' lead when we fear the consequences. I think great leaders are frequently afraid—afraid of failure, of not being heard, of losing respect. The idea of not having fear in difficult situations is a little like a young child who doesn't understand the consequences of walking into traffic and therefore is unafraid. The point is, courageous leaders understand the risks and acknowledge their fears, but they don't let their fears prevent them from taking action.

Part of the internal work of becoming a leader is learning how to *assume responsibility* for our own development, actions, knowledge, and deficiencies. The capacity and willingness to *serve the greater good,* the purpose at hand, and those for whom you lead, will move the agenda past the limits of personal ego. By *challenging* the prevailing or popular outlook and inviting others to challenge our positions, we can bring needed energy to a debate or dialogue. Transforming or changing a system, a set of practices, a philosophy, or a person's beliefs is a long, arduous process that begins with personal transformation. A leader must be willing to examine her own abilities and attitudes in order to positively influence the transformation of others. Every journey begins at home. And finally, when all other avenues have been exhausted and staying would mean compromising personal principles or integrity, a leader must have the *courage to leave.* The belief that one can't leave, that there is nowhere to go, is inhibiting and oppressive; it stifles the ability to be a courageous leader.

Leadership in the early childhood profession: A personal perspective

Over the course of years spent trying to realize a dream of creating wonderful, magical programs for young children, my own leadership abilities have often been tested to their limits. I have discovered that there is a cost to the exercise of responsible leadership but that there also are external as well as internal rewards.

Time

There is no question that the demands of leadership require time. In a field that is primarily female, mostly young, and chronically underpaid, the time it takes to attend meetings, give speeches, develop plans, or organize events is a major cost—for this is time not spent with your own child but working to improve conditions for all children. I remember once when I was leaving on yet another weekend to deliver another speech, my young daughter asked me to "Be rebellious and just don't go." Most of us are already working full time, raising families, and struggling with the delicate balance of work-family demands; to an overloaded plate, we now add the demands of leadership. (See Galinsky, chapter 16, p. 144.)

An unanticipated benefit is the pleasure and joy of working with professionals who exemplify the very qualities described in this chapter. By developing our own abilities and being willing to accept the responsibility of leadership, we enter the ranks of others who inspire us to be our best.

Stamina

I don't know if personal stamina and high energy are a cost or a requirement of leaders, but I do know that one must have the energy as well as the willingness to work long hours and then get up and do it again. Nothing we accomplish of lasting value is easy or quick. I personally have found that I need a regimen of nutrition, vitamins, exercise, and freedom from distractions to keep up with all the demands on my time. Effective leaders find reservoirs of energy—perhaps by strength of will—that fuel their efforts over time.

Optimism and orientation toward the future

To provide a vision that captures and holds the attention of others, one's message must lead somewhere others want to go. The vision offered must excite one about the possibilities of the future and present a view of humanity that is uplifting. We must share in the belief that we can do better, that we are capable of rising above our personal limitations. There is much to be celebrated in the field of early childhood and there is much to be improved. The optimism is born of our faith in the long run and keeping our sights on the future targets. I also think it is necessary to understand the tools of the future, such as technology, electronic communication, and easily accessible information for all.

Overcoming obstacles

The obstacles to identifying and developing leadership in early childhood are numerous, both in the personal and professional arenas. From the personal perspective is the issue of the type of people drawn to working with young children as a profession. We are predominantly women, we often have a nurturing urge, we derive satisfaction from being involved in the growth of others, and we are emotionally sensitive in our relationships. It has been my experience that these qualities contribute to a desire to please and yet an unwillingness to subject oneself to the rigors and hardships of leadership. We must include in our early professional training the vision, the urgency, and the tools to prepare all members of our field to accept the challenge and responsibility of leadership. Often, it is a matter of developing a personal identity of strength and competence that prepares one to emerge as a leader.

Professional obstacles are even more difficult to overcome. Our field is socially undervalued, chronically underpaid, plagued by high turnover rates, and inclined to underinvest in professional development—clearly not an ideal breeding ground for future leaders. Yet our field possesses a strength of conviction and depth of belief in our mission that propels individuals to rise above their circumstances and become a voice for children. One of the most compelling reasons for taking a personal risk is the opportunity to improve conditions for the young and defenseless. The belief that our cause is right and that our profession must move forward can be highly motivating, despite lack of external support.

In summary, a critical aspect of leadership development rarely mentioned is the need to nurture personal character—the imperative to help young leaders develop a set of personal principles that will fuel their professional contributions. We must work on our inner selves as well as master the knowledge of our field.

References

Chalfee, I. 1995. *The courageous follower: Standing up to and for our leaders.* San Francisco: Barrett-Kohler.

Covey, S.R. 1990. *Principle-centered leadership.* New York: Fireside.

Gardner, H. 1995a. *Leading minds: The anatomy of leadership.* New York: Basic.

Gardner, H. 1995b. *On leadership.* New York: Free Press.

Kohlberg, L. 1976. Moral stages and moralization: Cognitive-developmental approach. In *Moral development and behavior: Theory, research, and social issues,* ed. T. Lickona. New York: Holt, Rinehart, & Winston.

Phillips, D.T. 1992. *Lincoln on leadership: Executive strategies for tough times.* New York: Warner.

Commentary

by Richard M. Clifford

Discussion of the concept of leadership is particularly important in the early childhood field at the present time. We are at a pivotal point in the history of services to young children and their families. After decades of change in the makeup and economic structure of families in the developed countries of the world, we are about the task of inventing new ways of rearing and educating children in our societies.

During the last century and into the current one, we developed a public education system as an adjunct to the family to prepare our children to enter the newly organized world of work. The development of schools as we know them today was influenced by changes in the family during the industrial revolution, when newfound manufacturing methods moved jobs out of homes and neighborhoods to factories, taking men and women away from immediate contact with their children during the day.

Today, as more and more women with young children move into the paid workforce and as the number of single-parent families with young children dramatically increases, we must figure out how to modify our social institutions to assist parents in adapting to the new realities of life. Leadership in this environment is critical to the development of services that are good for both the adults and their children. As we approach a new century, we are making decisions that will have very long-term consequences—affecting generations of young children and ultimately all of us.

In discussing the personal dimensions of leadership, Linda Espinosa presents a picture of the ideal leader as moral, compassionate, kind, accepting of others, open to new ideas, visionary, courageous, and possessing great integrity and the ability to communicate effectively with others. But the real world operates far from that ideal. I cannot help but think of Watergate, the United Way scandal, and tax evasion in the proprietary sector. And of course it is not just in the recent past that we have experienced failures in the personal side of leadership. Our history books are full of stories of ruthless and cruel leaders. Indeed, most of the conquerors of the world have been murderers, allowing their followers to bring untold misery on the conquered and generally failing to show any trace of the traits described above. To paraphrase Emerson, what we see in leadership behavior gets in the way of hearing what leaders should be like.

So, does this mean that true, real-life leaders are corrupt, immoral, lacking in integrity, and just plain mean?

Has Linda Espinosa missed the point of leadership? Is it measured only by actual accomplishments, with no regard to the means used to accomplish the goals? I do not think so. In fact, it is the failure of personal dimensions of leadership that often brings down otherwise great leaders. These failures often get the press, and the good works of leaders get lost in the hype about their shortcomings. Another quote from Emerson is a good reminder: "To be great is to be misunderstood." It should be clear, however, that powerful leaders often do not possess many of the traits Espinosa presents as being important for leaders.

Another possible problem with discussing the personal side of leadership is that we think of leadership in several ways (see Katz & Kahn 1966). Leadership can be characterized as residing in a position. For example, George Bush, Margaret Thatcher, and Pope John Paul I led by virtue of the authority of the positions they occupied. Leadership may also be thought of as a type of behavior. As Espinosa stated, leadership may be thought of as the act of influencing others. Leadership thus requires at least two people. It is a relational concept. Leadership also may be viewed as a characteristic of a person. It was Marian Wright Edelman's personal leadership—not just the fact that she was president of the Children's Defense Fund (CDF)—that inspired so many people, most of them not members of CDF, to come to Washington, D.C., for the Stand for Children rally. The concept of the personal dimensions of leadership are discussed in this chapter in the context of the latter two conceptualizations of leadership.

In defining leadership, Espinosa contends that "knowledge, experience, and training are necessary but not sufficient requirements for early care and education leaders—and in some cases these are not even necessary." This position troubles me. It is hard to think that true leadership can be blind to the needs of the people or institutions being led or to the environments in which it functions. While it is true that Dwight Eisenhower knew little of politics when he became president, his leadership reflected his knowledge of how to organize and unite an organization to seek and use information to make progress. This knowledge was honed through a sound education and much experience with military operations. Leaders are not born. People learn to lead.

In the classic *On Becoming a Leader*, Warren Bennis says, "Becoming a leader isn't easy, just as becoming a doctor or a poet isn't easy but each of us contains the capacity for leadership" (1993, 3). He goes on to discuss the role of instinct and luck for leaders, stressing that these are actually based on knowledge. Restating a dictum attributed to Vince Lombardi, Bennis asserts that luck is a combination of preparation and opportunity.

Espinosa correctly cites three major characteristics of successful leaders—possessing moral principles, vision, and courage. Each of these play pivotal roles in the lives of leaders. I would add two others from Bennis's list. The best leaders have a good understanding of who they are. They are able to separate others' perceptions of them from the reality. Bennis puts it this way: "Know thyself, then, means separating who you are and who you want to be from what the world thinks you are and wants you to be" (1993, 54). A final aspect of leadership is what is often referred to as *drive*. This concept differs somewhat from the usual meaning of the word, which is the desire to accomplish. Drive, as I use it here, is also about curiosity and integrity. Successful leaders must have a compulsion to learn and understand reality in a way that goes to the root issues of whatever they are examining. Leaders must not turn from failure but must see the opportunity to learn from mistakes. This drive for the truth also means leaders welcome dissent and see it as means toward a more complete understanding.

I was particularly pleased that Espinosa's chapter deals with the concept of the teacher as leader. Dokecki and Heflinger (1989) write about the importance of understanding the impact of policy both from the top down and from the bottom up. As we define and develop the services that are effective in assisting families with preparing the youngest citizens of our country and world for an uncertain future, our best hope is for those most intimately involved in the provision of those services to have their voices heard. We are now experimenting in an open market of a wide array of services, provided unevenly to families who have little ability to choose and vastly different resources for selecting among the choices that are available. We must rely on our teachers and directors of local programs to use their knowledge to help shape services that are effective for both parents and children and to help identify mechanisms for ensuring equity in the delivery of these services. Parents, teachers, and directors all have pivotal roles as leaders in this great endeavor.

References

Bennis, W. 1993. *On becoming a leader.* Reading, MA: Addison-Wesley.

Dokecki, P.R., & C.A. Heflinger. 1989. Strengthening families of young children with handicapping conditions: Mapping backward from the "street level." In *Policy implementation and PL 99-457: Planning for young children with special needs,* eds. J.J. Gallagher, P.L. Trohanis, & R.M. Clifford. Baltimore: Paul Brookes.

Katz, D., & R.L. Kahn. 1966. *The social psychology of organizations.* New York: John Wiley & Sons.

New Directions in Fostering Leadership

SECTION 4

Chapter 12

New Directions in Higher Education

Barbara T. Bowman

The field of early child care and education has changed greatly over the last 25 years. Early childhood programs are an increasing public concern, and policies regarding them are now debated in halls of Congress, corporate board rooms, and family living rooms, as well as in colleges and universities. Leadership must be inextricably tied to these debates because of its link to program quality (Phillips 1986; Howes, Phillips, & Whitebook 1992). One would expect colleges and universities to play a predominate role in developing professional knowledge and training professional leaders for careers in early childhood care and education, as they do in other professions. However, the early childhood profession is not structured in the same way as other professional groups, making it difficult for colleges and universities to respond to its leadership needs.

Most professions are organized along a career ladder with clear demarcations regarding the kind and amount of training required for leadership opportunities. A license to practice (based on a standard program of study) is the baseline for most professional practitioners, with graduate and postgraduate education providing pathways to leadership. This is not the model for the early childhood field, where there is little agreement regarding the kind or the amount of training needed for direct service providers, managers, trainers, or advocates. Despite 10 years of research that points to training as a critical variable in program quality (e.g., Ruopp 1979; Phillips 1986; Bloom 1990; Bloom & Sheerer 1992), the field has yet to define the different roles and responsibilities of early childhood leaders or the academic preparation and support needed to carry these out.

There are a number of reasons for the disorganized state. First, programs for children and families take place in diverse settings, operate under different auspices, deliver a variety of services, and are embedded in several different professions (such as psychology, education, special education, home economics, social work, health, and business administration). The field also responds to a number of institutional contexts (including public schools, child care centers, hospitals, community centers, and social service agencies), different delivery systems (commercial, governmental, and not-for-profit organizations), and different age ranges of children (infants, toddlers, preschoolers, kindergarten/primary graders)—each with its own outcome expectations and professional biases.

Second, the economic and regulatory pressures on the field discourage formal early childhood training, except for teachers and administrators in public schools. Licensing standards in most states have minimal educational requirements for staff, and wages in the field are low. Thus, there is little incentive to seek higher education.

Third, because early childhood programs are often used to encourage community action and provide employment for people in poor communities, there has been a traditional ambivalence regarding formal training and credentials. Many policymakers, parents, and members of the professional community do not see the benefit of baccalaureate and graduate degrees as the baseline for leadership positions. To require such degrees is often viewed as professional gatekeeping, unduly inflating educational requirements and driving up the cost of child care.

Shortcomings of professional preparation

In view of these complicating circumstances, the field so far has handled the leadership issue by designing a career ladder that has multiple entry points and alternative paths to practice and leadership and has avoided strict educational standards (Johnson & McCracken 1993). Unfortunately, this model does not mesh easily with the professional preparation traditions in institutions of higher education. In most professions the first requirement of leadership is mastery of a basic curriculum provided by a four-year college or graduate school, which leads to a license to practice. Professional leadership training builds on top of such a basic credential. The field of early care and education is different. Since few states have very stringent requirements for preschool teachers and caregivers' education, there is not a well-defined market for higher education. With the exception of public school teachers—who are required to get their first professional training in a four-year accredited teacher education program—students in early care and education may do their introductory work in high schools, vocational schools, or junior or senior colleges as well as in graduate schools.

Curricula for early childhood careers overlap at each of these academic levels (Bowman 1990). Teacher training at all levels contains similar content, and some community colleges provide leadership programs for administrators and directors of children's programs. This means there is not a large group of students at any level who have a core of academic experiences as a foundation for professional practice or movement into leadership positions. Therefore, most colleges and universities do not have standardized and well-defined leadership programs for those seeking careers in early care and education.

Not only does professional education overlap at different levels in colleges and universities, the knowledge base for early childhood career preparation overlaps different disciplines—education, psychology, and social service, to name a few. Thus, colleges and universities have trouble locating the appropriate department to provide training. As a consequence, preparation for careers in early childhood—when it has been included at all—is found in a variety of departments (home economics, education, child development, or social services) with different knowledge bases, different professional biases, and different principles of practice. This diversity of training enriches the field but fails to ensure a common core of professional knowledge, and potential leaders do not have a discipline or a college/university department deeply identified with their professional issues.

Despite these shortcomings, we should not be blind to the array of ideas in higher education that have relevance to preparing early childhood leaders. This chapter focuses on formal leadership programs in colleges and universities (primarily in four-year colleges and graduate schools) and notes some of their strengths and weaknesses as they affect early childhood leadership.

Professional preparation in colleges and universities

The interest of colleges and universities in leadership preparation is evident from the large number and types of programs described in catalogs as leadership oriented and from the amount of research on leadership in the academic literature. Although few of these are designed specifically for the field of early care and education, they do contribute to the training of early childhood leaders.

Definitions of leadership in the academy

As noted by Kagan and Neuman (chapter 7), interest in educational leadership is not new. The three most popular definitions of leadership in the academic literature are of visionary/inspirer, manager, and collaborator. The visionary/inspirer is characterized by Green (1994) as the "heroic" leader who has personal power and transcendent vision. In contrast, the management leader is best described as a technocrat who demonstrates such traits as decisiveness, efficiency, tough-mindedness, emotional blandness, and control (Rogers 1992). Both heroic and managerial leadership are characterized as top-down approaches.

Collaborative leadership is a more recent entry into the leadership literature. Having arisen from a new view of social, economic, and political relationships, it is described as transformational or empowering, acknowledging the usefulness of cooperation and teamwork. This view envisions a more diverse society in which people of particular castes and classes are not excluded from leadership roles and where professionals, paraprofessionals, and community members work as a team rather than in a rigid hierarchical order. Accordingly, collaborative leaders must be able to create partnerships between disparate groups and individuals (Green 1994), functioning as enabler, servant, collaborator, facilitator, and meaning-maker (Rogers 1992). Characterized as a bottom-up leadership style, collaborative leadership emphasizes consensus building, shared responsibility, and relationships.

All three aspects of leadership are needed by leaders (Lomotey 1993), whether they be in early childhood or in other fields. However, the configuration of early childhood programs—goals that promote the development of children *and* family, staffing patterns that make extensive use of paraprofessionals and volunteers, overlapping staffing roles, resource constraints, and egalitarian social missions—propels the field toward a definition of leadership that is collaborative, distributive, and consensual (Rodd 1994). It is reassuring that this definition is gaining ground in higher education among researchers, teacher educators, and school reform advocates, and many colleges and universities are moving their leadership programs toward teamwork, mutuality between home and school, interprofessional collaboration, and site- and community-based management.

Leadership and academic achievement

Colleges and universities place school achievement high on their list of desirable leadership traits. Judging from catalogs and applications for admission, most programs base acceptance of candidates primarily on prior educational achievement and the results of standardized tests rather than on evidence of other possible leadership characteristics. Presumably, good leaders are to be found among those individuals of great intellectual merit. Those who do not meet formal standards (test scores and grades) are unworthy of leadership opportunities. Less attention gets paid to other traits associated with leadership, such as the ability to "develop or inspire in others an ideological commitment to a particular point of view" (Frank 1993, 383), and leadership opportunities are limited by prior educational achievement.

Economically disadvantaged individuals and people of color are disproportionately blocked from leadership training because of their more limited access to higher education (see Moore, chapter 8). Thus, leadership programs in colleges and universities often act as gatekeepers, effectively excluding people who may have an affinity for leadership but do not have the required academic preparation. One of the challenges for the field is to build a pipeline to leadership programs for racial/ethnic minorities, particularly African Americans and Latinos (Castle 1993). Toward this end, colleges and universities will need to expand recruitment and retention of students, faculty, and administrators from underserved groups.

Leadership in public schools

By far the most common leadership programs are found in departments and schools of education, typically leading to a master's or doctoral degree and/or an administrator's certificate for practice in public schools. Good management predominates as the raison d'être of these programs, and the corporate model, emphasizing pragmatism and the bottom line, is widespread. These programs stress professional and administration courses; educational psychology, curriculum, research, pedagogy, school finance, school law, personnel management, and technology are among those most frequently offered. A review of course offerings in such programs substantiates what is often noted in the literature on leadership: *manager* and *leader* are terms used interchangeably.

Educational leadership tends to be generic and not specific to the institution to be led. For instance, the University of San Diego's doctor of education program is described as follows:

> Doctoral students develop their understanding of leadership through the study of current research and models of organizational behavior, change, policymaking, ethics, adult development and future studies. . . . Graduates can then use this leadership expertise in any professional area of society and in any organization, public or private, for-profit or not-for-profit. (University of San Diego 1994, 52)

Few educational administration programs identify early childhood as a target for leadership training. A review of recruitment catalogs shows that leadership programs offer courses in curriculum without mention of how the characteristics (philosophical, theoretical, or pedagogical biases) of programs for young children and families might affect leadership. Leithwood (1994) explains the disinterest in early childhood as reflecting the belief that leadership training is more important for secondary-school leaders than for those in elementary, much less primary, education. He contends that the size and complexity of the secondary-school curriculum and the amount of pedagogical content knowledge required for expert teaching require extensive and unique preparation. Early childhood programs are evidently viewed as being simpler because the content (caregiving and curricula) is more widely understood. It is not at all clear, however, that directors of early childhood settings require fewer skills and less knowledge than school administrators; certainly no case can be made that their positions are less important. Although many of the practices in colleges and universities are not supportive of early childhood leadership, some aspects resonate well with the needs of leaders in the field of early care and education.

Probably the most significant change in the thinking about leadership for public schools is the increasing emphasis on teachers as leaders. The traditional top-down approach that is the norm, particularly in large urban school districts, has been challenged by reformers who want to vest greater power in the hands of teachers. Central to this movement is the National Board for Professional Teaching Standards (NBPTS), formed to certify expert teachers as professional leaders. The goal of this organization is to "elevate the teaching profession, educate the public about the demands and complexity of excellent practice, and increase our chance of attracting and retaining . . . talented college graduates with many other promising career options" (NBPTS 1995, preface). The early childhood standards call for expert teachers to not only provide exemplary education in their own classrooms but also to be able to

> evaluate school progress and the allocation of school resources in light of their understanding of state and local educational objectives. They are knowledgeable about specialized school and community resources that can be engaged for their students' benefit, and are skilled at employing such resources as needed. (NBPTS 1995, 4)

These standards imply a much broader definition of teacher role than is traditional in public schools, vesting teachers with leadership responsibilities for curricula, school improvement, and community relations. While there is considerable enthusiasm in colleges and universities for an expanded role for teachers, it is unclear how teacher education programs will respond to this new definition. Whether the content of teacher training and graduate work in education will change substantively as a result of the new standards is yet to be seen.

The knowledge base for early childhood leadership

An essential component of effective leadership is a sound knowledge base. The care and education of young children was not sufficiently widespread to command much attention from academic researchers until 25 years ago. With an explosion of research on young children and their families, program qualities, and collaborative planning and service integration, a new theoretical framework is developing (Bowman 1993; Stott & Bowman 1996). It crosses discipline boundaries and draws on a broad range of social and biological sciences to explain the complexity of human development and lay the basis for professional practice. In the past, university researchers frequently were not concerned with the practical implications of their research or with how it could guide practice in the real world. New perception of the role of research requires balancing experimental methods with real-life and meaning-derived models and creating partnerships among field-based researchers, practitioners, and the subjects themselves, with the goal of improving the lives of the people being studied. Thus, data is increasingly collected and interpreted in the context of program, making it more relevant and applicable to

practitioners and advocates. The new transdisciplinary, collaborative research fits well with the family-supportive and culturally responsive approach of many early childhood programs and has strongly influenced the development of early childhood practice guidelines (Bredekamp & Copple [1987] 1997).

The school reform movement also has spawned a wealth of early childhood research that has become part of the knowledge base of the field. This research, showing the potential of early childhood programs to change outcomes for vulnerable children (e.g., Berrueta-Clement et al. 1984; Hubell et al. 1985; NASBE 1988; Schorr 1988), has become pivotal, providing conceptual frameworks for policy analysts; coalescing support for early intervention, preschool education, and child care for young children at risk of educational failure; and providing a foundation for professional training.

Diversity and leadership

The consequences of racial and class divisions are seen by many as inimical to the country's economic and social well-being. A segment of American society still yearns for simpler days when lip service to democratic values was the hallmark of leadership and the realities of inequality were ignored, but many reformers in the last half of the 20th century have warned of the need for a more egalitarian, moral, and ethical society if we are to maintain world leadership. Since many early childhood programs are designed to address class and caste inequities, the field has a vested interest in how higher education responds to this issue (Zigler & Valentine 1978; Comer 1980; Arends 1990; DHHS 1993).

Giroux (1992) would place schools of education in the forefront to ensure the survival of the United States as a vibrant, democratic society. He says they should act as a "catalyst for a more inclusive and democratic model of society" (p. 5).

> The most important task facing educators is not collecting data or managing competencies but constructing a pedagogical and political vision which recognizes that the problems with American schools lie in the realm of values, ethics, and vision. Educating for democracy begins not with test scores but with the following questions: What kinds of citizens do we hope to produce through public education? What kind of society do we want to create? This involves educating students to live in a critical democracy and suggests a view of empowerment in which learning becomes the basis for challenging social practices that produce symbolic and real violence, that make some students voiceless and powerless, and that also implicate teachers in forms of bigotry, colonialism, and racism. (p. 8)

It is apparent that most colleges and universities have not taken Giroux's (1992) advice seriously.

Studies characterized by critical analysis do not show up in education and/or leadership curricula descriptions. On the other hand, the need of leaders to balance the world views, developmental norms, and codes of conduct of diverse groups with the goals and objectives of children's programs is receiving more attention than it has in the past. In the effort to help leaders meet the challenges inherent in diversity, many programs have added courses to leadership curricula that stress cultural sensitivity. Many schools and departments of education now require courses in multiculturalism, antibias practice, and school/home relations that focus on parent and community involvement in school and center activities.

In recent years, many colleges/universities, government agencies, and foundations have organized supportive services to encourage disadvantaged students to matriculate in and complete higher education programs and to join the pool of potential leaders. Recruitment and retention programs generally include special scholarships, mentoring, tutoring, and supportive groups. However, pressure to derail affirmative action presently threatens the ideal of diversity in institutions of higher education.

Innovations in leadership programs

Colleges and universities are beginning to infuse their courses with new concepts of leadership that are of particular interest to early childhood professionals. These include interdisciplinary education, problem solving, relationship-based education, reflective practices, performance assessment, and continuing education.

Interdisciplinary education. New interdisciplinary and transdisciplinary professional education programs are gaining a toehold as a few colleges and universities experiment with joint training programs in various combinations of social work, education, nursing, business, and law (Manthey 1992; Seltz 1995). The purpose of interdisciplinary programs is for students to learn to negotiate in multiservice organizations and develop collaborative relationships with other professionals. Characteristics of collaborative leadership include collegiality and mutual respect and trust, and the development of a community of learners. Team building also has been given high priority in both the school reform and collaboration literature.

The collaboration movement was stimulated by the 1995 Conference on Interprofessional Education and Training sponsored by the University of Washington's Human Services Policy Center, the University of Southern California's Inter Professional Initiative, and California State University's (Fullerton) Center for Collaboration for Children. This conference, attended by representatives of a number of colleges and universities, addressed effective interprofessional programs: goals, curriculum models, community/practice issues, evaluation, university change, and systems reform.

Problem-based instruction. Another strategy for developing leadership capabilities has come to be known as problem-based learning. Case material permits students to learn in the context of solving real problems. For instance, Stanford University's Prospective Principals Program provides hands-on training for would-be principals, who share their problems and solutions with one another, thus creating their own simulations. In programs such as these, leadership is redefined as collaborative rather than authoritarian, inclusive of all stakeholders and encompassing a common vision (Asayesh 1993).

Relationship-based education. Much of early childhood leadership revolves around relationships with deep personal meaning. Caring for other people's children is a complex activity, and the relationships among the various players are often emotionally charged. Leaders of early care and education programs must have highly developed ability to interact with parents, staff, children, and community members and be able to tolerate the uncertainty and frustration that often come with these relationships. Relationship-based education views interactions between and among people as the primary vehicle of change in organizations and contends that leadership in the social services requires a personal experience with and understanding of human interaction. Therefore, leadership programs ideally promote opportunities to form relationships with both supervisors and peers, permitting the student to extrapolate a parallel process for children, families, and colleagues (Stott & Bowman 1996).

Reflection. Reflection on practice is increasingly considered an essential attribute of effective practice and therefore of professional leadership (Schon 1983, 1987; Bowman 1989; Ellis & Macrina 1994). Through reflection and discussion with peers, teachers, and mentors, the professional transforms theoretical and general ideas into a meaningful practice framework. Schon (1983, 1987) notes that the practice of teaching is an art that eludes technical description, analysis, and systematization. The art of practice is not merely a means to an end or a search for solutions; rather, it weaves means and ends, with a goal of transforming through understanding. With reflection in and on action, one can intelligently, even intuitively, adjust one's practice. Reflective strategies focus on helping potential leaders reorganize how they think about a problem, integrate new information (without distorting it) to serve old theories, and encourage practitioners to generate and check explanations for their behavior and that of others (Stott & Bowman 1994). Reflection that draws on one's past experience has long been important to teachers of young children. A number of models for thoughtful inquiry or teacher reflection are used in early childhood programs (Jones 1986; Bowman 1989).

Values are critical to any discussion of leadership, but Asayesh (1993) points out that the central values for schools are practical skills designed to promote high-quality education for all and in an environment in which everyone is respected and valued. He advocates focusing on site-based management, collaborative relationships, and linkages of schools to social services. These innovations move the field away from simplistic, standardized models of education and toward complex, flexible, and diverse solutions—models better suited to early childhood education.

Performance assessment. Leaders invariably encounter competing priorities, clashes between approaches to practice, poorly conceived policies, and differences in cultural experiences and values. New assessment strategies are being developed that are more consistent with definitions of leadership as complex and situational. Instead of sampling knowledge and skills, leadership programs see the need to evaluate students in real contexts. Performance assessment, or measuring the ability of a person to apply ideas and concepts by relating them to real-life situations or simulations, is gaining adherents. Portfolios are an increasingly popular vehicle for leadership students to demonstrate their competence (Barnett 1995). Portfolios might include case studies, educational platforms or philosophies, term papers, journals, budgets, economic forecasts, video/audiotapes, memos, letters, professional development plans, or student handbooks.

Continuing education. University participation in continuing education in schools, centers, and other human services organizations through nondegree or noncredit courses also has increased over the past decade—e.g., the University of North Carolina Leadership Training Program at Chapel Hill. Higher education programs for practitioners vary from one-day workshops and yearlong certificate courses to taking responsibility for entire schools and school systems. Frequent topics for continuing education programs include team building, home/school/community relationships, collaboration skills, and school restructuring—topics central to early childhood leadership.

New directions for early childhood leadership preparation

Without a related career ladder, colleges and universities are likely to continue to squeeze potential leaders of the early care and education field into their already existing programs. If this is to change, the field itself must take the lead in conceptualizing leadership roles in relationship to professional education in institutions of higher education (see recommendations in chapter 18).

The author makes the following recommendations for consideration by the field:

1. Focus on leadership. In the past, through licensing standards and government funding of the Child Development Associate credential and training, emphasis has been placed on preparing entry-level employees to work in centers and schools. However, the economics of the field make this an increasingly less viable approach as turnover among new workers escalates, amounting to a training hemorrhage. A new way of structuring the career ladder for those not participating in a degree program might be to offer entry-level training as inservice and delay formal academics until workers are sure of their interest and commitment. Such a change would necessitate leadership personnel able to provide introductory training and to supervise new workers, thereby placing the onus of responsibility on the leaders rather than on new teachers/caregivers.

2. Clarify the professional career ladder and its relationship to formal education. For the field to flourish and exert effective leadership, it must come to grips with its traditional ambivalence on academic preparation. One option is to tie leaders at different levels (classroom, center, organization) and of different types (professional, advocacy, managerial, and policy) to specific formal education and experience. This would require collaboration between higher education and professional leadership organizations, such as the National Association for the Education of Young Children and the Council for Professional Recognition, to differentiate the career ladder and advocate for its acceptance by schools, government, and not-for-profit organizations.

3. Develop a consensus regarding the levels for professional knowledge. Given the diversity of the field, what are the skills and knowledge that should be incorporated into each level of professional education? As pointed out, a remarkable similarity exists among professional preparation programs at the junior, senior, and graduate levels (NAEYC 1996). While it is legitimate to be open and share knowledge with all people who work with children, our haphazard preparation model often inadequately grounds potential leaders in professional knowledge. For instance, many organizations routinely place teachers with B.A. degrees in leadership positions, yet courses in administration of early childhood programs are not usually a part of baccalaureate programs, particularly in colleges of education, where training is likely to be directed almost entirely toward classroom teaching. Thus many potential leaders complete their bachelor degrees with little understanding of their role in working with parents and supervising adult assistants. How much and what kind of knowledge leaders should have and at what level of academic complexity are serious questions. Perhaps we should wait until the graduate level to focus on theory and research, mainly addressing principles of practice during the first few steps of the career ladder. This might avoid the mindless devotion to poorly understood theories and research that leads many practitioners to be simplistic in their views on practice. The National Association for the Education of Young Children has revised its *Guidelines for Preparation of Early Childhood Professionals* (NAEYC 1996), distinguishing the competencies to be achieved at each educational level. However, by focusing on competencies, which may indeed overlap in practice, the curriculum content necessary for each level is ignored. A more rigorous effort is needed to delineate the content and complexity for each level.

4. Develop a graduate-level leadership knowledge base. The scope of early childhood leadership curricula has had little attention either in the field or in colleges and universities. Only a few institutions specifically focus on graduate-level leadership for early childhood programs (see Morgan et al. 1993)—one notable exception is the Bank Street College, Erikson Institute, Pacific Oaks College, and Wheelock College consortium formed to strengthen their ability to do research, share innovative practices, and contribute to the discussion of public policy and professional development. The following components, I believe, should be included in all graduate-level early childhood leadership programs:

• child development, from which appropriate program strategies are derived;

• family support and guidance and community culture;

• working knowledge of the role of allied professionals (social workers, health care providers, adult educators, community and career development specialists) as well as of different early childhood systems (day care, early intervention, preschool, and parent education and support);

• supervision and adult education;

• management and finances; and

• advocacy.

5. Develop a national leadership credential. Although many organizations give preference for leadership positions to candidates with advanced degrees, there is little similarity in the skills and knowledge such degrees represent. This flexibility permits exceptional individuals to rise to leadership positions, but it also means that many inadequately prepared people are in leadership roles. If the field is to move forward in a unified way, it is essential to create quickly a system that requires and validates higher education requirements.

Before colleges and universities can be more responsive to the needs of the field, we must resolve our own differences. Changes such as those noted above will require considerable work by the field itself. We must stabilize a career ladder and organize a system to encourage and facilitate leadership training. Perhaps this volume will stimulate thought and action in these areas.

References

Arends, R. 1990. Connecting the university to the school. In *Changing school culture through staff development* (1990 yearbook), ed. B. Joyce. Alexandria, VA: Association for Supervision and Curriculum Development.

Asayesh, G. 1993. Cultivating educational leadership. *Journal of Staff Development* 14 (3): 12–16.

Barnett, B. 1995. Portfolio use in educational leadership preparation programs: From theory to practice. *Innovative Higher Education* 19 (3): 197–205.

Berrueta-Clement, J., L. Schweinhart, W. Barnett, A. Epstein, & D. Weikart. 1984. *Changed lives: The effects of the Perry Preschool Program on youths through age 19.* Ypsilanti, MI: High/Scope.

Bloom, P.J. 1990. The child care center directors: Policy perspectives on increasing requisite qualifications. *Early Education and Development* 1 (3): 185–204.

Bloom, P.J., & M. Sheerer. 1992. The effect of leadership training on child care program quality. *Early Childhood Research Quarterly* 7 (4): 579–94.

Bowman, B. 1989. Self-reflection as an element of professionalism. *Teachers College Record* 90 (3): 444–51.

Bowman, B. 1990. Recruitment and retention of teachers. In *Early childhood teacher preparation*, eds. B. Spodek & O. Saracho. New York: Teachers College Press.

Bowman, B. 1993. Early childhood education. In *Review of research in education*, Vol. 19, ed. L. Darling-Hammond. Washington, DC: American Educational Research Association.

Bowman, B., & F. Stott. 1996. Understanding development in a cultural context: The challenge for teaching. In *Diversity and developmentally appropriate practices: Challenges for early childhood education*, eds. B.L. Mallory & R.S. New. New York: Teachers College Press.

Bredekamp, S., & C. Copple, eds. [1987] 1997. *Developmentally appropriate practice in early childhood programs*. Rev. ed. Washington, DC: NAEYC.

Castle, E. 1993. Minority student attrition research: Higher education's challenge for human resource development. *Educational Researcher* 33 (7): 24–30.

Comer, J.P. 1980. *School power: Implications of an intervention project.* New York: Free Press.

DHHS (U.S. Department of Health and Human Services). 1993. *Creating a 21st century Head Start: Final report of the Advisory Committee on Head Start Quality and Expansion.* Washington, DC: Author.

Ellis, A., & A. Macrina. 1994. Reflection and self-appraisal in preparing new principals. *Journal of Staff Development* 15 (1): 10–14.

Frank, M. 1993. The essence of leadership. *Public Personnel Management* 22 (3): 381–89.

Giroux, H. 1992. Educational leadership and the crisis of democratic government. *Educational Researcher* 21 (4): 4–11.

Green, M. 1994. Not for wimps or cowards: Leadership in the post-heroic age. *Educational Record* 75 (3): 55–65.

Howes, C., D. Phillips, & M. Whitebook. 1992. Thresholds of quality: Implications for the social development of children in center-based child care. *Child Development* 63 (2): 449–60.

Hubell, R., L. Condelli, H. Ganson, B. Barrett, C. McConkey, & M. Plantz. 1985. *Final report of the impact of Head Start on children, families, and communities: Head Start evaluation, synthesis, and utilization project.* Washington, DC: Administration for Children, Youth and Families, Office of Human Development Services, Department of Health and Human Services.

Johnson, J., & J.B. McCracken, eds. 1993. *The early childhood career lattice: Perspectives on professional development.* Washington, DC: NAEYC.

Jones, E. 1986. *Teaching adults: An active learning approach.* Washington, DC: NAEYC.

Leithwood, K. 1994. Leadership for school restructuring. *Educational Administration Quarterly* 30 (4): 498–518.

Lomotey, D. 1993. African-American principals: Bureaucrat/administrators and ethno-humanists. *Urban Education* 27 (4): 395–412.

Manthey, M. 1992. Issues in practice. Leadership: A shifting paradigm. *Nurse Educator* 17 (5): 5–14.

Morgan, G, S. Azer, J. Costley, A. Genser, I. Goodman, M. Lombardi, & B. McGimsey. 1993. *Making a career of it.* Boston: Center for Career Development in Early Care and Education, Wheelock College.

NAEYC. 1993. A conceptual framework for early childhood professional development. In *The early childhood career lattice: Perspectives on professional development,* eds. J. Johnson & J.B. McCracken. Washington, DC: Author.

NAEYC. 1996. Guidelines for early childhood professional preparation programs at the associate, baccalaureate, and advanced levels. In *Guidelines for preparation of early childhood professionals.* Washington, DC: Author.

NASBE (National Association of State Boards of Education). 1988. *Right from the start.* Alexandria, VA: Author.

NBPTS (National Board for Professional Teaching Standards). 1995. *Early childhood generalist standards for national board certification.* Detroit: Author.

Phillips, D., ed. 1986. *Quality in child care.* Washington, DC: NAEYC.

Rodd, J. 1994. *Leadership in early childhood: The pathway to professionalism.* New York: Teachers College Press.

Rogers, J. 1992. Leadership development for the '90s: Incorporating emergent paradigm perspective. *NASPA Journal* 29 (4): 243–52.

Ruopp, R. 1979. *Children at the center: Summary findings and their implications.* Cambridge, MA: Abt.

Schon, D.A. 1983. *The reflective practitioner: How professionals think in action.* New York: Basic.

Schon, D.A. 1987. *Educating the reflective practitioner: Toward a new design for teaching and learning in the profession.* San Francisco: Jossey-Bass.

Schorr, L. 1988. *Within our reach: Breaking the cycle of disadvantage.* New York: Anchor.

Seltz, J. 1995. A collaborative approach to professional development. *Journal of Continuing Higher Education* 43 (1): 44–53.

Stott, F., & B. Bowman. 1994. Child development knowledge: A slippery base for practice. *Early Childhood Research Quarterly* 11 (2): 169–83.

University of San Diego. 1994. *University catalogue.* San Diego, CA: Author.

Zigler, E., & J. Valentine, eds. 1979. *Project Head Start: A legacy of the War on Poverty.* New York: Macmillan.

Chapter 13

New Directions for Professional Organizations

Sue Bredekamp

Professional organizations play a unique and key role in leadership development. This chapter describes the current and potential roles in leadership development for the various early childhood professional organizations. Following a brief description of the existing organizations and their missions is a framework for conceptualizing early childhood leadership functions. The chapter concludes with a discussion of some possible new roles for professional organizations.

In this chapter, *leadership* is defined as the capacity to influence the opinions and/or actions of others. The framework suggested here identifies three key areas of influence for early childhood leaders: quality for children, knowledge about children, and advocacy on behalf of children.

Early childhood professional organizations

In general the mission of any professional organization is to improve the quality of services provided on behalf of the profession. Organizations typically achieve this mission by providing educational opportunities for members—the professionals—most often through publications such as regular journals and books, conferences, and affiliation opportunities in local communities that provide networking and advocacy for shared goals. The more traditional professional organizations in medicine, law, and education establish the criteria for and control admittance to the profession through specifying the credentials required to practice.

Early childhood education has a strong history of professional organizations, although not of the traditional variety. The largest such organization, the

National Association for the Education of Young Children, founded in 1926, has more than 96,000 members, most of whom belong through one of more than 425 local, state, and regional Affiliate groups. NAEYC publishes a refereed journal, *Young Children*, and more than 200 books, videotapes, and brochures, and it sponsors one of the largest educational conferences in the country. NAEYC also sponsors a national accreditation system for early childhood programs, promotes standards for professional preparation of early childhood educators, and promulgates a code of ethical conduct for the field.

NAEYC is not strictly a professional organization because it has no qualifications for membership. Traditional professional associations such as the American Academy of Pediatrics or the National Association of Social Workers require that members be qualified physicians or social workers respectively; NAEYC, on the other hand, welcomes not only early childhood educators with vastly different backgrounds in the field but also pediatricians and social workers and parents with no early childhood training.

But NAEYC is only one of many organizations serving the early childhood profession; for example, more than 100 liaison organizations regularly meet in conjunction with the NAEYC Annual Conference. Most of these professional organizations have similar missions—improving quality for children through education and advocacy—for a more focused sector of the profession. Among the many early childhood professional organizations are some, such as the National Head Start Association, the National Black Child Development Institute, and the Division for Early Childhood of the Council for Exceptional Children, that have been in existence more than 25 years. They serve important functions of education and advocacy through publications, conferences, and projects. Their local and state affiliate groups provide essential vehicles for acquisition and demonstration of leadership skills at multiple levels.

The National Association of Child Care Resource and Referral Agencies has a shorter history but is now well established as the professional organization for resource-and-referral personnel. The National Association of Early Childhood Specialists in State Departments of Education, in existence since the mid-1970s, is a relatively small organization, but it provides important collaboration opportunities to members who serve in key policy-related leadership positions in each state. The Society for Research in Child Development promotes research in human development and fosters the exchange of information among researchers and professionals of various disciplines.

Another group of early childhood professional organizations with a shorter history (10 to 15 years) is growing rapidly and contributing important professional development for members, through publication of journals or newsletters and at regular meetings. These organizations, which rely almost entirely on volunteers for support, include the National Association of Early Childhood Teacher Educators (NAECTE); American Associate Degree Early Childhood Educators (ACCESS); the National Association for Family Child Care (NAFCC); and the National School-Age Care Alliance (NSACA). NAFCC sponsors a national accreditation system for family child care homes, and NSACA is piloting an accreditation system for school-age care programs.

Leadership development in early childhood education is also stimulated by other organizations that are not professional organizations because they do not have membership structures, but they serve many of the same purposes of education and advocacy. These include the Children's Defense Fund, the Council for Early Childhood Professional Recognition (which administers the Child Development Associate credentialing program), the National Center for the Early Childhood Work Force, the Center for Career Development in Early Care and Education at Wheelock College, and ZERO TO THREE, the National Center for Infants, Toddlers, and Families.

Finally, in recent years the field has seen proliferation of many specialized organizations that may or may not survive long term but that clearly identify the need for leadership development and support of various sectors of the field. Among these are the Early Childhood Directors Association and the Primary Grades Interest Group.

Leadership development functions for professional organizations

Before we can identify roles for professional organizations in leadership development, we must first identify the kinds of leadership positions that exist in the various institutions serving the diverse field of early childhood education. In an oversimplification of the highly complex and diverse delivery system that characterizes the field, early childhood professionals hold leadership positions in three general types of institutions: (1) programs or schools that care for and educate young children from birth through age 8; (2) programs, including institutions of higher education, that prepare adults to work with young children; and (3) organizations and agencies that provide indirect services designed to support the delivery of high-quality care and education for young children and their families. Each of these types of institution requires a somewhat different type of leadership ability.

Programs for children require administrators whose primary role beyond management is to be educational *quality* leaders. Research demonstrates the key role that directors of child care centers play in influencing the quality of care and education provided for young children (Bloom 1992; Bloom & Sheerer 1992). Likewise, principals of primary schools are key figures in ensuring effective, high-quality education. They, too, must be educational quality leaders. Early childhood professionals need to see a school principalship as a legitimate career goal. Schools provide a potential career trajectory with much leadership potential: teacher, mentor teacher, principal, even school board member.

Programs that prepare adults to work with young children—institutions of higher education, for instance—require another kind of early childhood leader: a *conceptual* leader (see Kagan and Neuman's discussion of conceptual leadership in chapter 7). Faculty at these institutions not only translate knowledge into practice for their students but also expand the base of knowledge and theory.

The third grouping of institutions requiring leaders—organizations and agencies—is somewhat harder to categorize because it includes diverse types of institutions ranging from resource-and-referral agencies to state departments of education to regulatory agencies, with varying missions, and includes the professional associations themselves. These types of institutions require another kind of leader: a *political* leader. Whether the politics are congressional or internal, the ability to influence the opinions of others, persuading them to take specific action or change their behavior, is a prerequisite for successful leaders of organizations and agencies.

Of course, this framework of educational quality and political leadership is overly simplistic. Child care center directors or school principals would immediately argue that their job requires far more political acumen than they ever anticipated. Likewise, the best college faculty member is not just a conceptual leader but also a quality leader, teaching prospective teachers to demonstrate standards of practice while also questioning current conceptualizations of quality. The truth is, the most effective leaders in every type of early childhood institution demonstrate ability in all three categories: educational quality leadership, conceptual leadership, and political leadership.

How is this type of leadership developed and whose responsibility is it? No one strategy is sufficient to develop leaders with these multiple capacities; such leadership can best be developed through experiences in multiple sectors. These experiences can be provided through identification with multiple role models and/or mentors; through meaningful work experiences, both paid and volunteer; and through higher education opportunities that combine experience with theory. Each of the three types of early childhood institution can support leadership development in all these ways. But professional organizations are perhaps the most likely vehicle through which all these leadership opportunities can be provided without the restrictions that necessarily accompany more formal institutions (for instance, financial barriers to higher education or experience prerequisites for certain jobs).

Early childhood professional organizations are especially suited for this purpose because they do not restrict membership officially. Nevertheless, inclusive membership policies do not necessarily ensure diversity of membership and participation—diversity of all kinds, including ethnic and racial, gender, age, and work role (NBCDI 1993; NAEYC 1994). Professional organizations cannot fully achieve their potential for identifying and developing leaders until they first tackle the issue of diversifying their own memberships. We turn now to a discussion of roles for professional organizations in providing leadership opportunities in multiple sectors for diverse individuals.

New roles for professional organizations

Because leaders of tomorrow will need to be quality, conceptual, and political leaders, leadership development initiatives should enhance capacity in all these areas. Professional organizations have specific roles related to each of these functions. First, through their consensus-building processes and perceived authority to act on behalf of a profession, professional organizations set the standards for quality practice. Several examples of this role currently exist or are evolving. Accreditation systems are the most obvious example of professional organizations assuming responsibility for defining quality by setting standards. In early childhood, NAEYC's accreditation system sets standards and recognizes programs that achieve substantial compliance, but it also provides a career ladder of sorts for professionals to exercise leadership roles as directors of accredited program, validators, mentors, or commissioners[1] (NAEYC 1991). In addition, various community collaboration models, which assist programs in achieving accreditation, provide new leadership roles—mentor, consultant, trainer (see Bredekamp & Glowacki 1996).

Accreditation systems in family child care (Cohen & Modigliani 1994; Hollestelle 1994) and in school-age care (O'Connor 1994) provide or are developing similar professional development opportunities for those sectors of the field. The National Head Start Association sponsors a Quality Initiative that sets standards and evaluates performance of Head Start agencies, focusing on the administrative aspects of quality. NHSA also sponsors an administrative fellows program in collaboration with the University of California at Los Angeles and funded by Johnson & Johnson. For many years, the CDA credentialing program has provided leadership roles to implement the system: advisor, trainer, and CDA representative (who assesses candidates' competence). Initiatives such as these serve several leadership development functions. They provide guidance and focus for the paid role of the quality leader in programs for children and they also provide multiple volunteer roles for the members of the professional organization who participate in the various systems. To ensure that these opportunities include the fullest potential for leadership development, professional organizations have an additional responsibility to adequately train the volunteers for these roles.

Professional organizations play a key role in fostering development of conceptual leaders. One of the primary missions of a professional organization is to provide members with the most current, accurate knowledge about practice in their field. This service is an essential element in the development of conceptual leaders. Professional organizations provide vehicles for conceptual leaders to share as well as develop their expertise by publishing articles, making presentations at conferences, or conducting training sessions. At times, professional organizations assign themselves the role of conceptual leader, as NAEYC does when it develops position statements on issues of controversy (see, for example, NAEYC 1994; Bredekamp & Copple 1997), when NHSA advises policy leaders about the best ways of enhancing the Head Start program, or when NBCDI recommends appropriate classroom practices for African American children (NBCDI 1987).

In most professions, conceptual leaders are found primarily in institutions of higher education; faculty at colleges and universities are by definition conceptual leaders of their chosen fields. In early childhood, leadership development support is needed for faculty at two-year and four-year institutions. Unfortunately, early childhood faculty frequently work in isolation, lack colleagues with whom to develop new concepts, and work with limited resources, under difficult working conditions and with minimal status (Morgan et al. 1993). Within their own field, where they should be respected and venerated as role models, college faculty are sometimes vilified. At public meetings such as NAEYC conferences, professor bashing is common; early childhood educators who work directly with children in many different settings sometimes perceive college faculty as unrealistic or out of touch. A huge irony exists in this conflicting view of higher education, since the path to success as leaders is through higher education, as the NBCDI report (1993) emphasized. To ensure continued long-term production of conceptual leaders as well as legitimacy as a profession, the field of early childhood education must reinforce the leadership capacity of faculty in higher education and strengthen NAECTE and ACCESS, the organizations whose primary purpose is professional development of conceptual leaders.

In an era of tight resources and strongly competing voices, political leaders are needed at every level, especially at state and local levels as power and control of resources becomes more decentralized. The development of advocacy skills no longer can be reserved for the few whose job roles specifically demand it but rather must be considered an essential element of core content (Whitebook 1994; Bloom 1995). Professional organizations include advocacy as part of their missions and provide opportunities for public policy work through their local and state affiliate groups and in various volunteer roles.

The challenge for the future is for professional organizations not just to provide opportunities to demonstrate leadership but also to provide systematic strategies for recruiting and developing quality, conceptual, and political leadership skills. Ideally, to promote optimum results, these initiatives would be collaborative. Such initiatives have already begun in some professional organizations. For instance, NAEYC

and the National Head Start Association provide leadership training for their affiliate presidents, and both organizations plan to do more in the future. Through its National Institute for Early Childhood Professional Development, NAEYC conducts specific training institutes designed to help develop the capacity of Affiliate leaders to communicate and advocate for the positions of the association. In 1995 the Head Start Bureau of the U.S. Department of Health and Human Services announced a Head Start Fellows Program that provides mid-career fellowships for early childhood professionals in government agencies and professional organizations. These fellowships have the potential to provide a whole new cadre of early childhood leaders with mentors and meaningful work experiences in multiple sectors of the field. The National Black Child Development Institute has launched a new initiative with support from the Ford Foundation to develop action plans for increasing the number of African Americans in leadership positions in the early childhood profession. The project is an excellent example of how a professional organization can promote collaboration across various institutions; as its purpose states, "The project is designed to influence both institutions and organizations in the field, and will involve Historically Black Colleges, NBCDI's network of affiliates, as well as early childhood professionals" (NBCDI 1995, np).

Some initiatives sponsored through institutions of higher education have great potential for building collaborations with professional organizations. For example, the Robert R. McCormick Tribune Foundation is sponsoring a leadership development program at National-Louis University in which child care center directors obtain master's degrees and their programs achieve NAEYC accreditation (National Academy of Early Childhood Programs 1995). Such a program is an excellent model for combining experience with theory to improve practice. More higher education programs need to require or provide opportunities for internships, not just in programs for young children or as teachers of adults but in professional organizations and agencies. This strategy is strongly encouraged by NAEYC's revised guidelines for early childhood professional preparation at the basic and advanced levels, which are approved by the National Council for Accreditation of Teacher Education and thus required of institutions seeking NCATE accreditation (NAEYC 1995).

The most common and traditional role of professional organizations—establishing criteria for entrance to and promotion within the profession—has yet to be embraced by any early childhood organization. In fact, when NAEYC theoretically proposed such an entrance point and steps on a career lattice, the concept was met with considerable opposition (Bredekamp 1991; Bredekamp & Willer 1992). The field continues to embrace an inclusive view of itself (Morgan 1994) yet it also laments its perennial low status, inadequate salaries, and poor working conditions (Whitebook et al. 1990; Willer 1990). As long as there is an unlimited supply of unqualified workers for positions in the field, wages will be suppressed. Given this economic fact, some people argue that a legitimate role for professional organizations or government is establishment of required licensure for early childhood practitioners (Mitchell 1995; Kagan & Cohen in press). Such a move by any of the existing early childhood professional organizations would constitute a major departure from past practice. Gatekeeping, while not a particularly innovative idea among professional organizations in general, would be a new role for early childhood professional organizations, one that would take many years to gain acceptance and support.

Building personal relationships is not a new role for professional organizations either, but it is a critical one that needs considerable nurturing in every early childhood organization. So much of development of every kind is the result of personal relationships (Malaguzzi 1993; Berk & Winsler 1995). And mentoring is one of the most important strategies for developing leaders in any profession. Leaders of today commonly point to mentors as their most important professional influences. In fact, mentoring is so important to leadership development that professional organizations should not leave it to chance. Systematic strategies are needed for organizations to build mentoring skills in leaders, provide time and opportunities for mentor/protégé relationships to develop, and support efforts to recruit new and diverse leaders for the field.

Where will tomorrow's early childhood leaders come from? Most of them are already working or being trained in the field—in center-based and family child care programs, colleges and universities, and agencies. Certainly our field does not lack people with the capacity to become effective leaders, but individuals do not automatically develop the skills and knowledge they need to lead successfully. As a field we must find ways to provide training, mentoring, and other forms of support crucial to developing tomorrow's leaders. Recognizing that in the early childhood field our leadership needs to be as diverse as the children and families we serve, we must not only recruit broadly but also provide pathways to increased knowledge and skills for people from various backgrounds.

Note

1. Under the accreditation system, validators are on-site visitors, mentors are facilitators and disseminators of accreditation information, and commissioners are individuals who make accreditation decisions.

References

Berk, L., & A. Winsler. 1995. *Scaffolding children's learning: Vygotsky for early childhood educators.* Washington, DC: NAEYC.

Bloom, P.J. 1992. The child care center director: A critical determinant of program quality. *Educational Horizons* 70 (Spring): 138–45.

Bloom, P.J. 1995. Advocacy: An essential element of professional preparation. Paper presented at the annual conference of the National Institute for Early Childhood Professional Development, 7 June, San Francisco.

Bloom, P.J., & M. Sheerer. 1992. The effect of leadership training on child care program quality. *Early Childhood Research Quarterly* 7 (4): 579–94.

Bredekamp, S. 1991. A vision for early childhood professional development. *Young Children* 47 (1): 35–37.

Bredekamp, S., & C. Copple, eds. [1987] 1997. *Developmentally appropriate practice in early childhood programs.* Rev. ed. Washington, DC: NAEYC.

Bredekamp, S., & S. Glowacki. 1996. The first decade of NAEYC accreditation: Growth and impact on the field. *Young Children* 51 (3): 38–44.

Bredekamp, S., & B. Willer. 1992. Of ladders and lattices, cores and cones: Conceptualizing an early childhood professional development system. *Young Children* 47 (3): 47–50.

Cohen, N., & K. Modigliani. 1994. The Family-to-Family Project: Developing family child care providers. In *The early childhood career lattice: Perspectives on professional development,* eds. J. Johnson & J.B. McCracken. Washington, DC: NAEYC.

Hollestelle, K. 1994. Entrepreneurial skills for family child care providers. In *The early childhood career lattice: Perspectives on professional development,* eds. J. Johnson & J.B. McCracken. Washington, DC: NAEYC.

Kagan, S.L., & N.E. Cohen. In press. *Gearing up for quality: A vision for America's early care and education system.* Abridged report of the *Quality 200* initiative. New Haven, CT: Bush Center in Child Development and Social Policy, Yale University.

Malaguzzi, L. 1993. For an education based on relationships. *Young Children* 49 (1): 9–12.

Mitchell, A. 1995. *A proposal for licensing individuals who practice early care and education.* New Haven, CT: *Quality 2000,* Bush Center in Child Development and Social Policy, Yale University.

Morgan, G. 1994. A new century/A new system for professional development. In *The early childhood career lattice: Perspectives on professional development,* eds. J. Johnson & J.B. McCracken. Washington, DC: NAEYC.

Morgan, G., S. Azer, J. Costley, A. Genser, I. Goodman, J. Lombardi, & B. McGimsey. 1993. *Making a career of it: The state of the states report on career development in early care and education.* Boston: Center for Career Development in Early Care and Education, Wheelock College.

National Academy of Early Childhood Programs. 1995. Foundation supports professional development for directors and quality for children. *Academy Update* 9 (2): 8.

NAEYC. 1991. *Accreditation criteria and procedures of the National Academy of Early Childhood Programs.* Washington, DC: Author.

NAEYC. 1994. A conceptual framework for early childhood professional development. Position statement. In *The early childhood career lattice: Perspectives on professional development,* eds. J. Johnson & J.B. McCracken. Washington, DC: NAEYC.

NAEYC. 1995. *Guidelines for preparation of early childhood professionals.* Washington, DC: Author.

National Black Child Development Institute. 1987. *Safeguards: Guidelines for establishing programs for 4-year-olds in public schools.* Washington, DC: Author.

National Black Child Development Institute. 1993. *Paths to African American leadership positions in early childhood education: Constraints and opportunities.* Washington, DC: Author.

National Black Child Development Institute. 1995. NBCDI addresses glass ceiling in early childhood education profession. Press release. Washington, DC: Author.

O'Connor, S. 1994. Professional development for school-age child care. In *The early childhood career lattice: Perspectives on professional development,* eds. J. Johnson & J.B. McCracken. Washington, DC: NAEYC.

Whitebook, M. 1994. At the core: Advocacy to challenge the status quo. In *The early childhood career lattice: Perspectives on professional development,* eds. J. Johnson & J.B. McCracken. Washington, DC: NAEYC.

Whitebook, M., C. Pemberton, J. Lombardi, & E. Galinsky. 1990. *From the floor: Raising child care salaries.* Oakland, CA: Child Care Employee Project.

Willer, B., ed. 1990. *Reaching the full cost of quality in early childhood programs.* Washington, DC: NAEYC.

Chapter 14

New Directions for
Non-College/University Training

Marilyn Henry and Carol Brunson Phillips

Few professions allow entry into their ranks without rigorous postsecondary education preparation. The early childhood education profession is an exception, making it possible for nontraditional learners from diverse social, economic, and racial backgrounds to enter the field with little or no training or experience.

That the profession values these multiple entry points is established formally by the profession's career development scheme. In 1992 the National Association for the Education of Young Children presented a conceptual framework for the profession, symbolized by a career lattice (Bredekamp & Willer). The lattice represents the diversity of roles and levels of preparation within the early childhood field. To set upon a career path, the profession requires

1. completion of or enrollment in a credit-bearing early childhood professional preparation program that meets recognized guidelines, or

2. ongoing participation in formal training that may be credit bearing but is designed to lead to the acquisition of competency that could be assessed through mechanisms such as the Child Development Associate (CDA) credential and/or transformed into credit toward another professional credential or degree. (Willer 1994, 11)

This chapter focuses on the nontraditional training and education mechanisms that this framework supports and the ways that leadership can be afforded through such mechanisms. We examine the particulars of the CDA National Credentialing Program and the CDA Competency Standards and explore how each enhances the leadership capabilities of this population. Further, we describe how the profession is utilizing the creative solution of mentoring to move the entry-level worker and other early childhood professionals on to higher levels of achievement. Finally,

the concluding section reveals how linkages are being made on the national, state, and local levels to respond to the leadership development needs of all early care and education personnel.

The leadership potential of the Child Development Associate

Most definitions of leadership—and there are many—suggest sophisticated and complex skills for working with and leading other people. Yet leadership can be described *as a process* by which one person sets certain standards and expectations and influences the actions of others. As various forms of professional development contribute to this process, they also contribute to leadership development. In this light, let us look at the caregiver who seeks a CDA at the beginning stage of career development and examine CDA candidacy and training.

CDA Competency Standards support leadership development

When the CDA program was first conceived in the early 1970s, it was designed to be a new vehicle for career development that could be made available to the child care workforce at large, many of whom were poor and educationally disenfranchised, and that would provide the necessary access to professional status (Peters & Benham 1987). The competencies were constructed to describe what is required of both child care workers and the person responsible for training them. The competencies developed by a task force required the CDA candidate to

- support the interdependence of all children's development processes—acquisition of knowledge and skills, development of feelings and attitudes, applications of problem-solving techniques, and taking part in satisfying and meaningful life experiences;
- demonstrate sensitivity to the plurality of social, cultural, and regional family and child variations; and
- achieve an understanding between professional educators and parents by integrating the values and expectations of both. (Bouverat & Galen 1994, 18–19)

Ultimately, by 1975, six competencies for Child Development Associates were developed. And although there have been subsequent revisions and refinements in the wording of indicators and examples, the competency standards have remained virtually unchanged (see Figure 1). As you can see, the standards are delineated by 13 functional areas. The functional areas were created to direct the focus of observation within each of the competency areas.

Training programs that utilize the competency standards as the basis for preparing individuals to work with young children produce workers who are able to demonstrate skills in working not only with young children and their families but also in managing the child care program and advancing professionally as an individual. For example, inherent in the last three functional areas—families, program management, and professionalism—are skill areas that set the stage for leadership development: planning, organizing, communicating, cooperating, and making decisions.

CDA trainees generally are already working in child care, but because they are working in many different capacities, their level of responsibility in a program will vary. Classroom aides may have little or no independent responsibilities, whereas assistant teachers will likely share responsibility with other staff. Other candidates are center directors or those who have their own family child care homes. However, regardless of these variables in setting, at the time of assessment all CDA candidates must demonstrate their skills as Lead Caregiver and be able to organize, plan, keep records, and communicate with colleagues and co-workers in ways that enhance program operation. With a CDA credential, these individuals are expected to integrate all they have learned during training to make decisions about daily schedules, advise and support parents, select appropriate classroom materials and activities, implement discipline and teaching methods, and make significant contributions to the growth and development of the program. Therefore, the Competency Standards are supportive of leadership development in that they establish a uniform criterion for entry-level professional skill and prepare the individual to assume these behaviors and be able to articulate them to others.

CDA training itself is a motivator for further training. It has been demonstrated by national studies (Peters & Sutton 1984; Peters & Benham 1987) to provide participants with

- an increased knowledge of child development,
- more positive attitudes toward children's learning,
- stronger and more coherent beliefs in child-centered approaches toward early education,
- an increase in educational aspirations and further professional development,
- more active seeking of educational opportunities, and
- an increased sense of self-confidence in one's abilities to handle the complexities of the job. (Bank Street College of Education 1983, 22, 23)

Therefore, CDA training contributes directly to leadership development by setting the stage for the early care and education worker to believe he or she *can* make choices, achieve higher levels of responsibility, and assume leadership behaviors.

The role of the Council

In 1985 the Council for Early Childhood Professional Recognition was established by NAEYC and began administering the CDA National Credentialing Program. An essential component of the Council's mission was to increase the status and recognition of the credential and, with that, to increase the leadership development capacity of the profession. This effort has strengthened the involvement of college and university personnel who serve as CDA advisors and CDA representatives, who become advocates for articulation between CDA and college-based levels of preparation. Further, the Council has aggressively sought the involvement of child care and Head Start program directors to orchestrate training and career development opportunities, as well as staff in state offices such as human services and child care licensing to become advocates for continued upward mobility for CDAs.

The Council, through the CDA National Credentialing Program, contributes a diverse pool to potential leadership ranks because the CDA population encompasses all racial, cultural, and socioeconomic groups and educational backgrounds, ranging from a high school education through postdoctoral studies. CDAs are not all non-college/university trained. Three national surveys—conducted in 1983 (Bank Street College of Education), 1988 (Council 1990), and 1994 (Council 1996)—reveal that, on average, nearly half (48%) of CDAs have some college experience *before* applying to the CDA program, and nearly a quarter of them (24%) get two-year degrees *after* attaining the credential.

Figure 1. CDA Competency Standards and Functional Areas	
Competency standards	**Functional areas**
Establish and maintain a safe, healthy learning environment	• Safety: Candidate provides a safe environment to prevent and reduce injuries. • Health: Candidate promotes good health and nutrition and provides an environment that contributes to the prevention of illness. • Learning environment: Candidate uses space, relationships, materials, and routines as resources for constructing an interesting, secure, and enjoyable environment that encourages play, exploration, and learning.
Advance physical and intellectual competence	• Physical skills: Candidate provides a variety of equipment, activities, and opportunities to promote the physical development of children. • Cognitive skills: Candidate provides activities and opportunities that encourage curiosity, exploration, and problem solving appropriate to the developmental levels and learning styles of children. • Communication skills: Candidate actively communicates with children and provides opportunities and support for children to understand, acquire, and use verbal and nonverbal means of communicating thoughts and feelings. • Creativity: Candidate provides opportunities that stimulate children to play with sound, rhythm, language, materials, space, and ideas in individual ways and to express their creative abilities.
Support social and emotional development and provide positive guidance	• Self-concept: Candidate provides physical and emotional security for each child and helps each child to know, accept, and take pride in himself or herself and to develop a sense of independence. • Social skills: Candidate helps each child feel accepted in the group, helps children learn to communicate and get along with others, and encourages feelings of empathy and mutual respect among children and adults. • Guidance: Candidate provides a supportive environment in which children can begin to learn and practice appropriate and acceptable behaviors as individuals and as a group.
Establish positive and productive relationships with families	• Families: Candidate maintains an open, friendly, and cooperative relationship with each child's family, encourages their involvement in the program, and supports the child's relationship with his or her family.
Ensure a well-run, purposeful program responsive to participant needs	• Management skills: As a manager who uses all available resources to ensure an effective operation, the candidate is a competent organizer, planner, record keeper, communicator, and cooperative co-worker.
Maintain a commitment to professionalism	• Professionalism: Candidate makes decisions based on knowledge of early childhood theories and practices; promotes quality in child care services; and takes advantage of opportunities to improve competence, both for personal and professional growth and for the benefit of children and families.

In keeping with the career path strategy articulated by the professional development model (Willer 1994) as defined by the profession, the Council has made significant changes in the CDA program. In 1992 the Council implemented a one-year training program—the CDA Professional Preparation Program (CDA P$_3$)—for individuals with no child care experience or prior training. Candidates participate in supervised field experiences and seminar instruction at a postsecondary education institution.

The Council also revised the traditional CDA assessment process in 1993 to encourage more formal training experiences while still maintaining access through noncollege routes. And in 1996 the Council began implementing a revised CDA renewal process, requiring CDAs to participate in ongoing training and maintain active membership in an early childhood professional association. By setting new education standards for the CDA credential, the Council opened the doors to improve the credibility of the credential and put the CDA on the path for further professional development.

Although a Child Development Associate has set upon a career path and is poised for subsequent stages, not everyone in the child care workforce has access to CDA as a professional leadership-development launching point. More often, there is a lack of linkages between the employer or workplace and a training program. As a result, other professional and leadership initiatives are emerging. One such effort is mentoring.

Affording leadership through mentoring

Many professions and advocacy and consumer organizations are using mentoring to stimulate leadership development. Through the modeling of appropriate practices, mentoring allows for on-the-job nurturance. The term *mentor*[1] historically denotes a trusted guide and counselor, and the mentor-protégé relationship, a deep and meaningful association (Galvez-Hjornevik 1986). Mentoring has the potential to be an excellent vehicle for employers to use to move entry-level workers from one stage to the next along their career development path. For example, a noncredentialed early childhood professional at Level I (see Figure 2) could be guided by the Level II CDA, who can, by virtue of experience and knowledge, provide advice and direction. The CDA, in turn, could be guided by the Level III or IV teacher to the next stage of career development.

A popular proposal toward teacher improvement emphasizing support relationships comes from the National Center for the Early Childhood Work Force (NCECW). It was in the early 1990s that groups involved in mentoring programs in a number of states got together to share their ideas and experiences at the NAEYC Professional Development Institute. After that sharing session a Roundtable Discussion was formed. The roundtable group decided it would be beneficial to the field to establish a National Early Childhood Mentoring Alliance, coordinated by NCECW. Mentoring training for early child care and education, as envisioned by this group, creates a space for experienced teachers and providers to gain the adult training skills necessary for success in their current de facto role as on-the-job trainers for newly recruited providers. Further,

> These programs increase opportunities for a student teaching experience so often unavailable to the growing numbers of teachers who have not received preservice training, often due to financial need. Early care and education programs have a rich history of "on-the-job" training not only in lab schools, but also in Head Start programs and in parent cooperatives. Mentoring programs extend this practicum tradition to the many settings in our field that have been overlooked, such as family child care, infant and school care, and programs serving families from diverse linguistic and cultural backgrounds. (Whitebook, Hnatiuk, & Bellm 1994, 13)

According to Whitebook, Hnatiuk, and Bellm (1994), leadership development should be a natural outcome of a successful mentoring program; cultivating leadership is an inherent part of mentor training programs because mentors are called upon to act as leaders and role models for other caregivers. As mentors build their understanding of adult development and their skills in communicating and supporting others, they also build their capacity for leadership.

> Mentor programs create a new step in the early childhood career progression, allowing a teacher or provider to advance professionally while continuing to educate and teach children directly. [Mentor programs] also establish an incentive for caregivers to continue in the field, and by providing them with new opportunities for leadership development, mentor programs strengthen the voice of practitioners in efforts to upgrade child care services. (p. 13)

This leads to the second major impetus for the burgeoning interest in mentoring. The hope is to use this method to counter the high rate of turnover (estimated at 41%) among child care teachers (Morgan et al. 1993). There are sound reasons for trusting the potential validity of the mentoring concept to retain teachers. Research reveals that new teachers become socialized into their new roles and settings through relationships with adults who are more experienced (Lortie 1975; Kremer-Hazon & Ben-Peretz 1986). Relationships with colleagues also increase teachers' sense of efficacy (Parkay et al. 1988; Newman, Rutter,

Figure 2. Early Childhood Professional Categories and Qualifications

Early Childhood Professional Level VI

- Successful completion of a Ph.D. or Ed.D. in a program conforming to NAEYC guidelines; or
- Successful demonstration of the knowledge, performance, and dispositions expected as outcomes of a doctoral degree program conforming to NAEYC guidelines.

Early Childhood Professional Level V

- Successful completion of a master's degree in a program that conforms to NAEYC guidelines; or
- Successful demonstration of the knowledge, performance, and dispositions expected as outcomes of a master's degree program conforming to NAEYC guidelines.

Early Childhood Professional Level IV

- Successful completion of a baccalaureate degree from a program conforming to NAEYC guidelines;
- State certificate meeting NAEYC certification guidelines;
- Successful completion of a baccalaureate degree in another field with more than 30 professional units in early childhood development/education, including 300 hours of supervised teaching experience with 150 hours each for two of the following three age groups: infants and toddlers, 3- to 5-year-olds, or the primary grades; or
- Successful demonstration of the knowledge, performance, and dispositions expected as outcomes of a baccalaureate degree program conforming to NAEYC guidelines.

Early Childhood Professional Level III

- Successful completion of an associate degree from a program conforming to NAEYC guidelines;
- Successful completion of an associate degree in a related field, plus 30 units of professional studies in early childhood development/education, including 300 hours of supervised teaching experience in an early childhood program; or
- Successful demonstration of the knowledge, performance, and dispositions expected as outcomes of an associate degree program conforming to NAEYC guidelines.

Early Childhood Professional Level II

II. A. • Successful completion of the CDA professional preparation program; or
- Completion of a systematic, comprehensive training program that prepares an individual to successfully acquire the CDA Credential through direct assessment.

II. B. • Successful completion of a one-year early childhood certificate program.

Early Childhood Professional Level I

- Employed in an early childhood professional role, working under supervision or with support (e.g., linkages with provider association or network or enrollment in supervised practicum) and participating in training designed to lead to the assessment of individual competencies or acquisition of a degree.

& Smith 1989) and professional growth (Rosenholtz, Bassler, & Hoover-Dempsey 1986) and enhance awareness of resources, ideas, and skills (Reich 1986). A lack of support relationships leads to poor professional self-image (Cruickshank & Associates 1980) and low job satisfaction (Freisen, Prokop, & Sarros 1988), which are frequently cited as major reasons for teachers leaving the profession (Lortie 1975; Alexander, Adams, & Martray 1983).

If there is to be widespread acceptance of the mentor-teacher role for caregivers, a formal program design must be in place to ensure the success of the mentor teachers. Top management, of course, must support, publicize, and contribute to the mentor program. Ongoing staff and resources also must be in place to support the development and continuation of the program.

Administrators rarely expect or encourage leadership development of classroom teachers in any area of education. Those teachers with superior leadership abilities are often whisked away into administrative work. However, such teachers reinvigorate the workplace, since people strive harder when they are motivated and their work makes sense to them, and—when they are involved—everyone benefits (Barrick 1988).

Ingredients for a successful mentoring program

According to the National Center for the Early Childhood Work Force (Whitebook, Hnatiuk, & Bellm 1994), a successful mentoring program requires the following key ingredients. Programs are

• responsive to the developmental needs of those they serve and grounded in research on teacher and adult development;

• supportive in nature, rather than linked to formal evaluation processes;

• forums for improving collegial connections between mentors, protégés, employers, and trainers; and

• learning systems that examine themselves, improve how they function, and contribute to the collective health of the early care and education community.

The mentoring relationship and how it is established within the workplace are also key to successful programs. Research in this area in the early childhood field is virtually nonexistent, but guidance can be provided from those who have examined the issue with teachers in elementary and secondary schools. For example, Alleman and colleagues (1984) propose that a developmental group for potential mentors be formed and that separate educative sessions be designed to focus on such topics as benefits of the mentor relationship, ways to increase the protégé's self-esteem, and adaptations of mentoring practices to particular settings while gaining organization-wide support.

Kram (1985) suggests a sequence of programs and organizational changes that support, rather than force, the mentoring process. She outlines four steps:

Defining the objectives and scope of the project; diagnosing the individual and organization circumstances promoting or interfering with effective mentoring; implementing educational programs, changes in the reward system, task design, or other management practices; and evaluating the intervention to determine what modifications are needed. (p. 40)

A formal program, Kram argues, may have little relevance for individuals or organizations. Even with the methods utilized above, one should expect time, patience, and effort when an organizational approach to mentoring is utilized, she says.

Research (Erikson 1963; Schmidt & Wolfe 1980; Krupp 1984) suggests that workshops on effective mentoring can potentially enhance staff growth and development, allowing older, effective teachers to recognize the culmination of their years of experience in the profession and providing beginning teachers with some needed assistance in their first year (Galvez-Hjornevik 1986). Although still at the infancy stage of development within the early childhood profession,

mentoring as a tool for staff growth and development and as a tool for producing leaders clearly has tremendous potential.

National efforts to meet the leadership needs of the entry-level professional

While leadership exposure through CDA and mentoring can be accomplished at the level of child care centers and family child care homes, several national efforts are also under way. One of the newest is the Head Start Fellows Program. The purpose of this program is to support the growth and development of individuals who can make special leadership contributions to the Head Start and early childhood development communities in policy, program development, and research.

Authors of the Human Services Amendments of 1994 and the Advisory Committee on Head Start Quality and Expansion envisioned that the program would be part of a long-term quality-improvement initiative aimed at upgrading the skills and experiences of promising individuals. A new cadre of leaders can influence and bring about improvements in policy and practice at a variety of levels to positively affect the lives and circumstances of low-income children and families across the country.

Each year 10 to 15 individuals are chosen under no age or educational requirement but within the field of child development and children and family services. The 12-month program calls for the fellows to participate in an orientation program in Washington, D.C.; a fellowship placement in the Administration for Children, Youth, Families, a national nonprofit organization, an innovative Head Start program, or a university-based center; a mentoring relationship with leaders from national early childhood associations and other professional public interest groups and university-based centers; professional education and training programs; and on-line connection with fellows, mentors, and the fellowship program coordinator.

The National Head Start Fellows Program is a significant and welcome addition to the leadership development efforts in early childhood care and education. Federal support of such an effort can develop a new generation of early childhood leaders, improve the quality of early childhood programs and policy, and promote the status of professionals who work with young children and their families.

The profession's national organizations also have developed ongoing leadership training. Some are offered at annual conferences, such as the Leadership Institute for Affiliate presidents, sponsored by NAEYC, or Leadership, Education and Development (LEAD), sponsored by the National Head Start Association and open to Head Start employees who want to take a more active leadership role. Also, there is the preconference Early Childhood Institute at the National Black Child Development Institute's annual meeting, devoted exclusively to early childhood education leadership.

Other leadership training by national organizations is more specifically focused, such as that offered

• in policy/advocacy by the Children's Defense Fund's Expanding Advocacy for Child Care Project;

• in local leadership and community planning offered (through national technical assistance) by the Families and Work Institute's EQUIP (Early Education Quality Improvement Project), Child Care Action Campaign, and Council of Chief State School Officers' Child Care and Education: Forging the Link;

• in early care and education support and information services provided to legislators and staff by the National Conference of State Legislators;

• for senior Head Start managers by the Strategic Training for Administrative Responsibilities (STAR) Institute, which was developed by the National Head Start Association and the Entrepreneurial Studies Center at UCLA;

• for antibias education training provided by Pacific Oaks College's Culturally Relevant Anti-Bias Leadership Education Project (CRABLE); and

• for creation of career development systems and training opportunities by the Center for Career Development in Education's Partners in Change project.

Conclusion

We have provided brief glimpses into the wealth of potential for development of leaders in the early childhood profession, at all levels and in settings outside the traditional college campus. The early care and education worker who begins his or her career with no experience and no formal training can access career-track training and development through an increasing number of opportunities.

One of the hallmarks of the early childhood profession is that it constantly seeks and finds creative methods to maintain the dynamism of the profession. Developing tomorrow's early childhood leaders from the ranks of CDAs, for example, is a novel concept but within the realm of possibility. The CDA training programs that are mushrooming all over the country are utilizing the CDA Competency Standards to foster the skills candidates need to assume greater responsibility and to prepare for leadership roles. Mentoring programs are another method with tremendous potential

for training and retaining early care and education workers and providing them with increased self-confidence, higher salaries, and hope for the future.

Finally, the profusion of national organizations affording leadership opportunities for all levels of early care and education workers is unprecedented. These national efforts are instilling a vision of a profession that is inventive, vigorous, and worthy of emulation by other professions. The idea of developing leaders for this field in avenues never before explored has gained momentum and is certain to affect teacher quality as well as the quality of care that young children receive.

Note

1. The term *mentor* is derived from Homer's *The Odyssey,* wherein Athene took the image of Mentor, Odysseus's loyal friend, and was given responsibility for nurturing Telemachus (Odysseus's son) when his father ventured off to fight the Trojan War.

References

Alexander, L., R.D. Adams, & C.R. Martray. 1983. *Personal and professional stressors associated with the teacher burnout phenomenon.* Paper presented at the annual meeting of the American Educational Research Association, April, Montreal.

Alleman, E., J. Cochran, J. Doverspike, & I. Newman. 1984. Enriching mentoring relationships. *Personnel and Guidance Journal* 62 (6): 329–32.

Bainer, D.L., & C. Didham. 1994. Mentoring and other support behaviors in elementary schools. *Journal of Educational Research* 87 (4): 240–47.

Bank Street College of Education, CDA Credentialing Program. 1983. *Results of the national survey of CDAs—A preliminary report.* Washington, DC: Author.

Barrick, R.K. 1988. Teachers can lead and still be teachers. *Vocational Education Journal* (November/December): 29–32.

Bouverat, R.W., & H.L. Galen. 1994. *The Child Development Associate National Program: The early years and pioneers.* Washington, DC: Council for Early Childhood Recognition.

Bredekamp, S., & B. Willer. 1992. Of ladders and lattices, cores and cones: Conceptualizing an early childhood professional development system. *Young Children* 47 (3): 47–50.

Council for Early Childhood Professional Recognition. 1990. *The 1988 CDA national survey results.* Washington, DC: Author.

Council for Early Childhood Professional Recognition. 1996. *The 1994 survey of CDAs: A research report.* Washington, DC: Author.

Cruickshank, D.R., & Associates [J. Applegate, J. Holton, G. Mager, B. Myers, C. Novak, & K. Tracey]. 1980. *Teaching is tough.* Englewood Cliffs, NJ: Prentice-Hall.

Erikson, E. 1963. *Childhood and society.* New York: W.W. Norton.

Freisen, D., C.M. Prokop, & J.C. Sarros. 1988. Why teachers burn out. *Educational Research Quarterly* 12 (3): 9–19.

Galvez-Hjornevik, C. 1986. Mentoring among teachers: A review of the literature. *Journal of Teacher Education* 37 (1): 8–11.

Kram, K.E. 1985. Improving the mentoring process. *Training and Development Journal* 39 (4): 40–43.

Kremer-Hazon, L., & M. Ben-Peretz. 1986. Becoming a teacher: The transition from teacher's college to classroom life. *International Review of Education* 32 (4): 413–22.

Krupp, J.A. 1984. Mentor and protégé perceptions of mentoring relationships in an elementary and secondary school in Connecticut. Paper presented at the annual meeting of the American Educational Research Association, April, New Orleans.

Lortie, D.C. 1975. *Schoolteachers: A sociological study.* Chicago: University of Chicago Press.

Morgan, G., S. Azer, J. Costley, A. Genser, I.F. Goodman, J. Lombardi, & B. McGimsey. 1993. *Making a career of it: The state of the states report on career development in early care and education.* Boston: Center for Career Development in Early Care and Education.

Newman, M., R.A. Rutter, & M.S. Smith. 1989. Organizational factors that affect school sense of efficacy, community, and expectations. *Sociology of Education* 62 (4): 221–38.

Parkay, F.W., G. Greenwood, S. Olejnik, & N. Proller. 1988. A study of relationships among teacher efficacy, locus of control, and stress. *Journal of Research and Development in Education* 21 (4): 13–22.

Peters, D.L., & N. Benham. 1987. Research on Child Development Associate training. In *Advances in day care and early education,* ed. S. Kilmer. Greenwich, CT: JAI Press.

Peters, D.L., & R.E. Sutton. 1984. The effects of CDA training on the beliefs, attitudes and behaviors of Head Start personnel. *Child Care Quarterly* 13 (Winter): 13–14.

Phillips-Jones, L. 1983. Establishing a formalized mentoring program. *Training & Development Journal* 37 (2): 38–42.

Reich, M.H. 1986. The mentor connection. *Personnel* 62 (2): 50–56.

Rodd, J. 1994. *Leadership in early childhood: The pathways to professionalism.* New York: Teachers College Press.

Rosenholtz, S.J. 1985. Effective schools: Interpreting the evidence. *American Journal of Education* 93 (3): 352–87.

Rosenholtz, S.J., D. Bassler, & K. Hoover-Dempsey. 1986. Organizational conditions of teacher learning. *Teaching and Teacher Education* 2 (2): 91–104.

Schmidt, J.A., & J.S. Wolfe. 1980. The mentoring partnership: Discovery of professionalism. *NASPA* 17 (3): 45–51.

Whitebook, M., C. Howes, & D. Phillips. 1989. *Who cares? Child care teachers and the quality of care in America.* Final report of the National Child Care Staffing Study. Oakland, CA: Child Care Employee Project.

Whitebook, M., P. Hnatiuk, & D. Bellm. 1994. *Mentoring in early care and education: Refining an emerging career path.* Washington, DC: National Center for the Early Childhood Work Force.

Willer, B. 1994. A conceptual framework for early childhood professional development. NAEYC position statement. In *The early childhood career lattice: Perspectives on professional development,* eds. J. Johnson & J. McCracken. Washington, DC: NAEYC.

Chapter 15

New Directions for Resource-and-Referral Agencies

Patricia Siegel

The leadership path of child care resource-and-referral agencies is winding and steep but relatively new compared to many parts of the diverse early care and education system. Unlike many parts of the child care world, the beginning of resource and referral did not come with leaders to follow, textbooks to read, or ready-made organizations to join. To establish the services essential to the child care delivery system, resource-and-referral agencies had to simultaneously create and evaluate a vision of service, fight for the resources necessary to implement it, and share and spread this vision with communities and states.

The individuals who developed the first child care resource-and-referral agencies (CCR&Rs) and services cultivated critical skills with which to catalyze the early care and education field toward positive change. These leaders have shared their knowledge and competences with others, thereby nurturing potential future leadership. Moreover, at the organizational level, CCR&Rs have become institutional leaders, setting the agenda and guiding early care and education policy and practice to better meet the needs of children and families.

This chapter explores the evolution of CCR&Rs from their fragile and uncertain beginnings to the strong leadership roles they play in the early care and education field today. CCR&Rs support parents in locating and using child care; compile, analyze, and share information; create new resources; collaborate with community agencies to articulate a vision for early care and education; and advocate with decision-makers in all phases of government. In examining the leadership role in each aspect of CCR&R service, the chapter suggests new opportunities and challenges for the future.[1]

The leadership path of CCR&Rs

The impetus for developing CCR&R services was great. The challenge of finding good, safe, reliable child care was daunting during a time when the child care delivery system was even more fragmented and far less evolved than it is today. The pioneers of resource and referral were parents, products of the '60s and committed to social change, who still believed they could change the world or at least transform their communities. Formidable tasks did not dissuade them. Many had worked in the civil rights and antiwar movements where they faced almost insurmountable barriers and still witnessed victories, sometimes large, sometimes small. The disarray, inadequacy, and fragmentation of the child care world invited activist zeal.

The rationale for the earliest CCR&Rs, then called information-and-referral services (I&Rs), was simple and direct, as described by Jim Levine, a Ford Foundation project consultant who worked with early organizers.

Put simply, child care information and referral services act as a "broker" to put parents in need of child care in touch with those who provide child care. Their services began emerging as a distinct type in the early 1970s when President Nixon's veto of the Child Development Act, limitations on Title IV-A, and state cutbacks in social service dimmed any prospects for rapid expansion of center-based care and made it necessary, in many communities, to explore new approaches to locating and supporting child care. Parent organizers of these new I&Rs—such as San Francisco's Childcare Switchboard or the Child Care Resource Center in Cambridge, Massachusetts—were often users of family day care (licensed and unlicensed), play groups, or other cooperative arrangements; many were not eligible for public subsidy, though they worked towards facilitating child care arrangements for all parents. Aside from helping parents find child care, their services typically engage in a wide variety of related activities: they offer technical assistance to start, sustain, or improve child care programs within their communities; they gather data for planning and advocacy purposes; they offer support groups for single parents; and they offer clearinghouses for people seeking jobs in the child care field. (Levine 1982, 380)

The first CCR&R leadership stretch came with the realization that sharing information about available child care and helping parents evaluate what services would best meet their family needs did not address significant gaps in care in many neighborhoods. Nor could the leaders easily deal with the almost universal shortage of care for infants and toddlers, the cost of care exceeding what families could afford, and parents' frustration over the uneven, sometimes disturbing, quality of the child care choices available to them. These frustrations were articulated in the early 1980s by Gwen Morgan, who described child care's "trilemma" as a "three-legged stool" delicately balanced on the legs of availability, affordability, and quality—with attempts to improve any one of these putting the other two at risk.

It was also during the early 1980s that a shift in CCR&R responsibilities occurred, and the child care *information*-and-referral label gradually but definitely became that of child care *resource*-and-referral. In the early years the distinction did not feel like a choice; it gradually became clear that for parents to have the child care programs and services they needed, CCR&R agencies would have to work on the problem from different directions. To ensure quality care and to enable providers to achieve professional status, work was needed to build supply and to identify new sources of support and encouragement. Doug Powell, who has written extensively on parents' searches for child care, observed this change:

> The experiences of well-established I&R services in this country challenge the assumption that a supply of quality child care exists in a given community, and the task of an I&R is to match day-care resources to parents' needs. The I in I&R is being transformed from *information* to *resource* in some operations. The change reflects the perceived need to take an active role in upgrading quality through training and developing new day-care options. (1987, 122)

Early CCR&R funders, including the Ford Foundation, urged leaders to document the requirements for supply building and to record what parents had to say about their search for and use of child care. It was this data that enabled CCR&Rs to help lead community planning and to initiate advocacy efforts in communities in every state (Adams, Foote, & Vinci 1996).

While many colleagues in the early care and education field have a focus on one or another sector of the delivery system—e.g., teachers and caregivers address the needs of the children served, college professors emphasize the needs of the teachers and caregivers preparing to teach, and policy analysts target legislation, finance, and regulation—CCR&R leaders work simultaneously across parent, provider, and community sectors. Their services crisscross many disciplines simultaneously—early childhood, social work, urban planning, and public policy—and require an inventive, imaginative, and flexible approach to making the child care system work better.

Without the security of clearly defined borders and boundaries, CCR&R leaders are compelled to take risks to achieve their goals. Developing leadership skills has been essential in a young service that began with limited assistance from academic and practical guidelines. CCR&R services emerged in a time when there was widespread interest in the concept of networking. The core function of local CCR&R services, state networks, and the National Association of Child Care Resource and Referral Agencies (NACCRRA) is connecting people, exchanging information, and sharing resources. These organizations also provide leadership in setting a policy agenda for the field. Theoretical roots for CCR&R service are found in the research and writing of Alice Collins, a social worker who taught at Portland State University in the 1970s. Her work on identifying "natural helping networks" within the community and developing neighborhood leaders through consultation practice were especially helpful to early CCR&R leaders in Oregon and California (Collins & Pancoast 1976). Today, CCR&Rs continue to employ leadership skills based on these core concepts of networking and consultation.

The current child care delivery system is often compared to a patchwork quilt composed of beautiful, but distinct, squares representing various unique contributions to the overall system. Even with the efforts of the Child Care and Development Block Grant to create a "seamless system" since its passage in 1990, no fully articulated national child care policy has emerged to bring all the pieces together. In the absence of a coherent child care policy, those concerned with creating a sensible delivery system—one easily understood by parents, providers, and community and business leaders—have come together for child care "quilting bees." CCR&Rs have taken on the role of "quilters." As articulated by Evelyn Moore, executive director of the National Black Child Development Institute, "For a fractured patchwork system to work, then, some coordinating mechanism like I and R must become an integral part of whatever structure does exist in the system" (1982, 436). With their documented perspectives on parents' needs, provider concerns, and available supply and cost, the CCR&Rs are able to stitch around and through the individual squares, creating a quilt that represents the diverse and sometimes conflicting elements of the child care delivery system.

Creating the child care quilt for each community requires both a vision for a completed quilt and the patience to revisit, rearrange, and adjust perspectives. Each contribution to the quilt must be carefully integrated into the whole through constant interaction with the maker of each square. CCR&R agencies seek to avoid clashes among the makers, knowing that the work of everyone will be affected by rearrangement of the binding that pulls it together. CCR&Rs work toward the production of a quilt large enough and so well crafted that it covers the needs of all the children who need child care in order to become fully functioning members of American society. CCR&R agencies now know how important skilled leadership is to successful quilting.

Leaders serve a dual role in organizing for the future. Not only must the leaders serve as quilters to hold the segments of the field together, but they also must see themselves as mentors to the next generation. They must pass on their techniques and skills and nudge potential talent along the path toward greater responsibility and success. Simple mentoring tasks and skills must become second nature so that new energy and competencies are brought along to the mainstream. Leaders resign, retire, and otherwise pass on to new fields of endeavor. Potential gaps brought about through inevitable loss must be filled ahead of time. Similarly, veteran organizations must be prepared to share their skills and expertise with newer agencies, whether they be fledgling CCR&Rs or other child care organizations. The nurturing role so obvious between adult and child is not always as evident between adults and among organizations who are on different levels of expertise and experience.

Leadership skills for CCR&R agencies

Efforts to be effective quilters, to improve and expand the child care delivery system, have stimulated nontraditional approaches to leadership. CCR&Rs work in circular rather than linear patterns. Their simultaneous efforts to help parents, support providers, and expand the supply of quality, affordable child care are interconnected. Working in this interactive, catalytic fashion requires leaders who are confident, articulate, flexible, and reciprocal, and who often rely on a good sense of humor.

CCR&R leaders must be open to new ideas, able to live with ambiguity, and unafraid of change. Because CCR&Rs' core work is grounded in a commitment to change, leaders must also deal with feelings of anger at the fragmentation of child care policies and the inadequacy of funding to meet the needs of the families they serve. Staying focused on a well-framed vision for the future of child care helps leaders maintain the passion to make improvements one day, one week, one month at a time.

Leaders in CCR&R have learned from experience that the power to influence policies, funding, and legislation stems from relationships. Establishing and maintaining relationships with parents, providers, and all sectors of the child care community has profound implications for CCR&Rs' ability to succeed in efforts to improve child care. The following sections explore these relationships further, focusing on the different leadership roles for CCR&Rs in each aspect of service.

Leadership opportunities with parents

Parents are the nucleus of all CCR&R services. All CCR&R roles and connections can be traced to parents in search of child care and related family services. CCR&Rs have come to understand—perhaps uniquely—the complicated, intimate nature of parents' search for good child care. Through state networks, NACCRRA, and national companies such as Work/Family Directions, CCR&Rs have refined counseling skills, improving their abilities to hear and address parents' most urgent concerns about child care. Methods of documenting parents' needs for child care are increasingly sophisticated, and dissemination of the resulting data helps bring the child care challenge to the public's attention. Documentation of community need also guides supply building and enhances quality improvement strategies.

The leadership role of CCR&Rs demands that agencies look beyond telephones, computers, and data profiles to determine how well they are keeping pace with parents and child care needs. At an NACCRRA-sponsored leadership retreat in August 1995, CCR&R leaders from around the country recognized once again the need to expand relationships with parents. The discussion of expanded service included several dimensions: reaching out to parents and communities who do not use CCR&R services, augmenting the information with which parents make decisions about quality, and going beyond telephone calls to better reach parents where they live and work. This "outposting" of services could take place in neighborhood storefronts, employment offices, churches, public housing, workplace cafeterias, hospitals and clinics, public schools, family resource centers, and other places where parents gather and do commerce. On-line hookups, Websites, and chat rooms provide another type of expanded access to child care information and assistance.

This expanded approach to serving parents poses some leadership challenges for CCR&Rs. Because CCR&R remains a young service, not fully institutionalized in many states, it may be difficult to secure the support and resources necessary to outpost services that are barely available in a centralized format. In states and communities where CCR&R services are more institutionalized, leaders may be resistant to changing service modes that are well established and adequately functioning. Seeking new outpost partners in the community requires trust, collaboration, and a willingness to share information and resources. CCR&Rs' need to be increasingly accessible and visible throughout the communities they serve is heightened by the pressures low-income families face under recently enacted federal welfare reform.

While they have made efforts to put these new strategies in place, CCR&R leaders understand that even with more than 20 years of service and solid advocacy efforts, overall progress toward meeting parents' needs has been limited and must be increased. Notably missing from child care advocacy efforts at every level have been the parents themselves. Even though no one speaks more convincingly for children's needs than parents themselves, busy schedules and harried lives leave many parents with little energy to work for long-term improvement and expansion of child care resources.

To address this void, the California Child Care Resource and Referral Network began to explore how CCR&R agencies could help parents build a stronger, more effective voice for child care in their communities. In 1994, with the invitation and support of the Jenifer Altman Foundation, the network convened a small group of CCR&Rs and other child care leaders to rekindle a parent voice for the child care movement. The group agreed that child care would continue to limp along without significant growth, and possibly encounter setbacks, if parents themselves did not speak up strongly and collectively for good, affordable child care. Later that year, the foundation offered seed money to the network and five of its member agencies to develop parent organizing efforts.

Like colleagues in the Oregon Child Care Resource and Referral Network and the Child Care Council of Suffolk County, New York, the California leaders realized immediately that taking on a new role required additional skills and leadership. The search for understanding and training in community organizing went beyond early childhood borders to the skilled organizers of the Industrial Areas Foundation. The network learned how community organizing differs from the service orientation that characterizes CCR&R work. The network came to understand that promoting parent organizing requires a midwifery approach; CCR&R agencies cannot own or direct parent organizing efforts. Rather, the job is to find capable parent leaders, support their leadership development, facilitate their connections to each other, and ultimately create powerful parent-led organizations that will involve and engage thousands of parents.

This organizing work is slow and challenging and represents another significant leadership stretch for CCR&Rs. Because the results of parent organizing efforts may not be felt for many years, this new work lacks the immediate and tangible results, reports, and products that CCR&Rs and those who traditionally fund them are accustomed to. Like all vanguard efforts, parent organizing requires intensive mutual support within the CCR&R world and continuing guidance from skilled community organizers outside CCR&R.

With parent organizing efforts, the work of CCR&Rs comes full circle. Many early CCR&R leaders were parents frustrated in their attempts to find good child care. CCR&R services were partially born out of parent advocacy. Today, new organizing efforts are helping to establish the next generation of parent leaders.

Data and leadership: CCR&Rs' blend

Early CCR&R leaders soon realized that their mission of helping parents locate good child care could not be accomplished without a simultaneous effort to build supply, improve quality, and enable affordability. This realization gave birth to one of CCR&Rs' key roles, that of documenting how child care functions in communities and among states. The data generated from CCR&Rs' daily contacts with parents and providers help produce a unique and much-needed "snapshot" of child care supply and demand. Like annual school photographs that chronicle a child's growth from preschool to high school graduation, the collection of CCR&R data "photos" over time help explain child care needs both to the field and to the public. They also remind decisionmakers of critical and continuing gaps in services (NACCRRA 1993; Adams, Foote, & Vinci 1996).

Sharing information in a timely manner and in a format that can be easily grasped and remembered by the child care field and leaders in the public and private sectors requires a combination of research, advocacy, and storytelling skills. In community meetings, state planning sessions, and national public hearings, CCR&R leaders report "tales from the field"—the real-life stories that make the data behind child care trends and issues come alive.

The role of storyteller is highly prized in direct work with children, but it is also critical to policy efforts. Anyone who understands that information is power knows the potential strength of the data gathered and reported by CCR&R agencies. To be leaders in the field and in the public arena, CCR&Rs must share their data willingly and generously with all sectors of the child care community, thus encouraging and empowering broad-based efforts to improve child care.

CCR&Rs' ability to generate useful child care data poses some unique leadership challenges. First, the data collected and made available may generate community expectations that CCR&Rs have all the answers to child care questions. The media and public officials sometimes press CCR&Rs to step over the line of what they can report with confidence and accuracy. The public wants a "one-stop" child care information source. This can lead to misunderstandings with other leaders in the field who are also eager to share their perspectives on child care needs and issues and may resent CCR&Rs' "hold" on child care data. As leaders, CCR&Rs therefore must honor their pledges to provide accurate data to parents and the public at large, and they must work to establish positive relationships with other leaders in the field.

The second challenge is related to CCR&Rs' urgent needs to nurture leaders with well-developed research, analytic, and computer skills. Many CCR&R leaders emerge with strong ties to early childhood education, but few have the full complement of research skills necessary to meet the community's increasing expectations. This point is illustrated by comparing the large volume of applicants for CCR&R jobs in parent counseling and provider training to a far smaller pool of applicants for jobs which require specific research and planning skills.

To meet these challenges, state networks and NACCRRA will need to be especially attentive to helping new CCR&R leaders understand the importance of their data-gathering, analysis, and presentation roles and to obtaining the resources necessary to make full use of available technology.

Shared leadership with the field: CCR&Rs' catalytic role in training and resource development

New leaders are emerging throughout the child care field, especially in the area of training and professional development. CCR&Rs help focus community and state attention on the supply of child care, highlight gaps in services, and identify unmet needs and quality issues that concern parents. In many states, such as California, Maryland, Michigan, and Oregon, CCR&R networks have stimulated new public-private partnerships dedicated to expanding and improving the supply of available child care. These partnerships and initiatives have allowed CCR&R agencies to play a leadership role in bringing training and resources to child care providers. At the national level, NACCRRA's leadership helped recruit major funding from Dayton Hudson for the Family-to-Family Initiative, which supported new family child care training across

the country, as well as the companion consumer education initiative, Child Care Aware.

Guided by data results and an understanding of community child care needs, CCR&Rs can be especially effective in uncovering areas of need that might not otherwise make it to the mainstream training agenda set by higher education and other training institutions. One example of a nontraditional effort is El Comienzo, the California CCR&R Network initiative to address the need for an expanded supply of Spanish-speaking family child care providers. Using the public-private partnership previously established through the Child Care Initiative Project, the network convinced funders to invest in the development of a curriculum specifically designed for Spanish-speaking family child care providers and a recruitment and training model geared specifically to meet their needs.

The leadership dividends of El Comienzo continue to multiply: new groups of Latino leaders have emerged within CCR&R agencies; Spanish-speaking family child care associations have developed in many communities; and funds have been secured to organize three national leadership seminars for Latino child care professionals. El Comienzo also provided an important CCR&R voice in the formation of the new National Latino Children's Agenda organization. It demonstrates not only the leadership ripple of good training but also CCR&Rs' potential for addressing the challenge of diversifying child care's leadership.

Action for Children Today, a collaborative AmeriCorps project developed jointly by NACCRRA and the National School Age Care Alliance, represents another facet of CCR&Rs' leadership role in training and development. In 1995, 63 AmeriCorps volunteers were working in 32 CCR&R and school-age sites in 10 states to improve the supply and quality of infant/toddler and school-age child care (Yasmina Zinci, executive director of NACCRRA, personal communition, Fall 1995). The AmeriCorps volunteers bring a strong commitment to public service and social change to their host agencies. Their volunteer energy and time help CCR&R agencies extend their presence in the community by providing on-site support and assistance. The successful model of two national associations working together to respond to an opportunity to expand and improve child care demonstrates the power and necessity of collaborative leadership.

Another example of CCR&Rs' collaborative leadership is the active commitment of many agencies to local Worthy Wage campaigns, including doing wage and benefit surveys on working conditions and compensation. CCR&Rs have willingly joined in the national effort to build and retain a stable, committed early childhood workforce.

A growing challenge for CCR&Rs is how best to provide information, training, and support to regulation-exempt care—which, depending on the state, may include family child care, church-based programs, part-day programs, and school-based programs. Regulation-exempt care became a new segment of the child care world in 1990, when federal legislation expanded the concept of parental choice. As noted in a recent study of regulation-exempt family child care (Child Care Law Center 1996), CCR&Rs employ many strategies for reaching this growing population, including providing information about becoming regulated. Resources for Child Caring in St. Paul, Minnesota, recently published the *Business of Informal Care,* which discusses the tax issues of being a regulation-exempt provider and highlights the benefits of becoming licensed. The Child Development Support Corporation, a CCR&R in New York, mails a quarterly newsletter called *Caring for Kids: A Newsleaf for Informal Providers* to all regulation-exempt providers receiving subsidy payment through their agency. The newsletter includes information on nutrition, health and safety, and developmentally appropriate activities.

Recognizing that parents can be an effective vehicle for reaching regulation-exempt providers, the California CCR&R Network recently produced a packet of materials that is given to parents who choose a regulation-exempt provider. The packet includes two miniposters, tax information, and information about TrustLine, California's registry of regulation-exempt providers. (CCR&Rs advocated for the TrustLine registry after parents whose children had been abused in regulation-exempt care sought help in getting information about the criminal and child abuse histories of providers they might consider hiring.) Parents are encouraged to discuss the contents with their providers and to give them the posters ("Be Safe at Home and in Child Care" depicts home health and safety, and "Ages and Stages: 10 Annoying Behaviors Which Show a Child Is OK" provides a humorous introduction to child growth and development).

The passage of welfare reform legislation in late 1996 requires expanded creativity for developing new and improved methods for reaching regulation-exempt child care providers. This in itself is a leadership challenge for CCR&Rs but one that is compounded by widespread concerns within the early childhood field over the quality and appropriateness of some regulation-exempt care and its increased utilization by many low-income families.

CCR&Rs walk a tightrope in this new arena. Their balance depends on their ability to realistically understand the nature and needs of this emerging provider population and why parents make a regulation-exempt choice. To find and maintain this balance— and effectiveness—CCR&Rs also need clear federal and state regulations and policies and sufficient funds to address the needs of exempt providers while main-

taining services and support to regulated providers. Finally, the CCR&Rs' success in this arena depends on the willingness of the broader child care community to acknowledge regulation-exempt caregivers as a legitimate part of the child care world.

Helping communities articulate a child care vision: CCR&Rs' leadership role in community planning

Many of the contributions of CCR&R agencies take place behind the scenes, not on center stage. For example, CCR&R data collection and analysis often provide the foundation for community planning efforts. These data help communities forecast and anticipate child care needs, chronicle changes in child care supply, and sound alarms whenever legislation or policy shifts threaten efforts to improve and expand the child care delivery system (Pardee 1996).

CCR&Rs' willingness to mobilize community resources for change is evident wherever child care resource-and-referral leaders are represented in state and national gatherings of child care advocates. Agencies have shown that parents and others can go to CCR&Rs to understand how the child care system works and what actions and efforts can improve it. The doll campaigns of 1995 and 1996 (see Blank, chapter 5) are examples of CCR&R leadership in community mobilization. To focus on proposed welfare reform legislation and its potential impact on children and families, NACCRRA and other national child care organizations adapted a Colorado advocacy tactic and brought thousands of life-size cut-out dolls to Washington, D.C., in conjunction with NACCRRA's annual Day on the Hill in February 1995. CCR&Rs throughout the county had mobilized parents, providers, volunteer groups, and community agencies to make dolls that represented children who need or benefit from child care. The spotlight on the dolls helped ensure that Congress significantly increased funding for child care in the welfare reform legislation. But the impact of the doll campaigns was also felt locally, where the child care community united in a massive, collaborative effort to impact and change federal policies that would harm children.

Leadership lessons from state CCR&R networks and NACCRRA

The leadership potential of individual CCR&R agencies in parent involvement, data collection and analysis, training and development, and community planning, as described above, is encouraged and supported by voluntary associations of

CCR&Rs at the state and national level. These state networks and the national association, NACCRRA, are unusual in the child care world. To support each other, craft their service, and discover their place in the broader child care world, CCR&Rs have had to be extraordinarily collaborative and communicative with each other. Unlike child care teachers, administrators, and providers who have access to several state and national organizations that promote professional leadership, CCR&R staff have looked to state networks and NACCRRA as important resources for leadership development.

Since 1975, when the Ford Foundation first convened a small group of pioneering information-and-referral agencies for a two-day meeting at Bank Street College in New York, CCR&R providers have understood the stimulus, joy, and necessity of sharing information, meeting challenges, and supporting each other. At that first national CCR&R gathering, participants met around the clock, eager to share how parent complaints were handled, what kind of relationships to develop with regulatory agencies, strategies for achieving public support, and other information. This historic meeting was the foundation of CCR&Rs' deep and abiding commitment to mutual support.

Those early leaders from Alabama, California, Illinois, Massachusetts, Michigan, New York, and South Carolina maintained communication with one other, sharing newsletters and phone calls and always welcoming the opportunity to meet at conferences. Beginning in 1976, CCR&R leaders took responsibility for organizing preconference gatherings at the NAEYC Annual Conference. These initially small seminars grew gradually; by 1982 they had attracted more than 100 participants.

Another critical juncture for CCR&R leadership development came in 1982 when Wheelock College in Boston added an intensive CCR&R seminar to its popular summer Advanced Day Care Seminar Series. Drawing on the newly emerged leadership in the field, seminar organizer and instructor Gwen Morgan put together an exciting week of skill-building and leadership training for CCR&Rs. This first and subsequent seminars have played a pivotal role in bringing new and existing CCR&R leaders together for more than one or two days. The mutual support and friendships established in the Wheelock seminars nurture CCR&R leaders and help them explore and envision the need for a national CCR&R organization. Wheelock's vision and leadership in reaching out to a very young segment of the child care field helps give CCR&R professional status and recognition.

Meanwhile, organizing the NAEYC preconference days had become an increasingly collaborative effort by CCR&R leaders from numerous states. As issues, needs, and funding challenges emerged in the preconference seminars, organizers and participants recognized the need for a national organization devoted exclusively to supporting and promoting CCR&R services. In 1984 a core group of leaders began work on the structure and definition of the NACCRRA and formed an incorporating, voluntary board of directors with regional and at-large representation. Incorporated in 1987, NACCRRA opened its Washington office in 1993, building on its previous years of work governed by a volunteer board and shepherded by an executive coordinator located in Minnesota (Ranck in press).

The relative youth of CCR&R as a field within early care and education, combined with limited resources, has required CCR&Rs to be exceptionally attentive in fostering affiliation and trust with one another. Both the structures of state networks and NACCRRA's organization have been remarkably democratic and open in seeking a balance between regional and at-large concerns. A "CCR&R culture" has emerged to nurture, inform, and support new and existing CCR&R agencies. Maintaining a congenial culture is not easy, and like colleagues in this and other fields, NACCRRA and state networks constantly struggle to find the resources needed to simultaneously increase the services to the membership agencies and develop and support new leaders.

Perhaps CCR&Rs take their greatest strength, the capacity to support and strengthen each other, too much for granted. As new leaders emerge, it would be wise to understand and remember what leadership support and skills are most valuable to the acknowledged leaders. Mutual support would most likely rank high, for it is unlikely that the CCR&Rs would have succeeded in building the new genre of child care service without mutual support and respect and the willingness to help and to share knowledge. It is interesting to note that many parts of the corporate community are now stimulating the creation of networking and team-building practices that are apparently second nature to CCR&R agencies and similar early care and education organizations (Helegesen 1990; Morgan et al. 1993).

Conclusion

During the past 20 years, child care resource-and-referral leaders have forged a new component of the child care delivery system, making significant progress in achieving public support for services for parents, providers, and local communities. To achieve this, leaders worked creatively and responsively—first creating services to help parents find child care, then branching out to find out what was needed to ensure a supply of safe, quality child care.

In 1975 there were fewer than 25 CCR&Rs throughout the country. What they had in common was their commitment to meet a local need. In starting something new, the early leaders realized that they had to go beyond what was simply possible at the time. To chart a new path, they had to be outspoken, they had to take chances, they had to be entrepreneurial, and they had to cultivate alliances.

Today, more than 450 child care resource-and-referral agencies, including 39 state networks and the National Association of Child Care Resource and Referral Agencies, exist throughout the country. These organizations work together to create an infrastructure in which innovative approaches are shared, successful programs are replicated, public policy information is communicated, and future leaders are developed.

As the number of CCR&Rs has grown, the range of services they provide has also grown. The early name of "information and referral" was shed in favor of "resource and referral," as organizations worked actively with parents and providers to develop a better-informed child care delivery system.

Today, CCR&R services are more shaped and defined. Many CCR&R directors come into their organizations with a well-arranged menu of services and an expectation that they will provide leadership in their child care communities. The challenge for leaders is twofold: First, they must resist the temptation to fall into a bureaucratic, service-provider mentality that focuses too acutely on providing services and in the process loses sight of the continual reinventing that dynamic organizations need to best serve their communities; second, they must resist the increasing trend in business and social service to assume more and more roles as they seek to maintain a competitive edge.

CCR&Rs have succeeded because they have been able to adapt to changes in their community while preserving their original focus. One challenge shared by organizations as they enter their second and third generation of leadership is that there are fewer obvious frontiers to explore; most CCR&R groundbreaking activity has been accomplished and much of what's left is the less inspiring task of maintaining an established process. But the communities of today have a completely different look from the communities of 20 years ago. While the day-to-day changes might appear extremely subtle, the composition of families and the issues facing them have changed dramatically. The challenges facing today's CCR&R leadership involve a constant reexamination of how a community's child care services meet family needs and how to make the system work better. Facing this leadership challenge requires CCR&Rs to stay rooted in the community, understand its dynamics, and develop vision for new and refined programs that respond to community needs.

CCR&R leaders, past and present, have demonstrated a willingness to work on some of the toughest challenges facing parents and providers in their communities. This work often takes them to the edge of issues, and working on the edge is never easy or comfortable. But the tension and activity that go hand in hand with working on the edge are what have inspired CCR&Rs' most dynamic and innovative work and have helped to define their leadership role with the broader child care community. Understanding this history will help prepare and position future CCR&R leaders for new roles.

Note

1. Appreciation goes to board members and staff of the National Association of Child Care Resource and Referral Agencies and the California Child Care Resource and Referral Network for their leadership examples and inspiration. Special thanks go to Yasmina Vinci, Edna Ranck, and Martha Roditti.

References

Adams, D., R.A. Foote, & Y. Vinci. 1996. *Making child care work: A study of child care resource and referral in the United States.* Washington, DC: National Association of Child Care Resource and Referral Agencies.

Child Care Law Center. 1996. *Regulation-exempt family child care in the public subsidy context: An exploratory study.* San Francisco: Author.

Collins, A., & D. Pancoast. 1976. *Natural helping networks: A strategy for prevention.* Washington, DC: National Association of Social Workers.

Helegesen, S. 1990. *The female advantage: Women's ways of leadership.* New York: Doubleday Currency.

Levine, J. 1982. The prospects and dilemmas of child care information and referral. In *Scientific and social policy issues,* eds. E. Zigler & E. Gordon. Boston: Auburn House.

Moore, E. 1982. Day care: A black perspective. In *Day care: Scientific and social policy issues,* eds. E. Zigler & E. Gordon. Boston: Auburn House.

Morgan, G., S.L. Azer, J.B. Costly, A. Genser, J.F. Goodman, J. Lombardi, & B. McGimsey. 1993. *Making a career of it: The state of the states report on career development in early care and education.* Boston: Wheelock College.

National Association of Child Care Resource and Referral Agencies. 1993. Infrastructure in place: Child care resource & referral agencies as sources of child care data. A panel presentation at the National Association for Welfare Research and Statistics, 7–11 August, Scottsdale, AZ.

Pardee, M. 1996. *Blueprint: Planning for the future.* Washington, DC: National Association of Child Care Resource and Referral Agencies.

Powell, D. 1987. Day care as a family support system. In *America's family support programs,* eds. S.L. Kagan, B. Weissbourd, & E.F. Zigler. New Haven, CT: Yale University Press.

Ranck, E.R. In press. *Our history, our vision: A history of the National Association of Child Care Resource and Referral Agencies.* Washington, DC: NACCRRA.

Chapter 16

New Directions for Mediating Organizations

Ellen Galinsky

It was not until I was invited to write this chapter that I thought of the Families and Work Institute, of which I serve as president, as a mediating organization. What is a mediating organization? It is an organization that stands between the larger institutions of society, such as government, and institutions that provide direct service. In early care and education, direct service organizations include schools, child care centers, family child care homes, child care resource-and-referral agencies, work-family vendors, family resource centers, colleges and universities, and parent education programs. By this definition, research, advocacy, membership, and professional associations are, in general, mediating organizations. So too are foundations. These categories, however, are fluid. Some types of organizations are both a mediating group and providers of direct service—for example, child care resource-and-referral agencies, membership organizations, family resource centers, work-family vendors, and colleges and universities.

Many of the mediating organizations formed to represent and serve members are older and well-established, such as the National Association for the Education of Young Children, the Child Welfare League, the Council of Chief State School Officers, and the National Association of State Boards of Education. Some of the advocacy organizations, such as the Children's Defense Fund, are also well established. Other organizations have been set up more recently to serve a constituency and/or to advance an issue (e.g., the School Age Child Care Project at Wellesley College, the National Center for the Early Childhood

Work Force, the Family Resource Coalition, the National Association of Child Care Resource and Referral Agencies, the National Association for Family Child Care, the Child Care Action Campaign, the National Center for Children in Poverty, and the Center for Career Development in Early Care and Education at Wheelock College).

These organizations do not fall into neat categories. This is probably because most of them continually invent and reinvent themselves—following the proverbial "flying the airplane while building it" analogy. As a board member of some of these organizations and as president of another, I have seen questions of identity and scope arise time and time again: What is our mission? What is our niche? How does the work of our organization fit with the work of others? How do we stack up against the competition? and even, Should we exist? Just as soon as some of these questions seem to be answered, the changing political landscape, changing staff, and changing boards recall the questions, pulling them back onto the table for renewed deliberation.

Although these organizations stand between the institutions of society and direct service providers, they are not passive links. To *mediate* means to intercede, step in, negotiate, and work out. Mediating organizations shape, study, broker, serve, and push the field of early education and care. Their work involves mediating on three levels: within one sector of the field (e.g., a family child care constituency), among sectors in the field (e.g., child care and the public schools), and among different fields (e.g., early care and education and the media or business).

Characteristics of the mediating function

Since many mediating organizations also offer direct services, it is useful to identify the characteristics of the mediating function.[1] Four characteristics seem particularly important:

1. Fairness. To mediate among groups, an organization must be perceived as fair and not aligned to any one specific group. In contrast, a group seen as biased is far less able to bring different groups to the table or to create linkages.

2. Credibility. Credibility is necessary in bringing groups together and in having an organization's work respected and heeded.

3. Expertise. Organizations that perform a mediating function successfully have unique knowledge and skills and a commitment to quality.

4. Connections. Mediating requires access to the significant stakeholders in various fields.

Leadership in mediating organizations

Mediating organizations offer one of the best breeding grounds for leadership in the field. If one looks at any list of conference keynote speakers, experts invited to participate on advisory committees or in field-shaping events, writers of key publications, and so forth, a disproportionate percentage of the individuals come from mediating organizations. The reasons for this are not surprising. From the platform of a mediating organization, one has access to numerous other leaders in the field and has experiences that require an understanding of the multiple perspectives of the stakeholders involved in any discussion or debate. Solutions have to work for the majority of stakeholders. In contrast, it is much easier for direct-service organizations to retain a singular focus, unless they participate in field-based activities such as community planning and mobilization, crossdiscipline task forces, or conferences.

The leadership requirements for mediating organizations are undoubtedly as diverse as the missions of the various types of organizations. During our seven-year collaboration, Dana Friedman, co-founder and former co-president of the Families and Work Institute (FWI), and I learned a great deal about how we define leadership and thus the kind of staff we hire in key positions. In the expectation that this experience is germane and instructive, I will share it.

When we first began FWI, we focused on knowledge and skills: Did the individual have the requisite skills and background to do his or her job? We learned, however, that knowledge and skills were necessary but not sufficient to do the kind of work we do and to thrive in the kind of organization we created. Certain skills are critical to success at the Institute and in other mediating organizations. These include the ability to be observant, to see patterns, and to look for the usual and unusual connections between pieces of information. In other words, leadership today calls for people who can "think outside the box."

A second but related aptitude is a comfort level with—indeed, enthusiasm for—ambiguity. At FWI, we describe this as not working in a world that is black and white but enjoying moments that are gray. Again, if our work calls for being on the cutting edge, we have to have leaders within our staff who can take risks, are willing to make mistakes and learn from them, and can go with the flow. As Nina Sazer O'Donnell of FWI puts it, "Working well is like playing jazz. You have to be able to follow the riffs."

When we take on a new project, the content as well as the methodology must be determined; they must have synergy—that is, the methodology must support a project's function or purpose. Two examples are illustrative. In one study evaluating the impact of parental leave laws on employers and employees in four states, we created state advisory boards of both the opponents and proponents of the laws and asked them what they wanted to learn. Because these two opposing groups worked together to identify the study questions and review the findings, the results were primarily seen as nonpartisan—a very important factor in the subsequent receptivity of policymakers to the study findings. Similarly, when we conducted a study for New York City's Human Resource Administration about whether the city should shift to an expanded use of vouchers as a payment mechanism for child care, we did not go off on our own, conducting an investigation and writing a consultant's report. With others, we developed a methodology whereby all of the vested interest parties—representatives from the city administration, advocacy organizations, unions, and providers—sat around a conference room table together and conducted telephone interviews with representatives from five cities that had moved to an increased use of vouchers. Because the city, providers, and advocates had the same information, a "we/they" stance was for the most part avoided, and mutual problem solving was possible. Thus, devising the means of conducting this project was more important to its success than simply providing the information. The leaders on our staff need to be comfortable with taking risks and trying new ways of doing things.

We also need individuals who are self-initiating, continuous learners. These people take responsibility to find out as much as they can about their work. They do not wait to be told but reach out to others to learn.

They exercise a rigor in their learning and thinking as well. They do not assume that what they have heard mentioned in a meeting is necessarily true but instead test assumption against data. Self-initiated learning makes it more likely that individuals will be extremely well-grounded in what they do and see the opportunities for next steps, new projects, and new tasks to be undertaken.

In addition, these individuals need to be able to communicate what they have learned in multiple ways—through speaking and writing as well as by the use of slides, computer graphics, and videos. The means of communication must fit the messages being communicated.

Finally, we see the ability to work in teams as critical to leadership at the Families and Work Institute. People need a balance between being entrepreneurial and being team players, learning from and supporting each other and taking and giving criticism constructively.

The characteristics just mentioned are not unique to the Families and Work Institute; they are the same qualities that progressive corporations have identified as integral to their competitiveness in the 21st century. Some companies such as Corning and Allstate conduct leadership scans—that is, they go through a process to identify the individuals who are particularly productive and effective. Through interviews with these individuals, their supervisors, and their co-workers, the characteristics held in common by the outstanding performers are unearthed. In these companies, risk taking, an entrepreneurial stance, teamwork, innovative thinking, continuous learning, and the ability to communicate have been identified as keys to success.

Each of these attributes has a downside. For example, people who think outside the box may ignore the box or accepted knowledge. Likewise, some people comfortable with ambiguity can dwell on it and sacrifice accomplishment. A self-initiating learner might go off and do his or her own thing, without regard for the needs and interests of others or the group norms for building consensus in decisionmaking. A team player sometimes becomes the group's emotional mother/father or sister/brother to a group in ways that become counterproductive. And finally, some communicators become slick, not grounded in what is rigorously known. Obviously, one must seek balance in each of these attributes.

It seems to me that the individuals who possess these characteristics are those who make the biggest difference not only at FWI but in our field—for it is the individuals within organizations who determine whether or not that organization takes a leadership role. We all have watched an organization recede

into the background or, conversely, move onto center stage when its leadership or staff members change.

Roles leaders play in mediating organizations

As I see it, leaders in mediating organizations assume four primary roles. They (1) monitor the field of early care and education's activities, from identifying problems to assessing the impact of interventions; (2) help shape the field; (3) share knowledge by teaching and developing materials; and (4) advocate for change. In taking these roles, leaders in mediating organizations use eight strategies. They

• conduct research,
• convene other leaders and/or hold conferences,
• network,
• teach and provide technical assistance,
• serve as brokers among organizations,
• set standards,
• develop materials, and
• work on shaping public opinion.

Monitoring the field

Research is the primary strategy that leaders in mediating organizations use to monitor the field. Such research takes different forms: assessing need, monitoring supply and demand, assessing quality, studying best practice, developing report cards and benchmarks, and evaluating practice.

Researching the need for and supply of services is one way that leaders in mediating organizations monitor the field. Typically, this is a local process—within a state, community, or organization such as a company. The Families and Work Institute routinely does needs assessments in its work with corporations. We have found that the process for developing a needs assessment is critical to its effectiveness. We convene focus groups and conduct management interviews with various constituencies, including some of the organization's "doubting Thomases and Thomasinas" to ensure that the questions asked are targeted at the issues perceived as most important. When employees and managers are involved in identifying the problems they face and the programs and policies that could help ameliorate these problems, they feel a sense of ownership for the results and also become more open to findings that contradict conventional wisdom.

Assessments of the need for and supply of services also can be national in scope. Studies on the supply of child care, conducted for the U.S. Department of Education by Mathematica Policy Research (Kisker et al. 1991), and on the demand, conducted by the Urban Institute for the U.S. Department of Health and Human Services (Hofferth et al. 1991), provided a national overview. When these data were compared with data collected by the government since 1965, patterns in child care cost, use, and supply and demand could be ascertained. The *Map and Track* report of state initiatives for children, conducted by the National Center for Children in Poverty (Knitzer & Page 1996), is very useful in helping policymakers see the patterns in state efforts on behalf of young children.

Research conducted by mediating organizations has been particularly important in delineating a picture of the quality of child care in the United States. The National Child Care Staffing Study (Whitebook, Howes, & Phillips 1989), the Study of Children in Family Child Care and Relative Care (Galinsky et al. 1994), and the Cost, Quality, and Child Outcomes in Child Care Centers Study (1995) not only assessed overall quality but also identified the characteristics most likely to be associated with better teaching and caregiving. This information enables policymakers and practitioners alike to shape quality intervention based on the knowledge of the features of child care that are linked to higher quality.

Mediating organizations also use research to document promising practice as another means of monitoring the field. The Family Resource Coalition, for example, has compiled information on best practice in family resource programs (1996). This information becomes very useful to practitioners in their daily work.

Another way that mediating organizations monitor is by using research to evaluate practice. Perhaps the best-known program evaluation is the Perry Preschool Project conducted by High/Scope (Berrueta-Clement et al. 1984). The finding that a year of high-quality preschool for low-income children was a cost effective investment has become legendary in our field. Evaluations also can be conducted on policy interventions, such as the mid-1990s' studies by Syracuse University of the role of child care in California's welfare-to-work program GAIN (Meyers 1994) or by the Families and Work Institute of Florida's regulatory changes (Howes, Smith, & Galinsky 1995).

Report cards have been used by mediating organizations. *Kids Count* and the *State of America's Children* yearbooks, published annually by the Children's Defense Fund, offer an easy-to-understand assessment of where states or the nation stands on a set of selected indicators. Likewise, leaders of mediating organizations have begun to use progress indicators and benchmarks to monitor the field. A progress indicator is a measure of position along an ordered continuum representing the amount, level, intensity, or prevalence of a result related to a stated goal or objective—for example, decreasing staff turnover in early care and education. A benchmark is a specific level of an indicator—for example, according to NAEYC, 25% of early care and education centers should be accredited by the year 2005.

Shaping the field

Shaping the field is a critical but often unspoken role of leaders in mediating organizations. Foundation leaders take on this role more visibly by what they fund and do not fund, but leaders of other organizations do so as well. One strategy used to shape the field is *setting standards*. For example, when it became obvious in the early 1980s that the Federal Interagency Day Care Requirements developed by the federal government were not going to become law, the National Association for the Education of Young Children began a process to improve program quality that led to the establishment of a voluntary accreditation system. A decade later, center accreditation is an accepted concept, and 20% of the center-based programs in the United States are either accredited or in the process of becoming accredited (Bredekamp & Willer 1996).

Another strategy used in shaping the field is that of *convening leaders*. The Carnegie Corporation of New York, the W.K. Kellogg Foundation, and Yale University's Quality 2000 project convened a two-day meeting in the summer of 1995 to examine the issue of child-based outcomes. That meeting and the publication based on its content are helping set an agenda in the states and among organizations. Still another example is the group convened in 1995 by the National Association of Child Care Resource and Referral Agencies (NACCRRA) to examine the notion of family support as a function of child care resource and referral. By bringing together a group of leaders and by writing a paper on this subject (NACCRRA 1996), the organization is strengthening promising practice within its member agencies to take more of a family focus in their work.

Shaping public opinion is a strategy used to help push the field forward. The Media Strategy Group, established in 1993 by the Child Care Action Campaign and the Communication Consortium, convenes leaders of more than a dozen early childhood organizations on a monthly basis to work together on more effective means of communicating knowledge about child care and shaping public opinion.

Conducting research also helps set the field's agenda. The National Child Care Staffing Study (Whitebook, Howes, & Phillips 1989), conducted by researchers at UCLA, the University of Virginia, and the Child Care Employee Project (now the Center for the Early Childhood Work Force), demonstrated a link between staff salaries, staff turnover, and child care quality and thus put the issue of salaries on the national agenda. The study of state preservice and inservice requirements for child care staff, conducted by Wheelock College's Center for Career Development in Early Care and Education in the early 1990s (Morgan et al. 1993), prompted states to take action to improve professional development activities and systems.

Finally, *developing materials* is important in shaping the field. The Carnegie Corporation of New York's *Starting Points* (1994) was instrumental in focusing public attention on the problems and needs of children from birth to 3 years old. Likewise, the 1991 report on school readiness, based on a task force convened by the National Association of State Boards of Education, helped publicize and define this concept and identify strategies for improving children's readiness for school and schools' readiness for young children. I also like to think that the Families and Work Institute's Family-Friendly Index in our *Corporate Reference Guide to Work-Family Programs* (Galinsky, Friedman, & Hernandez 1991) stimulated state and business action that addressed the family needs of employees.

Sharing knowledge

One of the key functions of leaders in mediating organizations is that of sharing knowledge. Although these organizations do not provide direct service, they reach practitioners through a variety of dissemination activities.

Virtually all mediating organizations *develop materials,* books, articles, fact sheets, film strips, videos, or films. The materials range from informational to specific. Over the past several years, mediating organizations in early care and education have become more sophisticated in communication strategies—offering on-line services, for example.

Holding conferences is a very important strategy used in sharing information in the field of early care and education. I remember talking with a young professional whose job it was to find the speakers for a particular conference. Whereas she saw her job as technical rather than educational, I saw it quite differently: Orchestrating a conference is like creating a book or a film. Good conferences are a work of art—emotionally compelling and intellectually challenging. The conferences of national membership groups, such as the National Association for the Education of Young Children, the National Association for Family Child Care, the National Black Child Development Institute, the

Child Welfare League, the National Association of Child Care Resource and Referral Agencies, are key events in the field that empower individuals by arming them with information to guide their future decisionmaking.

Increasingly, leaders in mediating organizations are teachers and purveyors of technical assistance, particularly on the state level. Some have projects specifically designed for this purpose. For example, the MOST (Making the Most of Out of School Time) project, run by the School Age Child Care Project of Wellesley College and funded in 1994 by the DeWitt Wallace Readers Digest Fund, enables three communities to improve before- and after-school programs.

Another activity of mediating organizations is that of *serving as brokers*. This is a role that FWI assumes when it convenes groups that typically do not work or talk frankly together. For example, we organize an annual "Corporations and Child Care" session at the NAEYC Conference. In this session, we share the most important trends in business involvement in child care. More importantly, we ask corporate representatives to reveal what it is like to work with the child care field, and we ask child care leaders to share their insights about what it is like to work with business. By making these perceptions more visible, FWI brokers more constructive relationships in the future.

Finally, mediating organizations use *networking* as a way of sharing information. For example, various organizations have scheduled telephone conference calls to inform state and community leaders about pending federal legislation and to prepare action strategies.

Advocating for change

Some leaders of mediating organizations see advocacy as central to their missions, while others take a more neutral stance, believing that the studies they conduct, the books and reports they write, and the speeches they give can inform others' advocacy efforts. Yet all these leaders in mediating organizations hope that their work results in positive changes for children.

Mediating organizations use numerous strategies to push for change. One of the most common is *developing materials*. The charts comparing various legislative bills, created since the late 1980s by the National Association for the Education of Young Children, come immediately to mind.

Another advocacy strategy used by mediating organizations is the creation of *networks and coalitions,* such as those set up state by state by the Children's Defense Fund state by state to push for passage of the 1990 Child Care and Development Block Grant.

Organizing *conferences* as well as speaking at conferences are approaches used to advocate. Studying the titles of conferences and of keynote speeches at early childhood events over the years would provide a picture of the ebb and flow of the strength of advocacy efforts over time.

Media campaigns are newer but growing in our field. Sometimes they occur within a mediating organization, such as the Full Cost of Quality campaign launched by the National Association for the Education of Young Children in the early 1990s or the Stand for Children campaign launched by the Children's Defense Fund in 1996. Increasingly, however, these campaigns will probably involve representatives from numerous organizations as well as partnerships with media experts. As an example, prominent entertainers, national media experts, leading foundations, and early childhood experts and organizations have launched an unprecedented public awareness and engagement campaign to focus on the importance of the first three years of life and on what families and communities can do to promote young children's healthy development and school readiness. Called the I Am Your Child Campaign (1997), it includes a prime-time ABC television show, public service announcements and fulfillment materials, reports on the brain development of young children (Shore 1997) and on business efforts to help new and expectant parents, a home video for new parents, a CD-ROM and on-line information, a special edition of *Newsweek* magazine, and state and local campaigns across the country.

Are these special leadership roles unique to mediating organizations? For the most part, yes. But I have also seen individuals within government or in direct service take these roles. For example, Joan Lombardi at the Child Care Bureau in effect uses the bureau as an organization that stands between the Department of Health and Human Services, other federal agencies, and state child care administrators. In other words, she and the bureau are taking on the role of a mediating organization.

Challenges

It is quite easy to chart the challenges faced by leaders in mediating organizations in the early childhood field. One has only to recall the conversations that occur when leaders find a few private moments to talk with each other—on the plane traveling to a conference, on a bus or taxi to an airport, during a break in the meeting, or on the telephone late at night. Although we all spend a great deal of time thinking about the content of our work, these challenges are the issues that truly plague us—the ones that cause us to wake up, consumed with worry, in the middle of the night.

Projects versus infrastructure

As all the leaders of mediating organizations that exist on soft money know, there is a terrible tension between funding projects and funding the infrastructure of the organization. Understandably, foundations (mediating organizations themselves) want to fund visible projects that bring recognition not only to the grantee but sometimes also to the funder. In addition, many foundations and governmental funders do not want to get in the position of providing ongoing organizational support to organizations because that leaves them less flexible to move on as national priorities or their own priorities change. Funding agents do not want to create dependency among the organizations they support. Yet the 15% overhead that foundations typically provide (a few provide more, but others provide less or none at all) does not support true overhead costs, which in my experience run in the neighborhood of 30% to 50%. Thus, nonprofit mediating organizations that are supported by government or foundations always have to figure out how to pay the receptionist or the fiscal office and how to replace old copying machines, fax machines, or computers. They also have to figure out how to pay for the ongoing interest in a project (e.g., for phone calls for information or requests for materials or other dissemination activities) once the funding period is over.

Mediating organizations that are supported with membership money or organizational activities such as conferences have a similar problem. Unlike soft money operations, they may have the cash to support their infrastructure, but they have to answer to their boards and their members about decisions to do so. Should they renovate their offices or initiate a media campaign?

This project-infrastructure tension is a profound one with no easy solutions unless the funding community and membership begin to change their views about how organizations operate and unless the leaders of mediating organizations begin to think more like entrepreneurs and seek creative ways of funding their infrastructures.

Strength versus fragility

The irony about many mediating organizations is that they are at once very strong and very weak. They help shape and monitor the field, pass on its collected learnings, and advocate for change yet, to their leaders, the organizations often feel quite fragile. For those organizations that are dependent on external funding, each new proposal submitted recalls this sense of vulnerability. Although most leaders put many irons in the fire (submit more proposals than they expect to be funded), they worry that proposal turndowns will lead to laying off staff or fundamentally changing priorities. The current conversation among some of the leaders of mediating organizations is about mergers and about which organizations are expected to survive and which may not. Should the organizations that feel more vulnerable be proactive and reach out to others? Since there are no seemingly easy fits, what would such a change do to their mission and activities? Mediating organizations are a crucial breeding ground for leaders in the field, but they are wondering, "At what price is survival?"

Change versus stability

Since many leaders of mediating organizations pride themselves on being on the cutting edge—they have to be to survive—change becomes a way of life. They are always reinventing themselves. Thus, there is an inevitable tension between the need to change and the need to have some constancy. If, for example, an organization begins a new line of work, it probably will have to phase out or decrease its emphasis on something else. As one executive director says, when the membership pressures for change, "Since we can't do everything, if we take on this new project, what *don't* you want us to do?"

Organizations that rely on foundation or government money also have to deal with what one head of a local nonprofit organization calls the "flavor of the month." Just when she had fully established a project, her funders changed their priorities. To save the project, she "repackaged" what she had been doing into the new flavor and prayed she would get funded again.

I see the tension between change and stability as a healthy one, but it calls for a specific set of leadership skills—of being a forward thinker yet being able to balance new adventure with enough constancy to retain staff and organizational stability. It also calls for business skills: reading quarterly reports, anticipating financial and field-based trends, and designing staffing patterns (such as hiring consultants rather than staff) for needed flexibility.

Competition versus collaboration

There are times when the leaders of mediating organizations must compete with one another. For those organizations that depend on soft money, competition over funding is unavoidable—some organizations will receive certain foundation or government

grants and others will be rejected. Membership organizations often vie for the same members. There is also competition over products. When an organization has established a certain line of work, other organizations, sensing a viable source of new income, will tread in, trying to establish themselves as more worthy. Finally, there is competition for recognition—who is quoted by the media, who is invited to a meeting, or who is asked to sit on a task force or commission.

But as competition becomes more fierce with diminishing funds and a larger number of players, collaboration increases. The message of the American Business Collaboration for Quality Dependent Care—a consortium of 22 major corporations that raised $100 million to invest in improving dependent care for their employees—seems most apt.[2] These business rivals realize that they can accomplish more together in improving dependent care in their communities than they can ever accomplish alone.

Few projects by mediating organizations these days are purely solo. Whether it is an equal partnership or whether collaboration involves an advisory function, there is little that mediating organizations can or should do alone. As one leader puts it, "There is no question about whether to collaborate these days. The question is about picking the right partners."

Collaborations are not easy, as anyone who has ever engaged in one knows. The ongoing joke is, "Collaboration is an unnatural act between two or more unconsenting adults." There are many issues to resolve: Who decides? Who does what? Who gets credit? The issue of credit can be complex. To survive, organizations need to establish what marketing people call "brand-name identity." On the other hand, survival also depends on sharing or even giving up public recognition. Thus, leaders of mediating organizations are learning how to balance competition with collaboration. There is a time to promote and a time to be humble.

Differences versus similarities

As leaders in mediating organizations collaborate either in direct projects or in field-based leadership activities, the question of similarities and differences arises. In the larger perspective, it is important for various organizations to bring diverse perspectives, competencies, and activities to the table. Yet there is the pull toward being the same. I see this tension arising most strongly around advocacy. Some organizations define themselves as advocates, while others do not. But when politics on a given issue becomes intense, there is the pressure to become advocates, even though the credibility of some mediating organizations rests on being seen as fair and accurate. One executive director insists that he wants his staff to be seen as expert witnesses rather than advocates.

The issue of "one size fits all" versus diversity is one that leaders of mediating organizations have to struggle with, both within their own organizations and in the early childhood field as a whole. Leaders have to find the right balance for their organization.

At home versus on the road

Success for a mediating organization requires that its leaders spend a significant amount of time on the road. Travel is necessary for keeping one's finger on the pulse of the changing landscape, for participating in field-based events such as conferences and meetings, for being in touch with funders, and for disseminating the results of the organization's work. Yet every leader of a mediating organization has an operation to run. Who decides how to respond to a problem with a landlord or a broken photocopying machine when the organization's leaders are traveling? How do the leaders who travel keep in touch with the staff back at home carrying out the work of the organization? None of us who heard Sue Bredekamp, director of professional development for the National Association for the Education of Young Children, say at a foundation-sponsored event that she sees more of us (other national leaders) than she sees her own staff, will ever forget it.

Some organizations try to resolve this tension by designating certain people to travel and others to remain in the office. Yet this division of labor can be imperfect. When an organization did not send its top leadership to a recent national meeting, there was speculation that the meeting must have been of low priority to the organization. And while the leaders back at the office can feel cut off, the leaders on the road can feel overburdened with 24-hour-a-day jobs.

Walking the talk

One of my most poignant memories as a young mother was trying to write *The Six Stages of Parenthood* (Galinsky 1987). I had taken a two-year leave from my job so that I could have the flexibility to write the book and be at home with my children. Although I had excellent child care available, my children understandably often wanted me. My daughter banged on my bedroom/office door one morning and I faced a painful choice: Should I go to her or should I stay on my writing roll to help other parents with their children? (I went to my daughter.)

The leaders of mediating and other organizations face that terrible split between helping other people's children or their own. Despite myths to the contrary, the choice does not become easier when the children get bigger or leave home. A few years ago, between flights en route to give an opening speech at a statewide early childhood conference, I called my daughter at college. She was sick and scared. So instead of going to the conference, I flew all night to be at her college dorm by morning. Fortunately, the leaders of that conference fully supported my decision. Unfortunately for those of us with children and families at home, most early childhood conferences and meetings take place in the evenings or on weekends. We are not a very family-friendly field. And in the car, plane, or bus going to a meeting, most early care and education leaders speak poignantly about what they are missing at home to be present at this event.

The leaders of the Families and Work Institute, an organization devoted to issues of work and family life, have had a special struggle. To create our organization, we have had to work very hard, but when we work long hours, we are not seen as good role models for others. We have concluded that there needs to be space for people in leadership positions to make the decisions that are right for them. If the decision is to be with their families, leaders should not be seen as less committed or productive. If the decision is to work hard, they should not be seen as poor role models. We need diversity in the leadership of mediating organizations and the understanding that careers will have their ebbs and flows. This is an emerging concept in the business world and one that should exist in our field as well.

Developing new leadership

Joan Lombardi, chief of the federal government's Child Care Bureau, is fond of assessing leadership development at early childhood gatherings. She asks the age of the participants and looks to see how many young people are in attendance. She questions the leaders about the extent to which they are mentoring new leaders. However, as she and the other leaders know, inhibitors work against the development of leadership. As funding gets tighter, some organizations are turning to expert consultants rather than mentoring younger staff. Because it is a poorly paid field, potential new leaders cannot always afford to participate in some of the annual conferences, where talent is spotted. And those of us who run mediating organizations know that we are not always appealing role models. Would others want the constant worry that is inherent in jobs like ours? And yet there is the unparalleled love for the work that we have the opportunity to do.

Conclusion

As technology blurs the boundaries between work and nonwork, as global competition speeds up the pace of work, as downsizing severs the employer-employee contract, corporate leaders are asking themselves what kind of organizations do they want in the 21st century. It is time for leaders of mediating organizations to do the same. Perhaps we should move the conversations that we have around the edges onto central stage. Is that possible? Is there enough trust to be honest and to problem-solve together? I think so, and I know we must try.

It is clear that today's successful organizations—whether they be large corporations, neighborhood businesses, government, direct-service providers, or mediating organizations—are learning organizations. We live in rapidly changing times. Leadership calls for being proactive rather than reactive, for discerning trends and responding appropriately, and for showing that new ways are possible.

Note

1. In this discussion, I am indebted to Dana Friedman, co-founder and former co-president of the Families and Work Institute, for her thinking.
2. For more information about the American Business Collaboration for Quality Dependant Care, call Work/Family Directions at 1-800-767-9863.

References

Berrueta-Clement, J. L. Schweinhart, W. Barnett, S. Epstein, & D. Weickart. 1984. *Changed lives: The effects of the Perry Preschool Project on youths through age 19.* Ypsilanti, MI: High/Scope Educational Research Foundation.

Bredekamp, S., & B. Willer. 1996. *NAEYC accreditation: A decade of learning and the years ahead.* Washington, DC: NAEYC.

Carnegie Corporation of New York. 1994. *Starting points: Meeting the needs of our youngest children.* New York: Author.

Cost, Quality, and Child Outcomes Study Team. 1995. *Cost, quality, and child outcomes in child care centers. Public report.* 2d ed. Denver: Economics Department, University of Colorado.

Family Resource Coalition, 1996. Guidelines for family support practice. Chicago: Author.

Galinsky, E. 1987. *The six stages of parenthood.* Reading, MA: Addison-Wesley.

Galinsky, E., D.E. Friedman, & C.A. Hernandez. 1991. *The corporate reference guide to work-family programs.* New York: Families and Work Institute.

Galinsky, E., C. Howes, S. Kontos, & M. Shinn. 1994. *The study of children in family child care and relative care: Highlights of findings.* New York: Families and Work Institute.

Hofferth, S.L., A. Brayfield, S. Deich, & P. Holcomb. 1991. *The National Child Care Survey.* Washington, D.C.: Urban Institute.

Howes, C., E. Smith, & E. Galinsky. 1995. *The Florida Child Care Quality Improvement Study.* New York: Families and Work Institute.

The *I Am Your Child* Campaign. 1997. Campaign materials. Washington, DC: Greer, Margolis, Mitchell, Burns, & Associates.

Kisker, E.E., S.L. Hofferth, D.A. Phillips, & E. Farquhar. 1991. *A profile of child care settings: Early education and care in 1990, Vol. 1.* Princeton, NJ: Mathmatica Policy Research.

Knitzer, J., & S. Page. 1996. *Map and track: State initiatives for young children and families.* New York: National Center for Children in Poverty.

Morgan, G., S.L. Azer, J.B. Costley, A. Genser, I.F. Goodman, J. Lombardi, & B. McGimsey. 1993. *Making a career of it: The state of the states report on career development in early care and education.* Boston: Center for Career Development in Early Care and Education, Wheelock College.

Meyers, M. In press. Cracks in the seams: Durability of child care in JOBS welfare-to-work programs. *Journal of Family and Economic Issues* 18 (4).

NACCRRA (National Association of Child Care Resource and Referral Agencies). 1996. *Supporting families and changing times: Child care resource and referral looks to the future.* Washington, DC: Author.

National Association of State Boards of Education. 1991. *Caring communities: Supporting young children and families.* Alexandria, VA: Author.

Shore, R. 1997. *Rethinking the brain: New insights into early development.* New York: Families and Work Institute.

Whitebook, M., C. Howes, & D. Phillips. 1989. *The National Child Care Staffing Study: Who cares? Child care teachers and the quality of care in America.* Final report. Oakland, CA: Child Care Employee Project.

Chapter 17

New Directions for Parent Leadership in a Family-Support Context

Judy Langford and Bernice Weissbourd

New understandings about children in the 20th century have led to the conviction that families are paramount in their children's early care and education. The knowledge that young children's development is inextricably tied to their parents' state of being has led to an emphasis on viewing children and families as a unit and to early childhood professionals working with both for the benefit of the child.

The focus on parents raises the question, What constitutes parent leadership? In family support, parent leadership has a meaning quite distinct from that of the sole dynamic leader or the leader who successfully builds teams of people to work together. Parent leadership rests on the assumption that all parents can be leaders in the lives of their children, doing so in the manner and to the extent that each chooses. Parents can be advocates at home, at school, in the community, and in society at large.

This construct of leadership, in which parents, both individually and collectively, influence the practices, programs, and policies that affect their children's lives, requires new approaches to fostering leadership development. It demands an understanding of parents' roles as parents as well as people functioning in the broader society. It challenges professionals to provide an environment in which parents recognize their singular importance to ensuring the child's opportunity for healthy growth both inside and outside the home. And the construct calls upon staff to analyze their own attitudes and expectations of parents and reorient their thinking toward the goal of building relationships that empower parents to function as leaders.

Frequently used phrases such as *parent involvement, parents as partners,* and *parent participation* reflect this understanding about the importance of parents and have led to changes in the relationship between parents and professionals. Parent involvement is a hot topic among educators who believe that children cannot easily succeed in school without parental participation. Sparked by the success of parent involvement in Head Start (Zigler & Muenchow 1992), parent involvement has been acknowledged as such a critical element of school success that virtually all school improvement efforts today include increased parent involvement as a primary goal (Comer 1984). The continuum of parent involvement activities ranges from doing learning activities at home with children to assisting with school activities and participating in school policymaking. *Parent participation* and *parents as partners* are alternative terms used both in early childhood and family support to describe the significant role of parents in their children's settings.

Parent empowerment refers to the important role of parents not only as participants in programs for children but also as change agents in those settings and the community at large. There is growing awareness among parents of the part they must play as advocates for themselves and their children, sometimes side by side with professionals and other times with their separate voices. Staff acknowledgment of parents being primary in the lives of their children leads to ensuring that they are critical players both in programs designed for them and in those designed for their children. The attention to parents also reflects the political climate of the moment, with a focus on personal responsibility for taking care of one's own family as well as greater community and neighborhood control over services and resources.

Parents' leadership roles

Engaging parents as leaders requires a concept of leadership consistent with the multidimensional roles parents play. Leadership is not quite the same as participation or involvement or empowerment. Leadership has implications of guiding, governing, managing resources, and making decisions about programs. Because parents function in a wide range of arenas, they may be viewed as exerting leadership in various aspects of their lives. In so doing, a concept of leadership evolves that is unique to parents. Instead of a focus on *styles* of leadership, the context becomes *domains* of leadership.

In the home the parent takes leadership in organizing the resources necessary to meet the needs of the child. It is the parent's responsibility to find a way to provide basic necessities such as food and shelter, and to ensure adequate health care, quality child care, a good education, and a safe environment. These can be complicated tasks. They often involve researching appropriate services; making arrangements for transportation, enrollment, ongoing contacts, and daily maintenance; and consistently serving as a knowledgeable advocate for the child's needs. In this sense, parents are expected to be the "case managers" for their children, responsible for organizing and managing the full range of resources needed for healthy development. This kind of leadership requires knowledge and skill on the part of the parent.

In the family system the parent also provides leadership in setting and maintaining the environment for family functioning. The way decisions are made, rules established and enforced, schedules coordinated, and tasks assigned and carried out are dependent on the parent's leadership within the family. Each family establishes its own culture, its own structure for functioning, with different members taking on different aspects of responsibility at different times. This family leadership requires skill in assessing who can do what; it requires negotiation and flexibility, as well as a collaborative commitment to making sure that the basic "work" of the family is done in a way that supports each member.

Another leadership role common to parents with young children occurs in the social and family networks around the family. In the extended family, each member has a defined role along with expectations for fulfilling the obligations of that role. Young parents are often expected to take responsibility for organizing family events, caring for cousins or nieces and nephews, providing housing or food for other family members in times of crisis, and responding to the needs of older members in the family who need their help. Similarly, in a network of friends or co-workers, parents often take responsibility for managing events; assisting others with child care, clothing, or transportation; and providing vital emotional support in times of need. These connections require sophisticated skills in juggling time and resources to meet expectations and in maintaining these important relationships over time.

Exerting leadership in these domains of home and family is key to the healthy development of children. An African American professor at an elite university noted that her mother never volunteered at school or talked to teachers, but she certainly communicated to her family that education was very important and that her daughter was expected to work hard in school and do well. The professor described her mother as strong, creative (because she made much out of few resources), and energetic, an initiator and builder of the kind of relationships that held the whole family together. This description captures the qualities defined traditionally as characteristic of leaders.

Some parents play leadership roles in the neighborhood through their relationship with other children as well as their own. A mother may offer milk and cookies to the children who regularly drop by her house after school. The children know she cares about them. A father may coach the local soccer team and become an advisor to children on and off the field. Members of a car pool can become trusted friends and confidants for the children they see on a regular basis.

In early childhood settings, parents choose varied levels of involvement. Some parents come to Head Start, child care centers, or family resource centers to assist the staff, serving as models for the children and expanding their sense of a caring community. Not all of these parents may attend parent meetings or advisory councils, but they are parent leaders in the classroom. Other parents share their skills with their peers, exerting leadership in their areas of knowledge—in such activities as craft making, baking, book reviewing, or budget management.

Parents as advocates for their families and children in public policy is the usual concept of parent leadership. Many parents who are active in neighborhood organizations, school councils, and Head Start have been effective in planning and policy development in communities around the country. Some parents mobilize for action on a specific issue, such as threats to Head Start funding, and their participation is a key factor in policy decisions. In communities in every state, it is by virtue of parent actions that school bond issues are passed or recreation programs are initiated or expanded. Although some parents start their involvement in the advocacy arena, others become advocates through a set of experiences in which they overcome a sense of helplessness and realize their power to make change. These experiences of leadership are often unrecognized in the larger community—and often unrecognized by the parents themselves.

When staff validate the many domains of parent leadership, parents are encouraged to develop their skills further. The skills these parents exhibit and practice in their everyday lives can be the basis for very effective leadership in a program or in the community at large.

The family-support model of parent engagement

In the field of early childhood education, as has been pointed out in this volume, the concept of shared leadership has replaced that of the sole dynamic leader. The focus on a charismatic, articulate leader who effectively motivates and rewards followers has recently given way to a more egalitarian focus on a leader who can build teams of people to make decisions and take responsibility collectively, as parents and professionals in early childhood settings are increasingly called upon to do.

Since the 1960s, community development and grassroots organizations have worked to identify natural leaders in a community, then provide them with skills and strategies to help them organize others to work toward change, usually economic or political change (Fisher 1984). This type of leadership development stems from a desire to put communities with fewer resources on a more equal footing in the political and economic structure to gain what they need to survive and thrive. This pattern is similar to family-support efforts to give parents more authority over resources needed by their children.

The root of the family-support view of leadership is in the relationship between program staff members and the families with whom they work. Establishing a mutually respectful relationship between staff and family is a primary goal of family-support practice. This relationship is based on an equal partnership, using unique resources contributed by each partner. The professional's expertise on children and families or available resources is not viewed as superior to the parents' expertise about their family and their children; it is seen as a resource to be used by the family at the direction of the family. The valued quality of staff

leadership is the capacity to relinquish power over program resources to parents as they express their needs and desires. The valued resources are combined knowledge and skills and shared commitment to the healthy development of children.

Revisiting early childhood programs from a family-support perspective

Over the past 20 years, the assumptions behind the family-support movement have substantially influenced many of the institutions that serve children and families. Because the original family-support programs focused primarily on supporting parents in the early years of their children's lives, early care and education programs were natural partners with family support in developing new avenues of support for both children and their parents. As early care and education programs have integrated family-supportive practices into their own work, the role of parents in these programs has shifted and grown.

The relationship between parents and early childhood professionals is heavily influenced by the culture of the program in which the professional works. Home child care providers, for example, often enjoy an intimate, supportive relationship with the parents of the children they serve. They usually have extensive knowledge of the family's life and the daily issues and problems that influence the child's development; they frequently serve as advocates for and supporters of parents.

Special parent roles and activities have been part of the Head Start program since its earliest days, with staff specifically assigned to do outreach and support for parents in addition to the involvement opportunities offered by classroom teachers. Training is provided for Head Start staff to increase their knowledge and skill in working with parents, and parents are viewed as partners with staff in program decisions (Zigler & Muenchow 1992).

Traditional preschools and child care centers tend to have a different kind of relationship with parents. Parents often have many choices of centers and preschools, and they choose their provider in part because of their comfort with the opportunities and support that particular program offers to the family. The specific ways that parents have input into the program and interact with staff differ widely among preschools and child care centers, and the extent to which parents participate directly in the governance of the program also varies. In some situations, parents are expected to play an active, involved role with their children and with staff, and regular individual opportunities are provided for consultation and feedback as well as for participation in program planning and policy. In other settings, parents may have limited contact with staff beyond picking up or dropping off children.

Early childhood programs under the aegis of public schools are likely to reflect the policies and attitudes of a school district toward parents. School districts that regularly reach out to parents in many ways and offer extensive opportunities for involvement in school affairs are likely to have early childhood programs that follow suit. Those that prefer that parents "leave the schooling to the schools" make it more difficult for early childhood teachers and administrators to institute extensive parent involvement.

As more family-supportive environments emerge, early childhood leaders in every setting will be challenged to take on new responsibilities for creating a program more responsive to parents. Early childhood leaders will be expected to respond to parents in new ways, which will require extensive changes in the preparation of leaders as well as in the ongoing programs of early childhood institutions.

Providing a family-support environment in early childhood settings

The first responsibility of an early childhood program leader is to create an environment in which partnerships with parents for the benefit of their children can flourish and grow. The second is to empower parent leaders to be full partners in governing the program and participating in the wider society beyond the program. Both of these responsibilities require new training and new perspectives for early childhood leaders and parents as well.

Creating a program environment for effective parent partnerships

Two essential elements of an appropriate environment are the attitude of the early childhood professional toward parents and the professional's ability to understand and reduce barriers to the parents' full participation in an effective partnership. The professional's attitude must be based on an informed commitment to the principle that parents are the most important people in a child's life. A mind-set that parents are primary creates an environment in which parents not only feel valued but they also recognize the child as their responsibility and seek to fulfill that responsibility well.

When staff are truly committed to this principle, patterns of relating to parents as teachers, judging parents' behavior, or focusing on "being nice" to parents give way to a new paradigm: the professional becomes a key partner whose role is to assist parents in "the best interests of the child." The staff-parent relationship is not helper-helpee or teacher-learner but rather a relationship in which the professional serves the needs of parents as they raise their child. With such an approach we may go beyond *parents as partners* to *professionals as partners*—a significant departure from the training and experience of many professionals today. Being a partner does not excuse the professional from providing the advice, counsel, and information parents seek. But it means doing so in a welcoming environment in which parents are appreciated, not depreciated, and in which parents' confidence is enhanced, not undermined.

In creating an environment that promotes parents as partners, staff need to look beyond the parent primarily as a vehicle for the child's growth and shift to understanding the parent as a developing person. Parenting is a pivotal stage in the life cycle, reflecting the events of childhood and presenting new possibilities for individual growth and development. Confidence is built in parents not only as they experience the satisfaction of seeing a child grow up well but also as they experience their own ability to manage their lives.

The staff's positive attitude toward parents leads to the second essential element of a supportive environment for partnerships: understanding and reducing the barriers to full parent participation. In a family-friendly program environment, staff are aware of the situation in which a family is living; whether the home is particularly stressful or isolated; whether a parent is struggling to balance work and family, trying to get off welfare, or adjusting to a different culture and language. Whatever the situation may be, staff communicate a belief that parents want to be good parents and do the very best they can for their children. Staff view parents as resources for themselves, their children, and their communities. In situations where parents do not function well, staff seek to understand the current problems or the childhood experiences that may be affecting the parents' behavior, and they do not further blame the victim. When staff do not fundamentally believe in the importance of parents and the desire of parents to do their best, their lack of genuineness is quickly perceived.

A major barrier that often prevents full and effective participation is the attitude of parents themselves, evident especially when they feel they have nothing to contribute, they are not sufficiently educated, or they are not fluent in English. Low self-esteem is further fostered by a society that does not value the role of parent as worthy of validation and support. Similarly, emotional barriers exist. Some parents may feel shy and unsure of themselves in groups. Some may have dropped out of school and feel uncomfortable in a school or social-agency setting. For other parents, there are practical barriers—lack of time, lack of child care, or lack of transportation. Some of these parents may want to participate but find it impossible to do so.

Past experiences also create barriers. Parents may have been excluded or demeaned by the authorities or the rules of a system that ignored their needs. Some of them long ago may have sworn oaths to avoid schools. Many families who have been heavily involved with public services have very good reason to be suspicious, hostile, noncompliant, and upset about human services in general and the way the system has treated them and their children in particular.

Recognizing these barriers is fundamental to creating an environment in which obstacles are overcome. In such an environment, staff believe every parent has something to contribute, and opportunities are provided for parents to use their particular skills. One parent may work wonderfully in the child care room, while another may share her secrets for great pies. A diffident parent who reads a great deal may be encouraged to give book reviews. Programs should offer or link parents to skill-building opportunities to learn English or acquire a GED. Whatever is necessary to encourage parents to use the skills they have and develop those they want should become part of the program plan. Similarly, staff help parents to face practical barriers and make decisions about how to overcome those problems so that parents are able to participate as they wish.

Empowering parents in the program

The capacities of parents to be leaders develop in an environment in which individual abilities, talents, and strengths are recognized and built upon and parents experience themselves as change agents. The key component is that parents, through the relationship built with practitioners and through meaningful involvement in planning and policy, learn that they have the capacity and power to make a difference.

The principles of governance for a program contribute to an environment in which parents feel comfortable and empowered. The program's organizing structure (boards, advisory councils, or program and policy committees) should be based on the assumption that parents play a major role in governance and are not merely "parent representatives." As staff encourage parents to feel—and be—competent, both as parents and as people, a community of parents emerges in which the members support each other and understand their individual and collective

strength. Parent leadership expands as parents become involved in governance and policy decisions and when they experience success in effecting change—whether it is within the program, procuring a stoplight for a dangerous intersection, or ensuring a more adequate statewide early childhood system.

Community-based programs that support and encourage leadership develop a powerful and subtle staff-parent partnership that goes beyond formal governance structures. For example, one parent participant in a Chicago program serving a very high-risk community recently explained, "Well, we have committees and all, but Gilda [the director] and Jewel [the program coordinator] know that if they send out somebody that talks down to me, I'll call right up and tell them not to ever send 'em over here again." This parent feels real power in this program; the program leadership is personally well-known to her, directly accountable to her, and responsive to her concerns. She—and other parents—has a major impact not only on the formal mechanisms established by the program but also on policy decisions in the program's environment. It is the normal way of doing business.

The interaction of early childhood leaders and empowered parents can sometimes be a new experience for both parents and professionals. When parents express needs and desires for their children that are not part of the professionally planned program or perhaps conflict with the program's mission or philosophy, the staff have to be ready to respond in a positive, constructive way. In child care programs, for example, staff often encourage parents to learn advocacy skills for supporting increased child care funding from public sources. When these empowered parents later decide that improved housing is a higher priority for them than child care, program leaders are challenged to balance their support for the parents' ongoing empowerment with the goals of the child care program.

Empowering parents in the community

There are many examples of a growing acknowledgment that parents are critical players in any programs designed to assist them. Consumer-driven services are now a goal of many human service agencies, including those that provide physical and mental health services and self-sufficiency programs. Following the lead of colleagues on the business side, where profits are determined by customers, human services professionals now recognize that their effectiveness often depends on their responsiveness to the needs of the people they serve. Community-based services are one result of the move toward consumer-driven services; essential services located in neighborhoods close to the people they serve are more accessible and responsive.

The new collaborative models of community-based governance for children and family services include recipients and parents in planning new services and deciding how resources are to be used. "Empowerment" describes the many different programs and approaches that offer participants new skills and opportunities to take charge of their lives. The goal of most empowerment programs, including the federally designated Empowerment Zones in several large urban areas, is to give local communities and the people who live there more control over the resources they need to survive and thrive.

The leadership capacities of parents outside the program are as yet underutilized by policymakers, but as the groundswell of parents' voices grows stronger, so does the expectation of closer connections between parents and policymakers. The commitment of parents to their children constitutes the strength of the parent voice and underscores the necessity for policymakers to listen. Parents could be a resource and partner with policymakers as they are with staff in early care and education programs, and do so in ways appropriate to the spheres of policy planning and decisionmaking. A recognition in the policy world of the importance of parent input could lead to a national environment that fosters parent leadership in much the same way as programs do.

Early childhood professionals have a responsibility to facilitate parent participation in policymaking beyond the scope of the early childhood program. One important avenue is assisting parents in taking on roles that are increasingly available to them in public settings. Legislation at all levels mandating that parents sit at the decisionmaking table has placed parents in new positions of authority in schools, state planning committees, and local advisory councils for all kinds of programs. Yet mandates are a poor substitute for real change. The legal formality of participation will remain a token gesture until parents are accepted as full partners by others at the table and until they gain the experience necessary to effectively use the power that they have. Mandates, however, have opened doors for some parents who have long wanted access. Other parents feel unsure of their abilities to function in settings where the procedures, rules, or language are unfamiliar. Engaging and maintaining families in participatory roles in policy decisions is a dramatic shift from the usual way of working with them, and it requires rethinking and retraining both families and professionals to make the partnership work effectively.

Meeting the challenges of empowerment

The focus in early childhood has moved from being solely on the child to including a consideration of the child's family, but there is not yet an acceptance of parents as being integral to the functioning of a program. Many early childhood professionals are not comfortable with the concept of building relationships of equality with parents and find it difficult to relate to parents in ways beyond the conventional types of communication—exchanges at drop-off and pick-up times, conferences, or occasional social and educational events. Encouraging parents as leaders requires that staff understand issues of parenthood as they understand those of childhood and that they are open to changing long-held notions of the professional's role as an authority. If the premise of family support—that parents are the primary people in the child's life—underlies early childhood education, then staff must learn how to work toward building empowering relationships with parents as well as with children.

There are four areas to consider in meeting the challenges raised by the view of parent leadership presented in this chapter.

1. **Inservice and preservice training.** Students in early childhood education are thoroughly trained in child development, developmentally appropriate practices, and classroom management, but little emphasis is placed on forming relationships with parents or ensuring that parents have a voice in the governance structure of the program. A knowledge base in adult development would enable early childhood professionals to be more skilled and confident in working with parents. Both preservice and inservice training should include information on parenthood as a developmental phase, adult development in general, and relationship-building with parents. In addition, information on program planning and governance structures designed to strengthen parents' capacities as leaders should be a component of professional development.

2. **Parent leadership training.** Parent leadership training has developed from parents' desire to learn the skills necessary to function in governance, planning, and policy roles. It is most effective when it is not a curriculum imposed on parents but an example of a partnership in which professionals meet the expressed needs of parents by providing the knowledge they seek as they assume responsibilities in new and different arenas. Various parent leadership training programs emerge as an increasing number of parents express an interest in acquiring the tools of participation in public policy and advocacy. These programs can be a referral source for early childhood educators to parents.

3. Consensus building. The conviction that early childhood programs and policies must target the child and the family, not the child alone, is not an understood nor widely accepted assumption among practitioners and policymakers. A concerted effort to have broad acknowledgment of an ecological approach to children is necessary. Just as preschool education once lacked public consent and the importance of the first three years of life was relatively unknown until recently, so must the limitations of viewing children as separate from their families move from its present status to become a generally accepted construct. Among the ways this can be accomplished is through professional conferences, public testimony by professionals and parents, media presentations, and inclusion by professionals of parents at meetings.

4. Advocacy. Professionals and parents, separately and together, should advocate for policies that include a parent component in all early childhood programs. Doing so requires a recognition that a more comprehensive parent-support program cannot function without additional funding. An already overworked staff must have assistance or more people to allow time for developing parent-staff relationships. Head Start, which assigns a special staff person to work with parents, can serve as a model.

Leadership for partnership

As we approach a new millenium, early childhood leaders have an opportunity to be at the forefront of a growing political and social movement: a society-wide push for parents to assume a position of power and responsibility in their children's lives and the life of their communities. Efforts to control what their children learn, experience, and observe, as well as the ongoing debates over the role of government in supporting families, are presenting parents new choices and challenges. The "attitude of involvement" that is emerging in both policy and program is not a legalistic, formal, formula-driven strategy. It is an assumption that the receivers of service—the families who are the primary advocates, protectors, and nurturers of their children—have something important to contribute. Parents become leaders when they have the opportunity to do so and when the environment is sufficiently supportive for them to claim it as their own.

Early childhood professionals already understand the importance of parents as full partners with them in helping young children develop, and they are working in many ways to create an effective partnership in both program and policy. The promise of parent leadership is a new era in which the resources of each community are focused on the well-being of all its children—and parents are the source of protection and hope for their community as well as their children.

References

Comer, J.P. 1984. Home-school relationships as they affect the academic success of children. *Education and Urban Society* 16: 323–37.

Fisher, R. 1984. *Let the people decide: Neighborhood organizing in America.* Boston: G.K. Hall.

Zigler, E.G., & S. Muenchow. 1992. *Head Start: The inside story of America's most successful educational experiment.* New York: Basic.

Advocacy Leadership

SECTION 5

Chapter 18

Moving the Leadership Agenda

Barbara T. Bowman and Sharon L. Kagan

This volume was inspired by the conviction that greater attention needs to be given to the development and support of leaders in the field of early care and education. At present, early childhood leadership is fragmented, uncoordinated, and inequitable in presentation, and it lacks clear guideposts for professionals seeking opportunies to advance. As a result, the needs of young children and their families are often unmet.

To redress this situation, extensive changes are needed—changes in practices, policies, incentives, and leadership development, to mention a few. This is so because—as is clear from the preceding chapters—the field is growing in its understandings and in its scope. The field needs leaders who not only have a well-formulated understanding of early development and pedagogy but also are able to fulfill roles with allied professionals, agencies, foundations, corporations, communities, and parents. We need new attitudes about leadership, changes in the organizational structures in the field, and a broader and deeper knowledge base than the one presently in use.

Many chapters in this volume have addressed these issues, providing extensive analysis of the need for new leadership. Many authors have suggested recommendations to advance the leadership agenda. In this final chapter, we present an array of recommendations, some of which emanated from the chapters, some from the ideas of others, and others from our own understandings of where the field might best be positioned to advance.

All of the preliminary ideas were carefully honed by a group of wonderful colleagues who formed a Leadership Working Group. Working over the duration of this undertaking were Sue Bredekamp, Dwayne Crompton, Linda Espinosa, Evelyn Moore, Gwen Morgan, and Carol Phillips, who each lent their experience, energy, and intelligence to the effort. Their work was crucial at several points—in conceptualizing the volume, in crafting their contributions, and in synthesiz-ing and adding conceptual clarity to the recommendations. While the final draft of the recommendations represents our work and tailoring, the ideas herein reflect the thinking of many, most notably the Working Group and the contributors to this volume.

Content

Several overarching themes recurred throughout the volume and in the discussions of the Leadership Working Group. These included (1) professional organizations must take an instrumental role in promoting change in the field, (2) leadership diversity must be supported by providing information and promoting opportunity, and (3) professional development should include a career ladder with multiple pathways to leadership. These ideas are so pervasive that they form a set of assumptions upon which the following specific and actionable recommendations have been based. Note that the recommendations are not listed in any order of priority; all are necessary if durable change is to be undertaken and real leadership advancement achieved.

1. Pioneer new definitions of and visions for leadership for early care and education professionals.

The early care and education field historically has approached leadership as something that happens to some people. Until recently, we have not tended to accord it the serious analysis and action that it deserves. This is true at practical and conceptual levels. We have underestimated the importance of leadership to the advancement of the field and to the children and families served. Moreover, we have been unclear about what is meant by leadership and where it can and should exist.

To that end, the field needs to broaden its understandings of what leadership is and how it is best produced. The new definition must take the increasingly diverse leadership demands of the field into consideration. For example, leaders are not only those individuals who hold directorship or administrative positions in frontline work. Leaders are not only those in certain jobs or those with certain degrees or skin colors. Leadership must include diverse individuals working in all the diverse settings in which decisions are being made about the care and education of young children. Leadership should be understood to include those individuals who contribute to the field through research, teaching, scholarship, and advocacy and those who work at local, state, and national levels, as well as those who provide direct services to children and families.

Attention should be accorded leadership venues in allied fields—health, education, and social work—and to less visible leadership roles from which early childhood professionals are often excluded, including reviewers for grant-making organizations, book and journal editors, and search firm recruiters. Moreover, emerging and new roles for those with an early childhood background should be explored— roles in business, industry, politics, science, and technology. Now is the time for the profession to consider new ways to conceptualize leadership that affects the decisions that touch children and families.

Action recommendations. Form a coalition of professional organizations to define a leadership agenda that includes

• raising awareness in the early childhood community about the need for and value of a formal leadership system,

• codifying understandings about leadership,

• conceptualizing a new definition of leadership,

• creating a vision for leadership and obtaining consensus about it, and

• exploring nontraditional roles for early childhood leaders.

2. Engage allied groups and organizations concerned about children and families in the development of a new emphasis on and vision for early childhood leadership; encourage their recognition and support.

A number of organizations and groups are concerned about, make policy for, and provide services to young children and their families. If policy and plans for service are to be informed by knowledge and un-

derstanding, allied groups must include early childhood leadership in a decisionmaking capacity. Allied groups include, among others, policy and advocacy organizations (such as the Children's Defense Fund and the American Association of Retired Persons), other professional groups (such as the American Medical Association and the National Association of Elementary School Principals), administrators in government agencies (such as health and welfare departments), representatives from business and industry (such as the Committee for Economic Development), and oversight and review organizations for colleges and universities (such as state, regional, and national accrediting associations). Outreach into all segments of society is necessary to raise awareness about the need for and the value of effective early childhood leadership.

Action recommendations. Professional groups should take the lead to

• call attention of allied groups and fields to the importance of informed leadership when planning programs for young children and families,

• awaken appreciation for the value of early childhood leadership in a number of domains, and

• develop strategies for getting early childhood leaders into positions in corporations, universities, government agencies, and other institutions.

3. Formalize a leadership structure for the field.

Currently there is no structure or agreed-upon process for systematically developing a new generation of leaders for the field. Different auspices and services have created a hodgepodge of licenses, certificates, credentials, and degrees required for leadership roles. To develop an infrastructure, a plan must be made that delineates leadership standards and credentials and makes sure that diversity and different paths to leadership are built into the system. This plan should be tied to the service delivery system, coordinated with training requirements, and promoted broadly within the profession.

Action recommendations. Professional organizations, allied groups, and institutions of higher education must work together to

• create a process for identifying potential leaders with a strong knowledge base and leadership skills,

• create mechanisms that will systematically nurture and prepare these individuals for leadership roles,

• develop new strategies for diversifying opportunities,

• create formal and informal support systems for potential leaders and those in leadership positions,

- develop various approaches for formal and informal inservice training in early childhood leadership,

- develop a rich array of strategies for promulgating the training, using—for example—mentoring, peer alliances, and technology, and

- arrange conference presentations that include tracks on leadership and bring business and foundation representatives to the field to encourage new and innovative leadership ideas.

4. Encourage higher education to match leadership training to the needs of the field.

Leadership programs at colleges and universities now are at every level of training, thereby providing a leadership pool that often lacks basic knowledge and skills. The knowledge base for the field is drawn from a variety of disciplines, including developmental psychology, education, infant studies, sociology, anthropology, and family support. Yet students frequently are exposed to subject matter content and experience in only one discipline or department. At present, the research base for early childhood practice is slim. Many researchers contributing to the field reflect the perspectives and approaches of other disciplines, such as psychology, social welfare, health care, or education. Collaborative research is needed to define the knowledge and skills necessary for leadership in the field of early care and education.

The relationship between what leaders do and the content and level of their training must be coherent, comprehensive, and available. Leaders in the field need a fundamental knowledge of the range of factors that affect how children develop and learn. The knowledge base must include theory, research, and best practices drawn from a variety of disciplines and departments within higher education. The goal is to ensure well-prepared leaders by tying the knowledge requirements to leadership roles. Therefore, institutions of higher education and the professional community must work together to design and evaluate effective leadership programs.

Action recommendations. Professional organizations should organize to

- define leadership roles and desired preparation,

- encourage institutions of higher education to rethink content for leadership training and promote collaboration among the academic disciplines that frame the field, and

- promote research on leadership roles and appropriate training.

5. Promote nonacademic opportunities for early childhood leaders to learn and gain experience.

To fully serve children and families, early childhood professionals need to broaden their experience and knowledge into domains of decisionmaking in which they currently do not participate. To better prepare early childhood leaders, both formal (apprenticeships and fellowships) and informal (mentors and support groups) opportunities need to be created. Such programs should help individuals already in the field gain exposure to and experience in policy arenas, government administration, research, and allied professions' culture and practice. Therefore, additional opportunities for leadership training must be created for early childhood leaders.

Action recommendations. Professional organizations, colleges and universities, government agencies, and foundations must create opportunities for early childhood leaders to extend their knowledge and experience by

- providing/seeking funding for early care and education leadership programs at each level of government—community, state, and national;

- establishing leadership fellows programs in advocacy organizations for individuals with demonstrated leadership capability at the local level; and

- organizing support groups for leaders facing new challenges—such as directors, researchers, and government administrators.

6. Advance diversity through opportunity and the elimination of bias.

Individuals working on behalf of children and families must be committed to fairness, inclusion, and mutual respect. However, many of our communities and institutions have a long history of exclusion and bias. An inclusive leadership cadre that reflects the diversity of the United States is essential if we are to make early childhood programs responsive to children's needs and backgrounds. Therefore, early care and education programs, as well as other community institutions, must work to include well-qualified individuals from the various groups that make up our society.

Action recommendations. Everyone must take responsibility to

- enlarge the leadership pool by encouraging early childhood workers at every level to strive for additional training and leadership positions;

• offer both formal and informal support to individuals from groups often excluded from leadership roles;

• insist on zero tolerance for racial, religious, gender, cultural, or sexual preference bias;

• encourage identification of potential leaders from underrepresented groups, such as through the National Black Child Development Institute's proposed data bank; and

• promote new leadership models that include diverse cultural perspectives and experiences.

*   *   *   *   *

While the above recommendations constitute a robust agenda, they clearly do not represent the full array of ideas and options open to the field. They should be regarded as suggestive of potential steps that must be taken. They, like the entire contents of this volume, are designed to signal the need for greater attention to be paid to the importance of leadership development in early care and education. It has been said that the strength of any institution or field is the strength of its leaders. Nothing could be more true for early care and education. It is to this end that this volume is dedicated.

Information About NAEYC

NAEYC is . . .

. . . a membership-supported organization of people committed to fostering the growth and development of children from birth through age 8. Membership is open to all who share a desire to serve and act on behalf of the needs and rights of young children.

NAEYC provides . . .

. . . educational services and resources to adults who work with and for children, including

• *Young Children, the* journal for early childhood educators

• **Books, posters, brochures,** and **videos** to expand your knowledge and commitment to young children, with topics including infants, curriculum, research, discipline, teacher education, and parent involvement

• An **Annual Conference** that brings people from all over the country to share their expertise and advocate on behalf of children and families

• **Week of the Young Child** celebrations sponsored by NAEYC Affiliate Groups across the nation to call public attention to the needs and rights of children and families

• **Insurance plans** for individuals and programs

• **Public affairs** information for knowledgeable advocacy efforts at all levels of government and through the media

• The **National Academy of Early Childhood Programs,** a voluntary accreditation system for high-quality programs for children

• The **National Institute for Early Childhood Professional Development,** providing resources and services to improve professional preparation and development of early childhood educators

• **Young Children International** to promote international communication and information exchange

For free information about membership, publications, or other NAEYC services, visit the **NAEYC Website** at **http://www.naeyc.org/naeyc**

National Association for the Education of Young Children
1509 16th Street, NW
Washington, DC 20036-1426
202-232-8777 or 800-424-2460